LOCAL STREET ATLAS

CHESTER WREXHAM

**BANGOR-ON-DEE · BUCKLEY · CHIRK · CONNAH'S QUAY · FLINT
HAWARDEN · HOLYWELL · HOPE · LLANGOLLEN · MOLD**

CONTENTS

Page Layout & Road Map................ 2-3
3½ Miles to 1 Inch

Chester Enlarged Centre....................4
6 Inches to 1 Mile

Wrexham Enlarged Centre 5
7 Inches to 1 Mile

Street Maps................................ 6-71
4 Inches to 1 Mile

Index to Streets..............................72

www.philips-maps.co.uk

First published in 2005 by
Estate Publications

This edition published by Philip's,
a division of Octopus Publishing Group Ltd
www.octopusbooks.co.uk
2–4 Heron Quays, London E14 4JP
An Hachette Livre UK Company
www.hachettelivre.co.uk

Second impression 2008
01/05-05

ISBN 978-0-540-09396-0

To the best of the Publishers' knowledge, the information in this atlas was correct at the time of going to press. No responsibility can be accepted for any errors or their consequences.

The representation in this atlas of a road, track or path is no evidence of the existence of a right of way.

Ordnance Survey and the OS symbol are registered trademarks of Ordnance Survey, the national mapping agency of Great Britain

Printed in China by Toppan

LEGEND

ute
Road
d
Pedestrianized / Restricted Access
Track
Built Up Area
Footpath
Stream
River
Lock
Canal
Railway / Station
Post Office
Car Park / Park & Ride
Public Convenience
Place of Worship
One-way Street
Tourist Information Centre
Adjoining Pages
Area Depicting Enlarged Centre
Emergency Services
Industrial Buildings
Leisure Buildings
Education Buildings
Hotels etc.
Retail Buildings
General Buildings
Woodland
Orchard
Recreational / Parkland
Cemetery

LIVERPOOL
Birkenhead
Bebington
Wallasey
HALTON
Runcorn
Widnes
Halewood
Speke
Garston
Ellesmere Port
Eastham
Whitby
Frodsham
Helsby
Neston
Heswall
Hoylake
West Kirby
WIRRAL
RIVER MERSEY
RIVER DEE
(AFON DYFRDWY)
Flint (Y Fflint)
Connah's Quay
Deeside Industrial Park
Shotton
Bagillt
Holywell (Treffynnon)
Greenfield (Maes-glas)
Mostyn
Buckley (Bwcle)
Mold (Yr Wyddgrug)
Hawarden (Penarlâg)
Saltney
Blacon
CHESTER
Hoole
Huntington
Waverton
Mickle Trafford
Guilden Sutton
Tarvin
Kelsall
CHESHIRE
FLINTSHIRE
Mollington
Saughall
Backford
Stoak
Moston
Broughton
Penyffordd
Higher Kinnerton
Mynydd Isa
Northop
Northop Hall
Soughton (Sychdyn)
Ewloe
Drury
Sandycroft
Garden City
Gwernaffield-y-Waun
Halkyn
Ince Banks
Manchester Ship Canal
LIVERPOOL JOHN LENNON

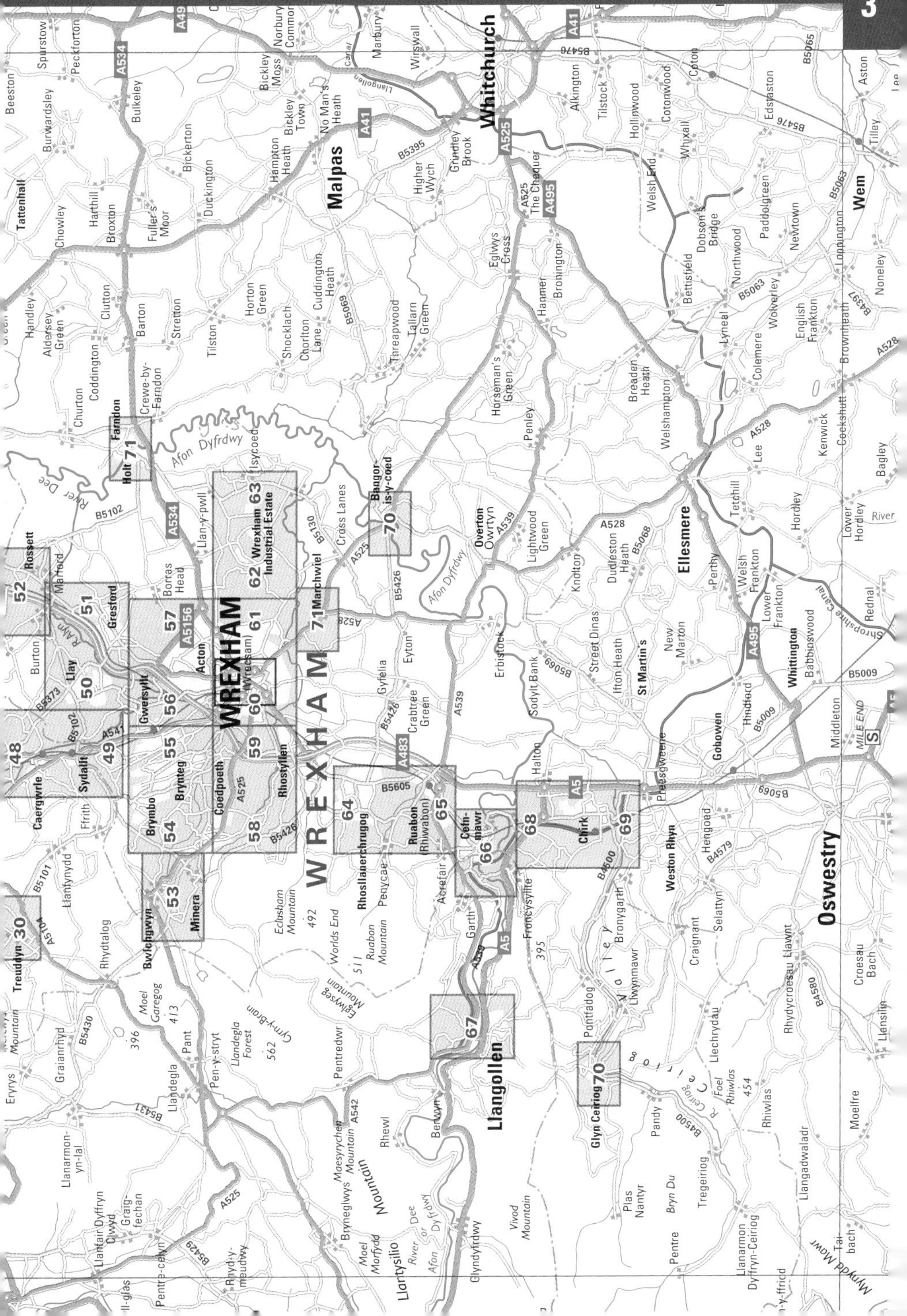
Whitchurch
Malpas
WREXHAM
(Wrecsam)
W R E X H A M
Wrexham Industrial Estate
Ellesmere
Oswestry
Wem
Llangollen
Overton
Owrtyn
Bangor-is-y-coed
Chirk
Ruabon
(Rhiwabon)
Rhosllanerchrugog
Cefn-mawr
Gresford
Rossett
Holt
Farndon
Coedpoeth
Brymbo
Brynteg
Gwersyllt
Caergwrle
Sydallt
Llay
Acton
Marchwiel
Rhostyllen
Minera
Bwlchgwyn
Treuddyn
Glyn Ceiriog
Weston Rhyn
St Martin's
Gobowen
Whittington
Llantysilio
Afon Dyfrdwy
River Dee
Shropshire Canal
Llangollen Canal
Ruabon Mountain
Esclusham Mountain
Eglwyseg Mountain
Llandegla Forest
Vivod Mountain
Maesyrychen Mountain
Mynydd Mawr
A5
A41
A49
A483
A495
A525
A528
A534
A539
A541
A542
A5156
Beeston
Spurstow
Peckforton
Bulkeley
Tattenhall
Handley
Tilston
Threapwood
Hanmer
Penley
Overton
Erbistock
Froncysyllte
Pontfadog
Llanarmon Dyffryn-Ceiriog
Llandegla
Glyndyfrdwy

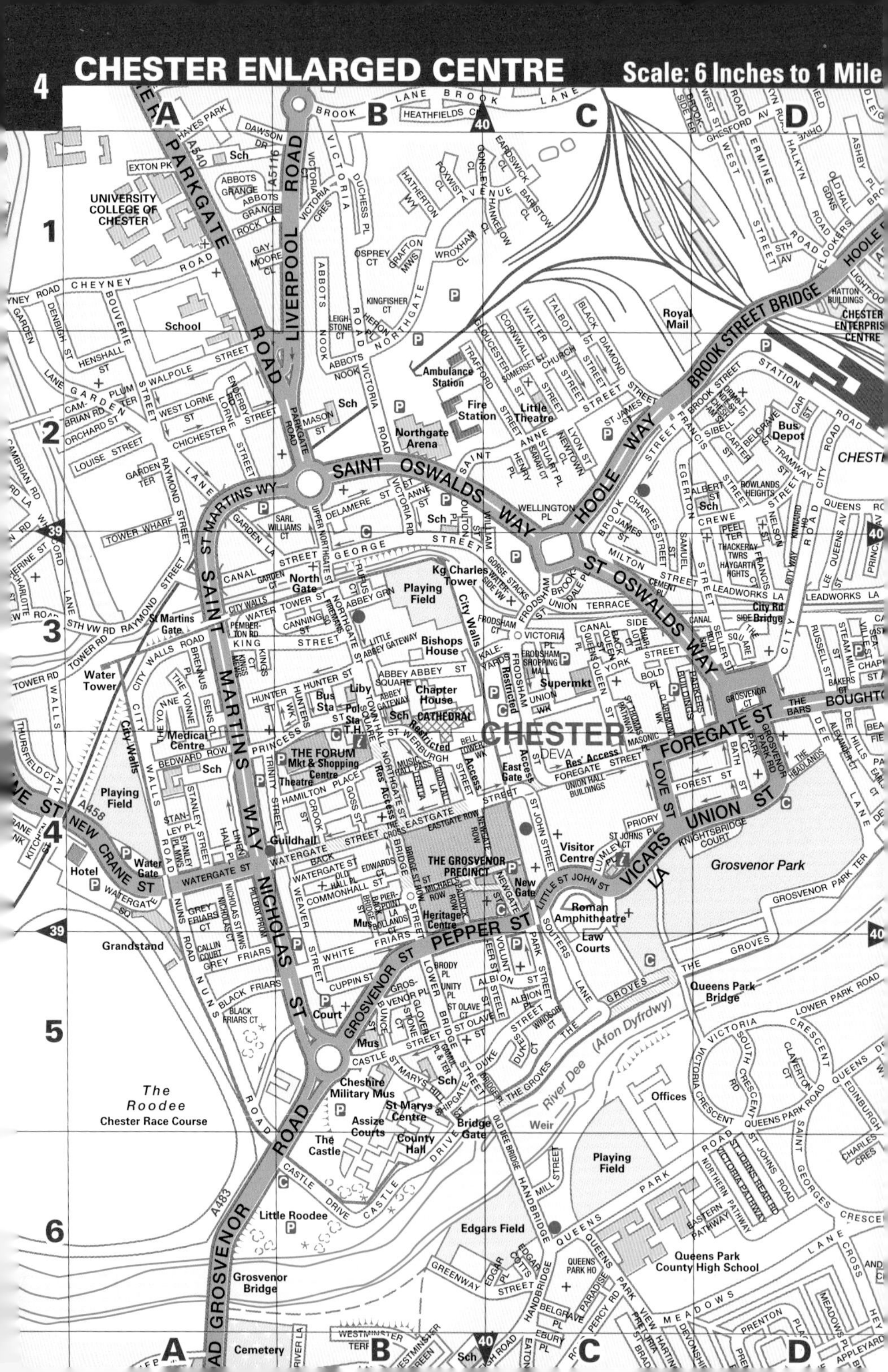
A
B
C
D
1
2
3
4
5
6
39
40
PARKGATE ROAD
LIVERPOOL ROAD
UNIVERSITY COLLEGE OF CHESTER
School
Royal Mail
BROOK STREET BRIDGE
HOOLE WAY
SAINT OSWALDS WAY
ST OSWALDS WAY
Ambulance Station
Fire Station
Northgate Arena
Little Theatre
Bus Depot
North Gate
Playing Field
Kg Charles Tower
City Walls
Bishops House
Chapter House
CATHEDRAL
CHESTER
DEVA
Supermkt
FOREGATE ST
Water Tower
Medical Centre
THE FORUM Mkt & Shopping Centre
Theatre
Guildhall
THE GROSVENOR PRECINCT
Heritage Centre
PEPPER ST
East Gate
New Gate
Visitor Centre
Roman Amphitheatre
Law Courts
Grosvenor Park
VICARS LA
UNION ST
LOVE ST
NICHOLAS ST
SAINT MARTINS WAY
WATERGATE ST
Water Gate
Hotel
Grandstand
The Roodee
Chester Race Course
Court
Mus
Cheshire Military Mus
Assize Courts
The Castle
County Hall
St Marys Centre
Bridge Gate
Weir
River Dee (Afon Dyfrdwy)
Queens Park Bridge
Offices
Playing Field
Edgars Field
Little Roodee
Grosvenor Bridge
GROSVENOR ROAD
Queens Park County High School
Cemetery
CHESTER ENTERPRISE CENTRE
HATTON BUILDINGS
City Rd Bridge
THE GROVES
QUEENS PARK ROAD
VICTORIA CRESCENT

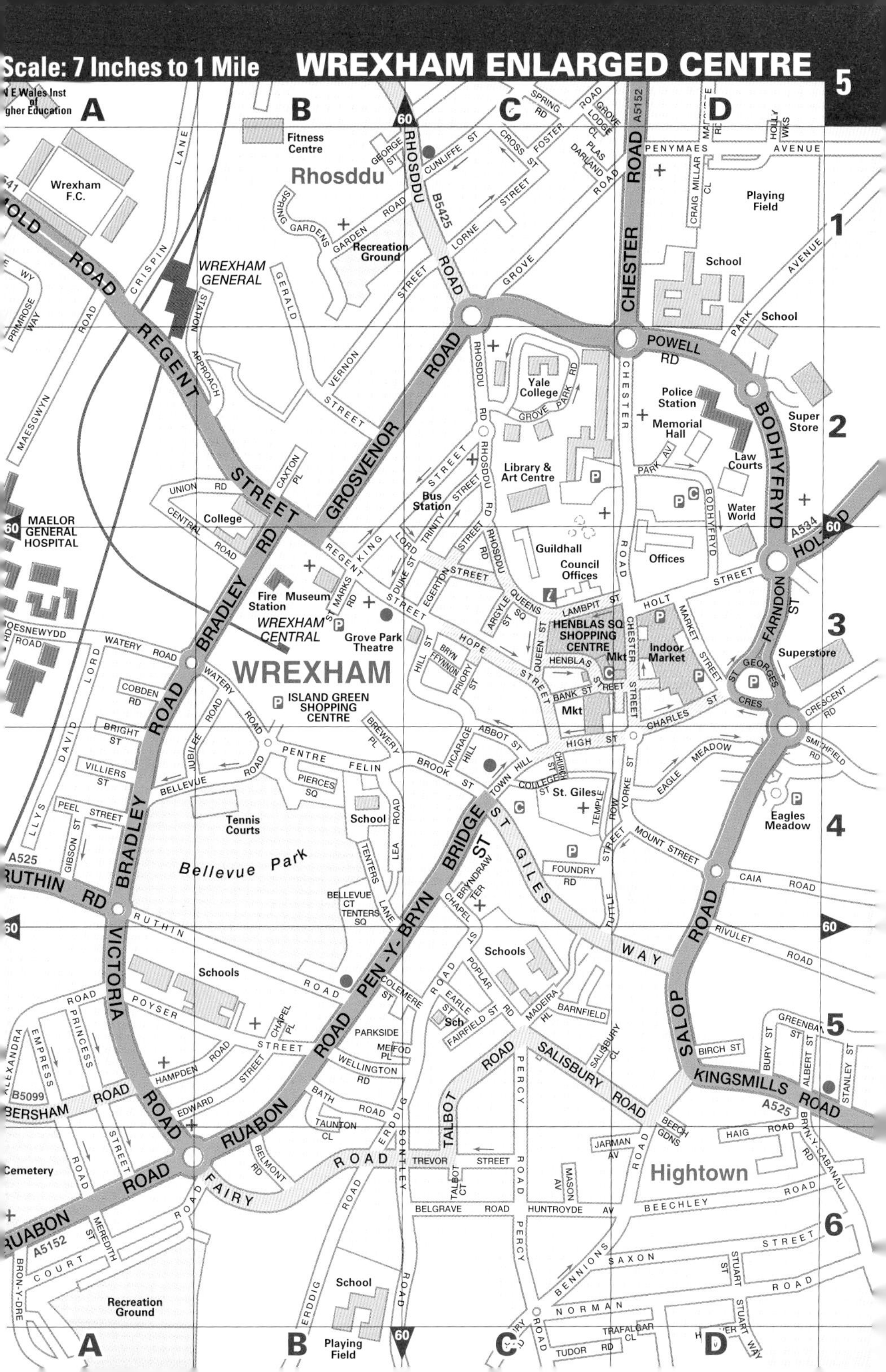
A
B
C
D
1
2
3
4
5
6
Wrexham F.C.
Fitness Centre
Rhosddu
Recreation Ground
WREXHAM GENERAL
Yale College
Police Station
Memorial Hall
Law Courts
Super Store
Library & Art Centre
Bus Station
Water World
Guildhall
Council Offices
Offices
MAELOR GENERAL HOSPITAL
College
Fire Station
Museum
WREXHAM CENTRAL
Grove Park Theatre
HENBLAS SQ SHOPPING CENTRE
Mkt
Indoor Market
Superstore
WREXHAM
ISLAND GREEN SHOPPING CENTRE
St. Giles
Eagles Meadow
Tennis Courts
School
Bellevue Park
Schools
Sch
Cemetery
Hightown
Recreation Ground
Playing Field
Playing Field
REGENT STREET
GROSVENOR ROAD
BRADLEY ROAD
CHESTER ROAD
POWELL RD
BODHYFRYD
FARNDON ST
HOLT ROAD
RUTHIN RD
VICTORIA ROAD
RUABON ROAD
PEN-Y-BRYN
BRIDGE ST
ST GILES WAY
SALOP ROAD
KINGSMILLS ROAD
SALISBURY ROAD
TALBOT ROAD
FAIRY ROAD
BERSHAM ROAD
MOLD ROAD
RHOSDDU ROAD
A5152
A534
A525
A5152
B5425
B5099
60

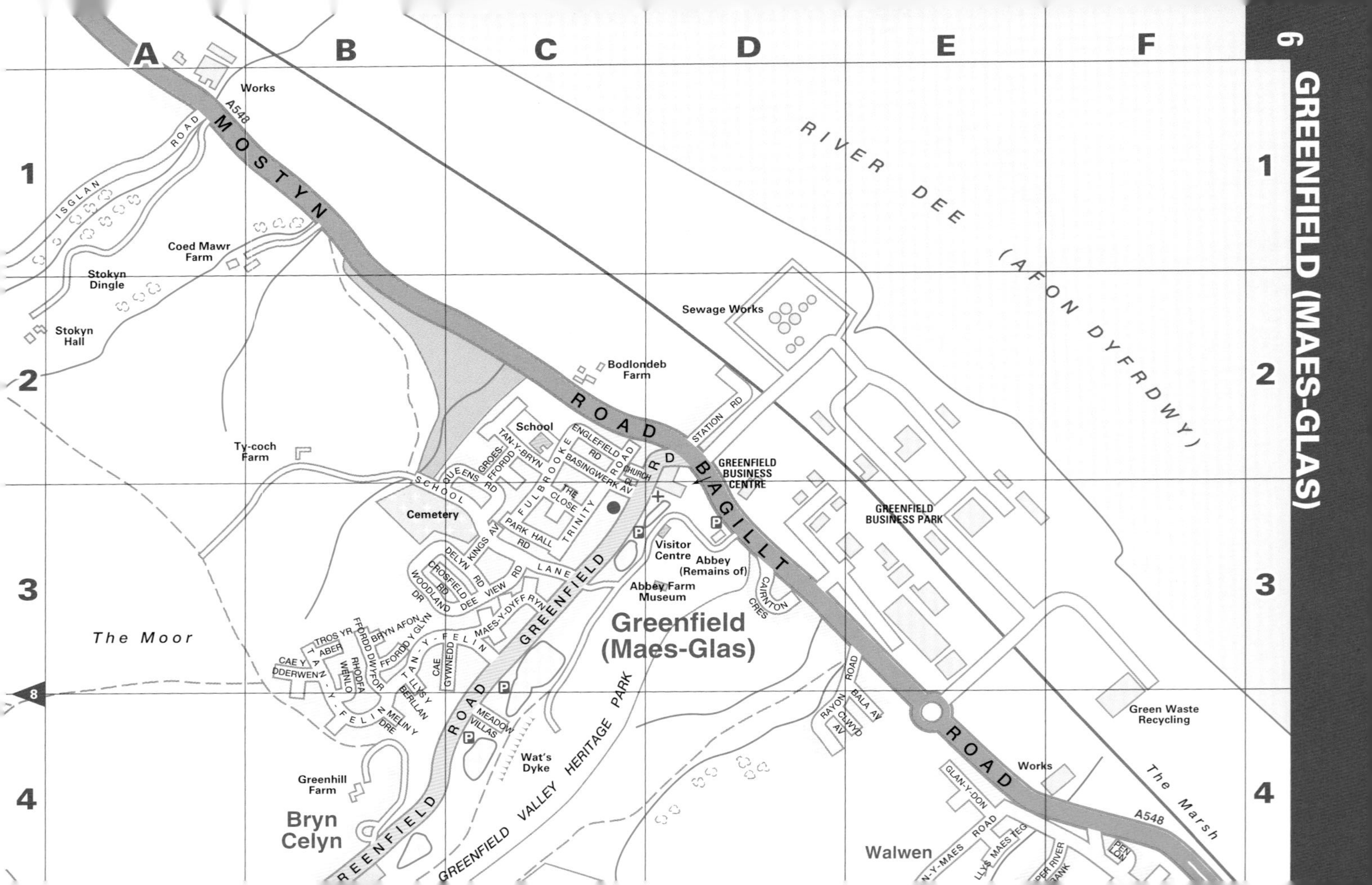
A
B
C
D
E
F
1
2
3
4
Works
A548
MOSTYN
ROAD
ISGLAN
Coed Mawr Farm
Stokyn Dingle
Stokyn Hall
RIVER DEE (AFON DYFRDWY)
Sewage Works
Bodlondeb Farm
ROAD
BAGILLT
STATION RD
GREENFIELD BUSINESS CENTRE
GREENFIELD BUSINESS PARK
School
Ty-coch Farm
SCHOOL
QUEENS RD
GROES-FFORDD
TAN-Y-BRYN
ENGLEFIELD RD
FULBROOKE
BASINGWERK AV
CHURCH CL
THE CLOSE
TRINITY
PARK HALL RD
KINGS AV
Cemetery
DELYN RD
CROSFIELD RD
WOODLAND DR
DEE VIEW RD
LANE
MAES-Y-DYFFRYN
GREENFIELD
Visitor Centre
Abbey (Remains of)
Abbey Farm Museum
CAIRNTON CRES
The Moor
Greenfield (Maes-Glas)
TROS YR ABER
CAE Y DDERWEN
FFORDD DWYFOR
RHODFA WENLO
BRYN AFON
FFORDD Y GLYN
TAN-Y-FELIN
CAE GWYNEDD
LLYS Y BERLLAN
MELIN Y DRE
ROAD
MEADOW VILLAS
Wat's Dyke
GREENFIELD VALLEY HERITAGE PARK
8
Greenhill Farm
Bryn Celyn
GREENFIELD
RAYON ROAD
BALA AV
CLWYD AV
ROAD
Works
GLAN-Y-DON
Green Waste Recycling
The Marsh
A548
Walwen
ROAD
LLYS MAES TEG
PEN LON

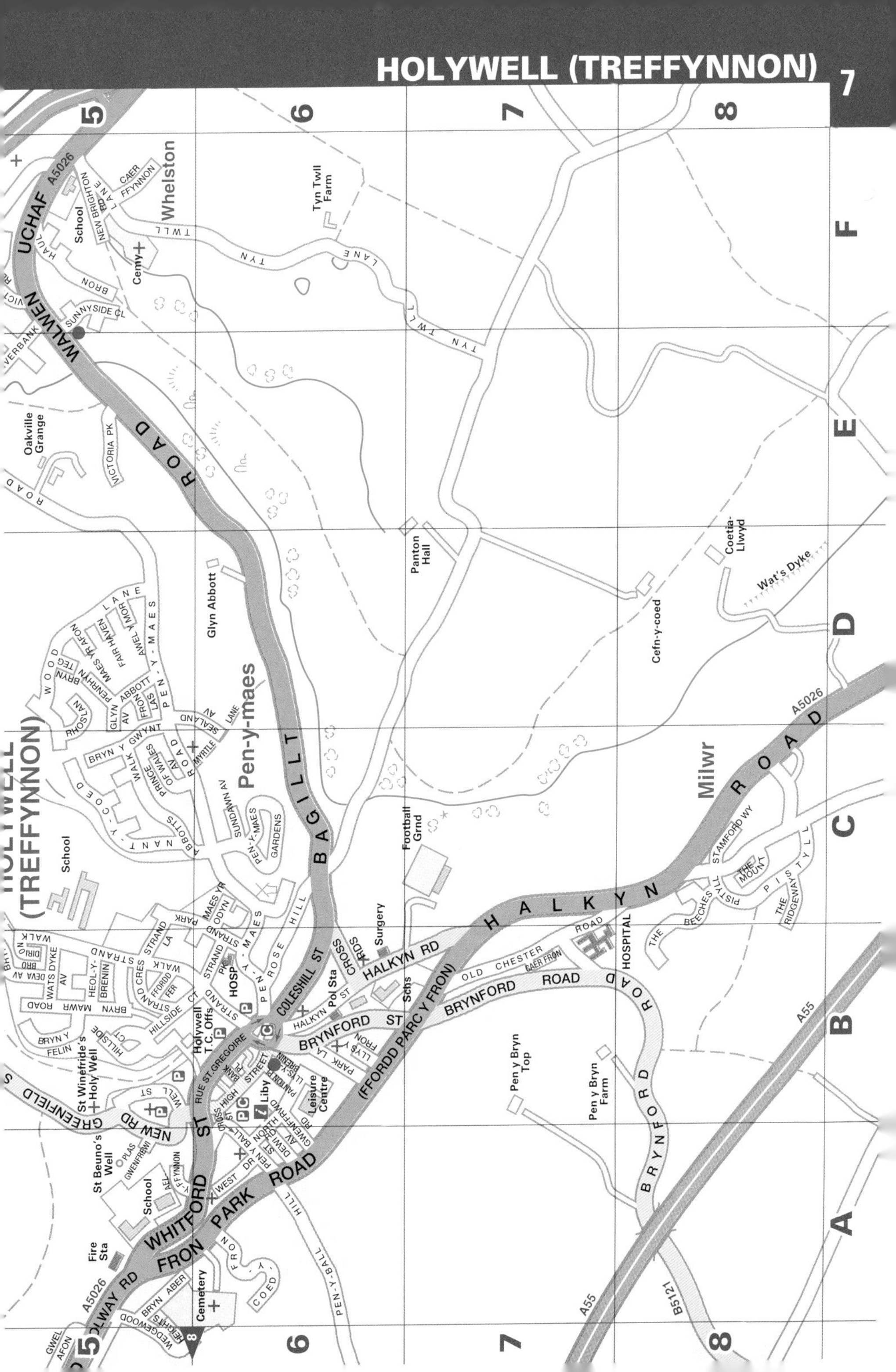
Whelston
Tyn Twll Farm
TYN TWLL LANE
School
Cemy
UCHAF
A5026
WALWEN ROAD
NEW BRIGHTON RD
CAER FFYNNON
SUNNYSIDE CL
BRON
HAUL
Oakville Grange
VICTORIA PK
Glyn Abbott
Pen-y-maes
Panton Hall
Coetia-Llwyd
Wat's Dyke
Cefn-y-coed
HOLYWELL (TREFFYNNON)
BAGILLT ROAD
PEN-Y-MAES
GLYN ABBOTT
BRYN Y GWYNT
PRINCE OF WALES AV
SUNDAWN AV
PEN-Y-MAES GARDENS
ABBOTTS
NANT-Y-COED
SEALAND AV
MYRTLE
LANE
PEN-Y-MAES LANE
FAIR HAVEN
AWEL Y MOR
MAES YR AFON
PENRHYN
BRYN TEG
RHOSLAN
WOOD
School
Football Grnd
Surgery
Milwr
HALKYN ROAD
A5026
STAMFORD WY
THE MOUNT
PISTYLL
THE RIDGEWAY
THE BEECHES
HOSPITAL
OLD CHESTER ROAD
CAER FRON
BRYNFORD ROAD
BRYNFORD ST
HALKYN RD
CROSS RDS
COLESHILL ST
PENROSE HILL
STRAND
MAES YR ODYN
PARK
Pol Sta
Schs
HOSP
(FFORDD PARC Y FRON)
Holywell T.C. Offs
RUE ST.GREGOIRE
HIGH STREET
Liby
Leisure Centre
GWENFFRWD RD
DEWI AV
ST NORTH
PEN Y BALL
WEST DR
St Winefride's Holy Well
St Beuno's Well
PLAS GWENFFRWD
WELL ST
NEW RD
GREENFIELD
FFYNNON
School
Fire Sta
WHITFORD ST
FRON PARK ROAD
A5026
HOLWAY RD
BRYN ABER
Cemetery
HEIGHTS
WEDGEWOOD
GWEL AFON
PEN-Y-BALL HILL
FRON-Y-COED
Pen y Bryn Top
Pen y Bryn Farm
BRYNFORD ROAD
A55
B5121
HEOL-Y-BRENIN
BRYN MAWR ROAD
WATS DYKE AV
DEVA AV
BRYN Y FELIN
HILLSIDE CT
STRAND CRES
FFORDD FER
WALK
5 6 7 8
A B C D E F

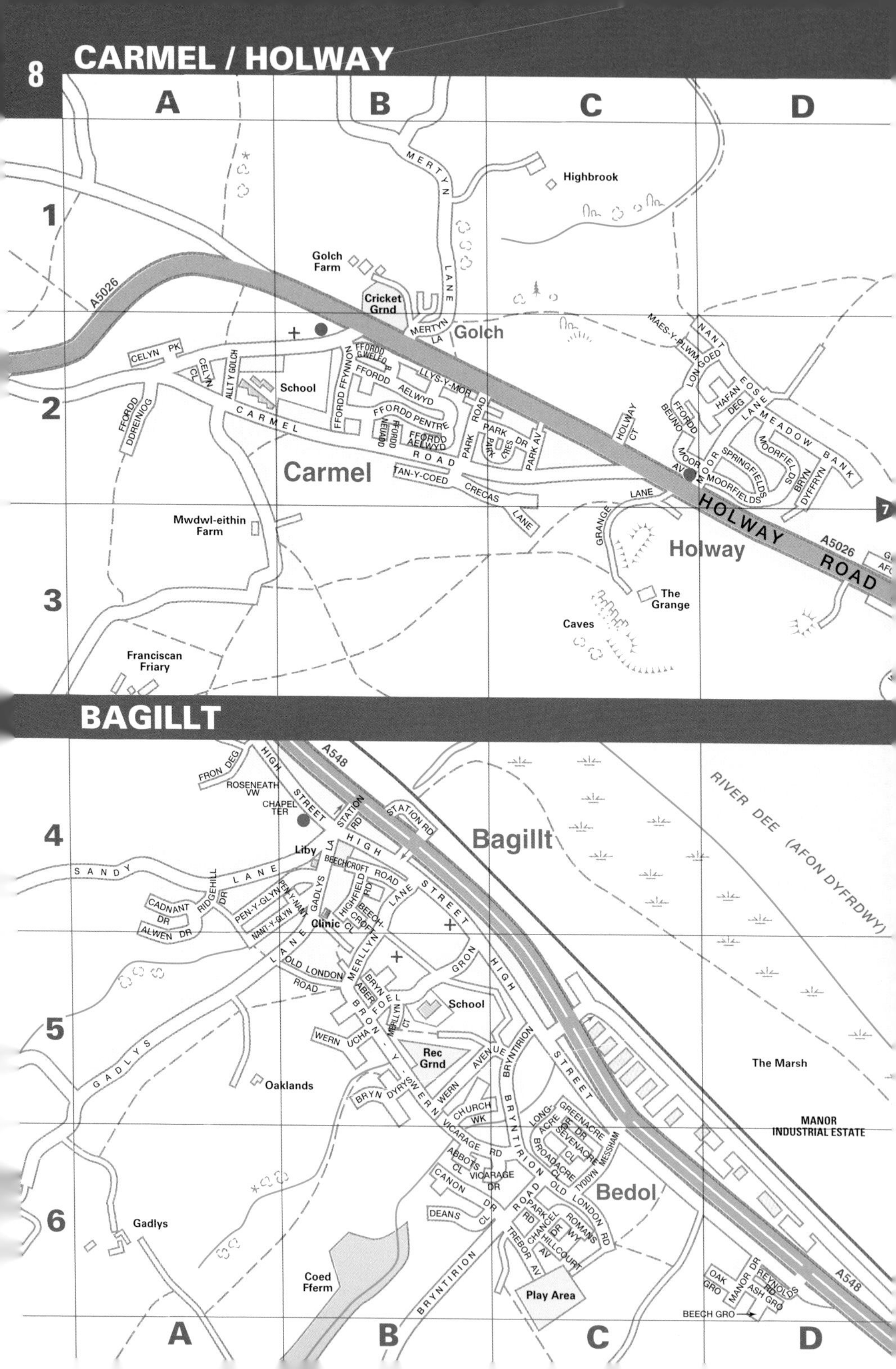
CARMEL / HOLWAY
A
B
C
D
1
2
3
Highbrook
MERTYN LANE
Golch Farm
Cricket Grnd
A5026
MERTYN LA
Golch
CELYN PK
CELYN CL
ALLT Y GOLCH
School
FFORDD FFYNNON
FFORDD G.WELEO
FFORDD AELWYD
LLYS-Y-MOR
FFORDD PENTRE
FFORDD NEUADD
FFORDD AELWYD
PARK ROAD
PARK DR
PARK AV
HOLWAY CT
FFORDD DDREINIOG
CARMEL ROAD
Carmel
TAN-Y-COED
CRECAS LANE
MAES-Y-PLWM
NANT
LON GOED
FFORDD BEUNO
HAFAN EOS
DEG
LANE
MEADOW BANK
MOOR AV
MOORFIELDS
SPRINGFIELDS
BRYN DYFFRYN
LANE
HOLWAY ROAD
7
Mwdwl-eithin Farm
GRANGE
Holway
The Grange
Caves
Franciscan Friary
BAGILLT
A548
FRON DEG
ROSENEATH VW
CHAPEL TER
HIGH STREET
STATION RD
RIVER DEE (AFON DYFRDWY)
Bagillt
4
Liby
SANDY LANE
RIDGEHILL DR
BEECHCROFT ROAD
HIGHFIELD RD
CADNANT DR
ALWEN DR
PEN-Y-GLYN
PEN-Y-NANT
NANT-Y-GLYN
GADLYS LANE
Clinic
BEECH-CROFT CL
OLD LONDON ROAD
MERLLYN
GRON
School
5
GADLYS
BRYN ABER
FOEL
BRON-Y-SWERN
MERLLYN CT
WERN UCHA
Rec Grnd
AVENUE
BRYNTIRION
Oaklands
BRYN DYRYS
WERN
CHURCH WK
The Marsh
LONG-ACRE
GREENACRE DR
SEVENACRE CL
BROADACRE
TYDDYN MESSHAM
MANOR INDUSTRIAL ESTATE
VICARAGE RD
ABBOTS CL
VICARAGE DR
CANON DR
OLD LONDON RD
Bedol
6
DEANS CL
ROAD
PARK RD
CHANCEL DR
ROMANS WY
HILLCOURT
Gadlys
TREBOR AV
BRYNTIRION
Coed Fferm
Play Area
OAK GRO
MANOR DR
REYNOLDS RD
ASH GRO
BEECH GRO

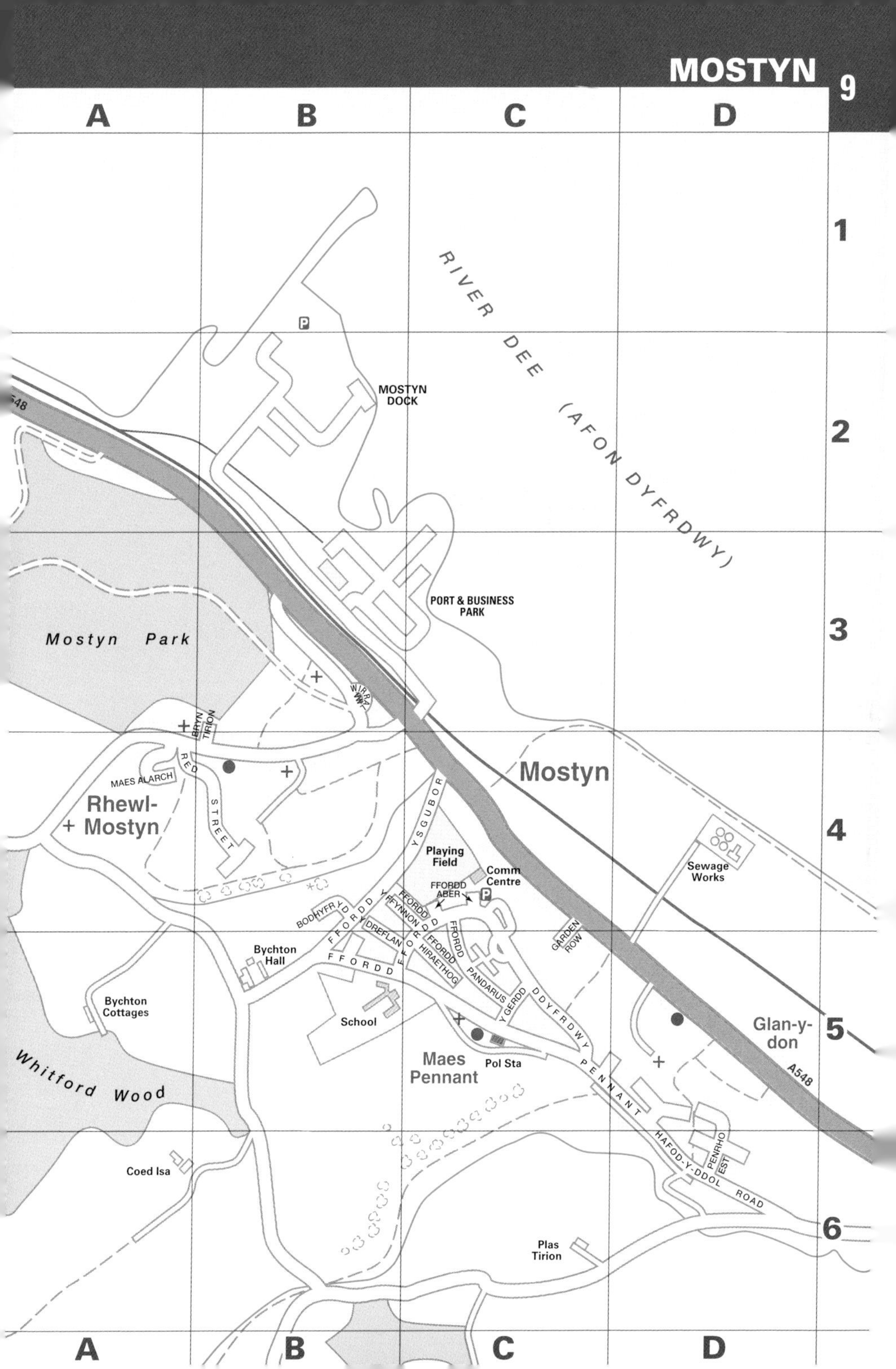
A
B
C
D
1
2
3
4
5
6
RIVER DEE (AFON DYFRDWY)
MOSTYN DOCK
PORT & BUSINESS PARK
A548
Mostyn Park
WIRRAL WAY
BRYN TIRION
RED STREET
MAES ALARCH
Rhewl-Mostyn
Mostyn
YSGUBOR
Playing Field
Comm Centre
FFORDD ABER
Sewage Works
BODHYFRYD
FFORDD Y FFYNNON
FFORDD DREFLAN
FFORDD HIRAETHOG
FFORDD PANDARUS
Y GERDD
GARDEN ROW
DDYFRDWY
Bychton Hall
Bychton Cottages
FFORDD
School
Maes Pennant
Pol Sta
PENNANT
Glan-y-don
Whitford Wood
HAFOD-Y-DDOL ROAD
PENRHO EST
Coed Isa
Plas Tirion

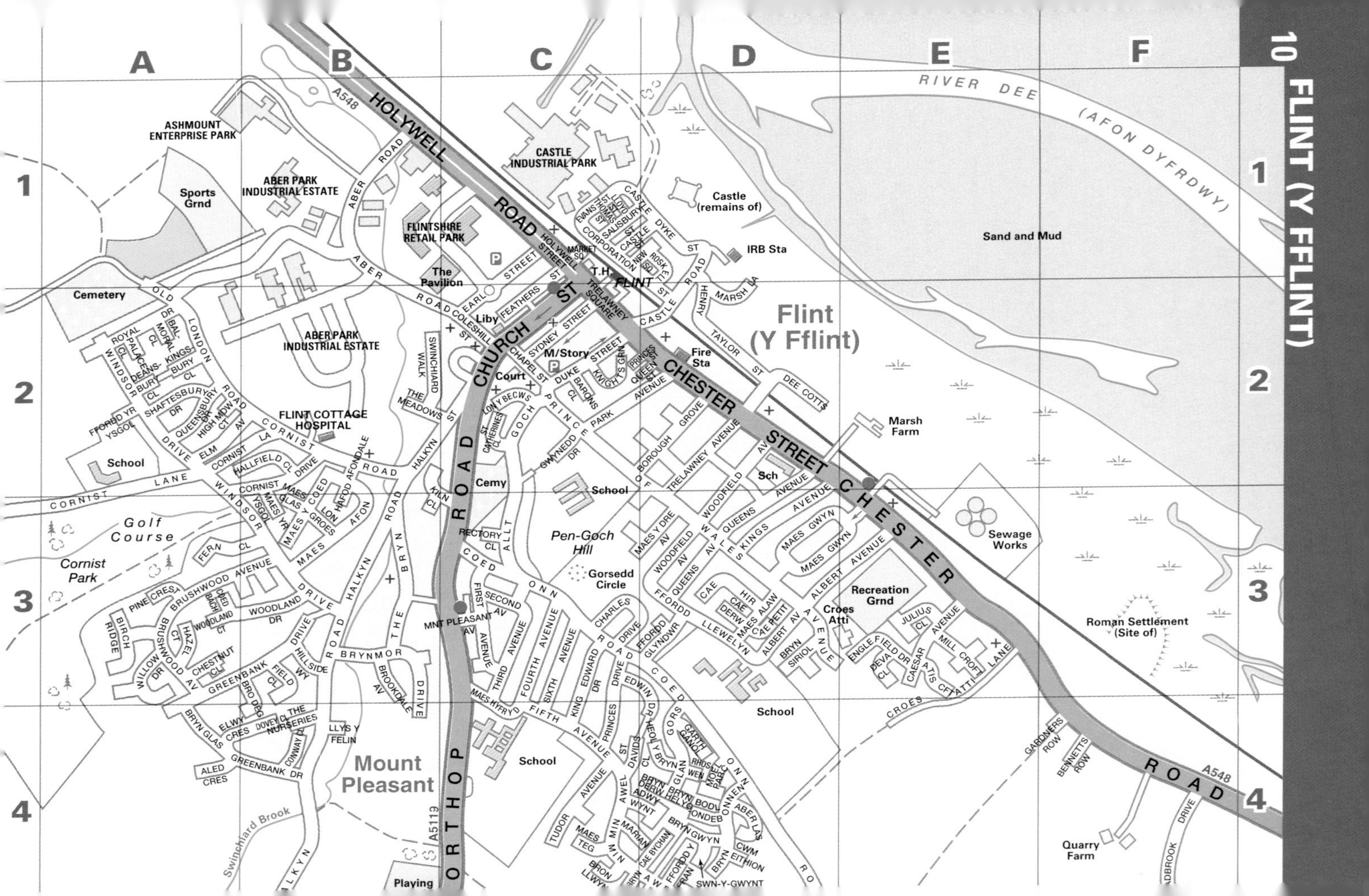
RIVER DEE (AFON DYFRDWY)
Sand and Mud
Flint (Y Fflint)
Castle (remains of)
IRB Sta
Fire Sta
Marsh Farm
Sewage Works
Roman Settlement (Site of)
Quarry Farm
Recreation Grnd
Croes Atti
School
Sch
Pen-Goch Hill
Gorsedd Circle
Cemy
Court
Liby
M/Story
T.H.
FLINT
The Pavilion
FLINTSHIRE RETAIL PARK
CASTLE INDUSTRIAL PARK
ABER PARK INDUSTRIAL ESTATE
ASHMOUNT ENTERPRISE PARK
Sports Grnd
Cemetery
FLINT COTTAGE HOSPITAL
Golf Course
Cornist Park
Mount Pleasant
Playing
Swinchiard Brook
HOLYWELL ROAD
CHESTER ROAD
CHESTER STREET
CHURCH ST
ROAD
A548
ORTHOP A5119
ABER ROAD
EARL ROAD
COLESHILL ST
SWINCHIARD WALK
THE MEADOWS
HALKYN ROAD
HALKYN ST
THE BRYN
DUKE ST
SYDNEY STREET
CHAPEL ST
FEATHERS
TRELAWNEY SQUARE
HOLYWELL STREET
MARKET SQ
CORPORATION ST
CASTLE DYKE ST
SALISBURY ST
THOMAS ST
LLOYD ST
EVANS ST
CASTLE ST
MARSH LA
HENRY TAYLOR ST
DEE COTTS
PRINCE OF WALES AV
GROVE AVENUE
TRELAWNEY AVENUE
WOODFIELD AV
QUEENS AV
KINGS AVENUE
MAES GWYN
ALBERT AVENUE
ALBERT AV
BRYN SIRIOL
CAE HIR
MAES LLEWELYN
FFORDD GLYNDWR
ALLT GOCH
COED ONN ROAD
CHARLES DRIVE
PRINCES AVENUE
KING EDWARD DR
SIXTH AVENUE
FIFTH AVENUE
FOURTH AVENUE
THIRD AVENUE
SECOND AV
FIRST AVENUE
RECTORY CL
MNT PLEASANT AV
KILN CL
BROOKDALE DRIVE
BROOKDALE AV
BRYNMOR ROAD
HILLSIDE DRIVE
WOODLAND DRIVE
WOODLAND CT
BRUSHWOOD AVENUE
HAZEL CT
BIRCH RIDGE
PINE CRES
WILLOW DR
GREENBANK DR
ELWY CRES
BRYN GLAS
ALED CRES
CONWAY CL
LLYS Y FELIN
AFONDALE ROAD
HAFOD
MAES Y GROES
MAES YR YSGOL
CORNIST LA
CORNIST DRIVE
CORNIST LANE
WINDSOR DRIVE
LONDON ROAD
OLD LONDON ROAD
BALMORAL CL
ROYAL DR
KINGS CL
SHAFTESBURY DR
QUEENSBURY CT
HIGH MDW
ELM CT
FFORDD YR YSGOL
HALLFIELD CL
TUDOR AVENUE
MAES TEG
GORS
EDWIN DR
ST DAVIDS CL
CAESAR AVENUE
JULIUS CL
ENGLEFIELD DR
DEVA CL
MILL CROFT
ATIS CROES
BENNETTS ROW
GARDNERS ROW
CROES
SWN-Y-GWYNT

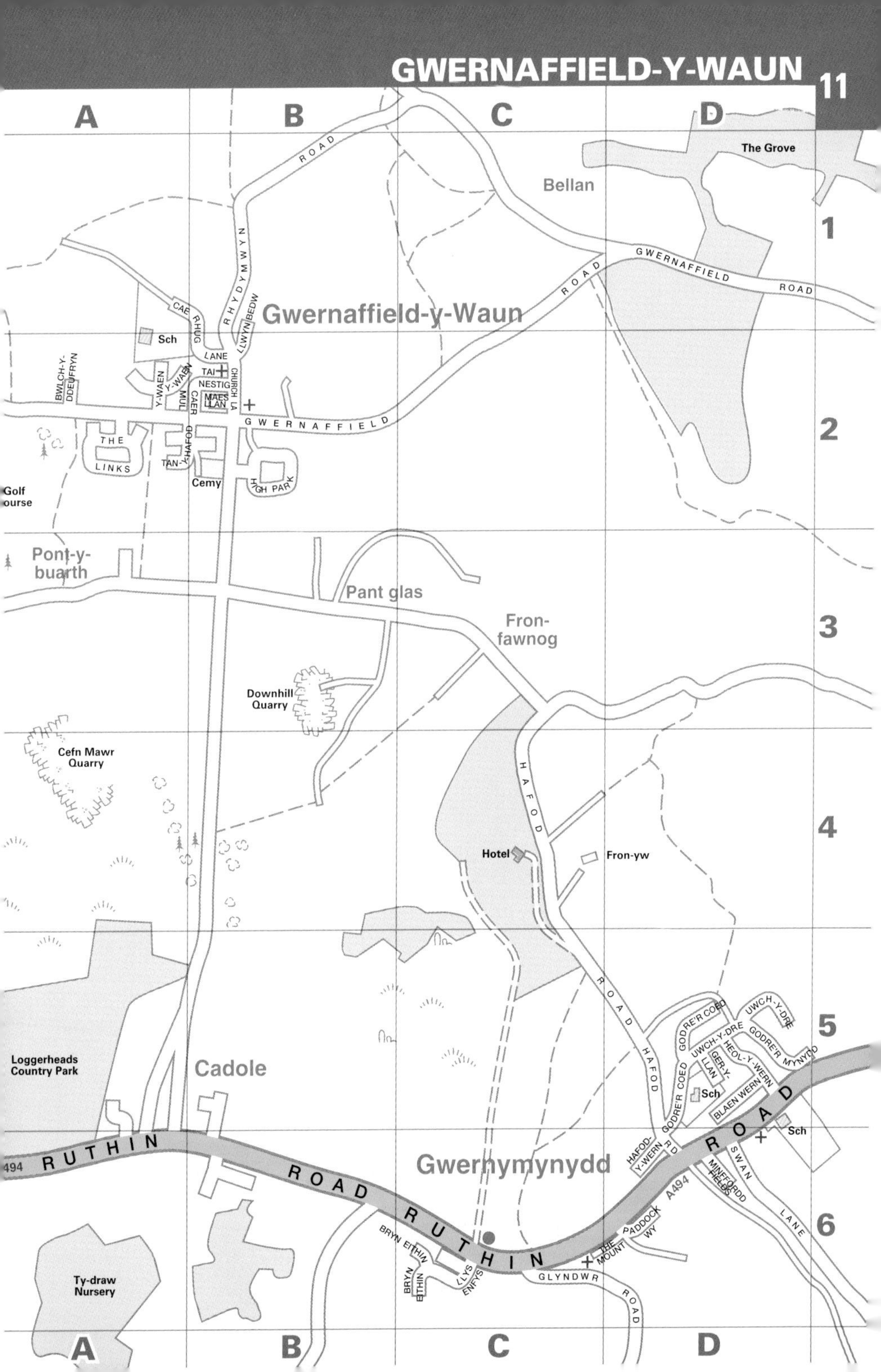

A
B
C
D
1
2
3
4
5
6
The Grove
Bellan
GWERNAFFIELD ROAD
ROAD
RHYDYMWYN
Gwernaffield-y-Waun
LLWYN BEDW
CAE RHUG
LANE
Sch
BWLCH-Y-DDEUFRYN
Y-WAEN
TAI NESTIG
MAES LLAN
CHURCH LA
CAER MUL
GWERNAFFIELD
THE LINKS
TAN-Y-HAFOD
HIGH PARK
Cemy
Golf ourse
Pont-y-buarth
Pant glas
Fron-fawnog
Downhill Quarry
Cefn Mawr Quarry
HAFOD ROAD
Hotel
Fron-yw
GODRE'R COED
UWCH-Y-DRE
GODRE'R MYNYDD
HEOL-Y-WERN
GER-Y-LLAN
BLAEN WERN
Sch
Loggerheads Country Park
Cadole
Gwernymynydd
HAFOD-Y-WERN
A494
RUTHIN ROAD
MINFFORDD FIELDS
SWAN LANE
PADDOCK WY
THE MOUNT
GLYNDWR ROAD
BRYN EITHIN
LLYS ENFYS
Ty-draw Nursery

A
B
C
D
E
F
1
2
3
4
White Sands
RIVER DEE (AFON DYFRDWY)
Breakwater
A548
WEIGHBRIDGE RD
DEESIDE INDUSTRIAL PARK
14
Gas Power Station
Power Station
A548
FLINTSHIRE BRIDGE
Hostel
Kelsterton
LANE
KELSTERTON ROAD
B512
Deeside College
Works

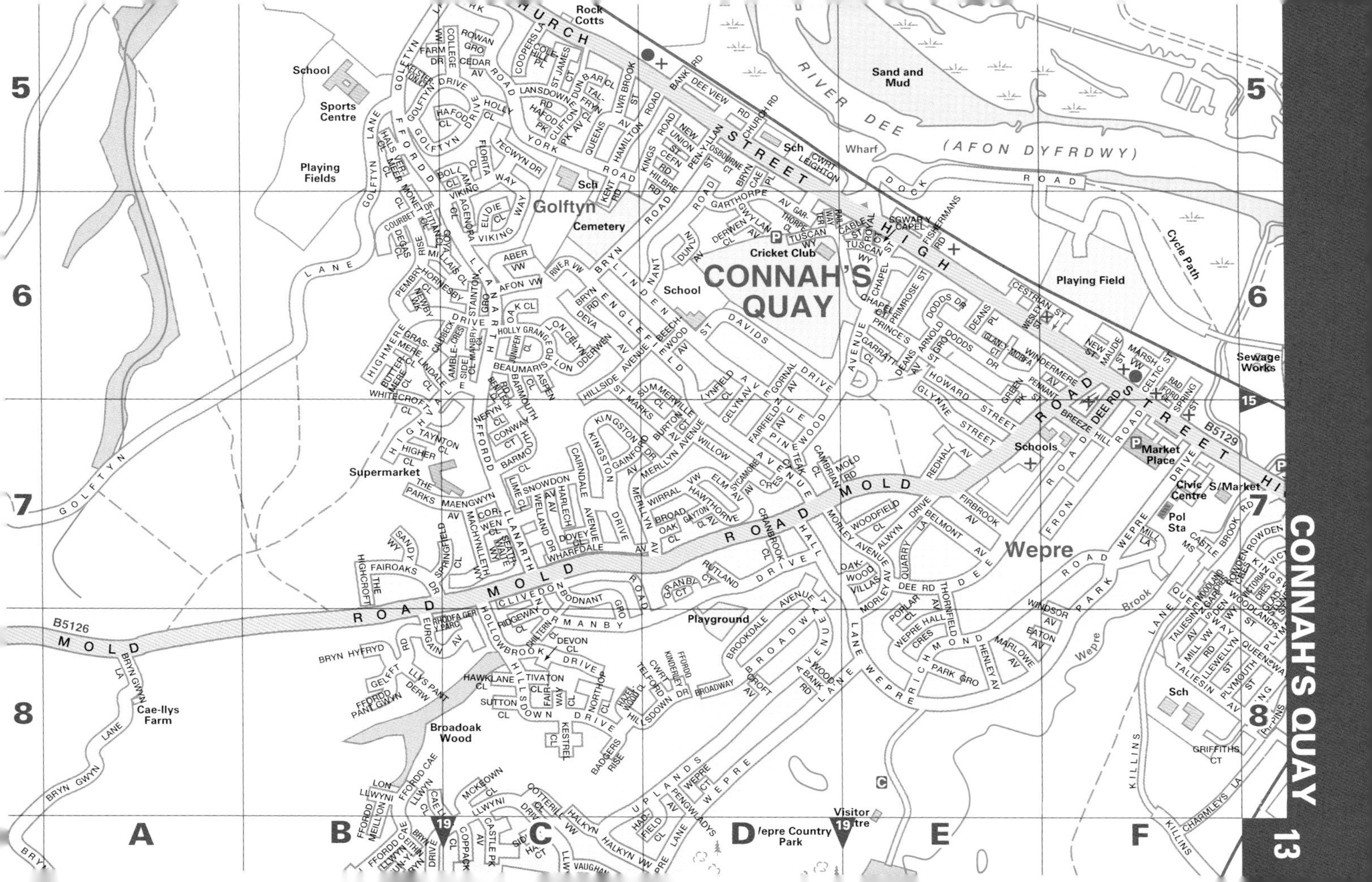
CONNAH'S QUAY
Wepre
Golftyn
RIVER DEE
(AFON DYFRDWY)
Sand and Mud
Wharf
DOCK ROAD
Cycle Path
Playing Field
Sewage Works
HIGH STREET
CHURCH
B5129
MOLD ROAD
B5126
WEPRE LANE
WEPRE DRIVE
KILLINS
CHARMLEYS LA
Civic Centre
Pol Sta
Market Place
S/Market
Schools
School
Sch
Cricket Club
Cemetery
Playground
Supermarket
Sports Centre
Playing Fields
Broadoak Wood
Visitor
Cae-llys Farm
BRYN GWYN LA
GOLFTYN LANE
LLANARTH
FFORDD LLANARTH
LINDEN
ENGLEFIELD AVENUE
NANT
ST DAVIDS DRIVE
Rock Cotts
5
6
7
8
A
B
C
D
E
F
15
19

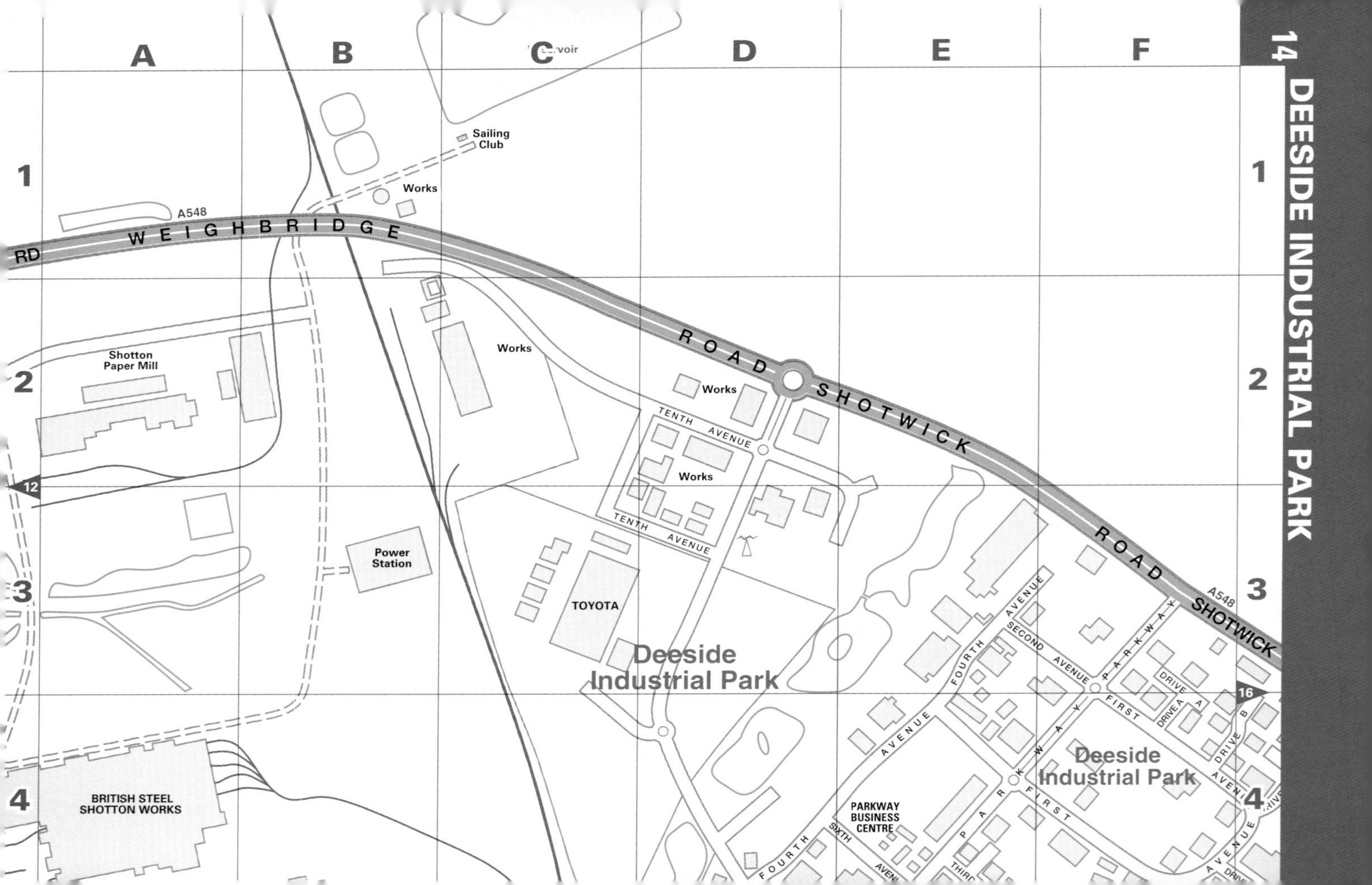

A
B
C
D
E
F
1
2
3
4
Sailing Club
Works
A548
WEIGHBRIDGE RD
ROAD SHOTWICK ROAD SHOTWICK
Shotton Paper Mill
Works
Works
TENTH AVENUE
Works
TENTH AVENUE
12
Power Station
TOYOTA
Deeside Industrial Park
SECOND AVENUE
FOURTH AVENUE
PARKWAY
FIRST
DRIVE A
DRIVE B
16
Deeside Industrial Park
BRITISH STEEL SHOTTON WORKS
PARKWAY BUSINESS CENTRE
SIXTH

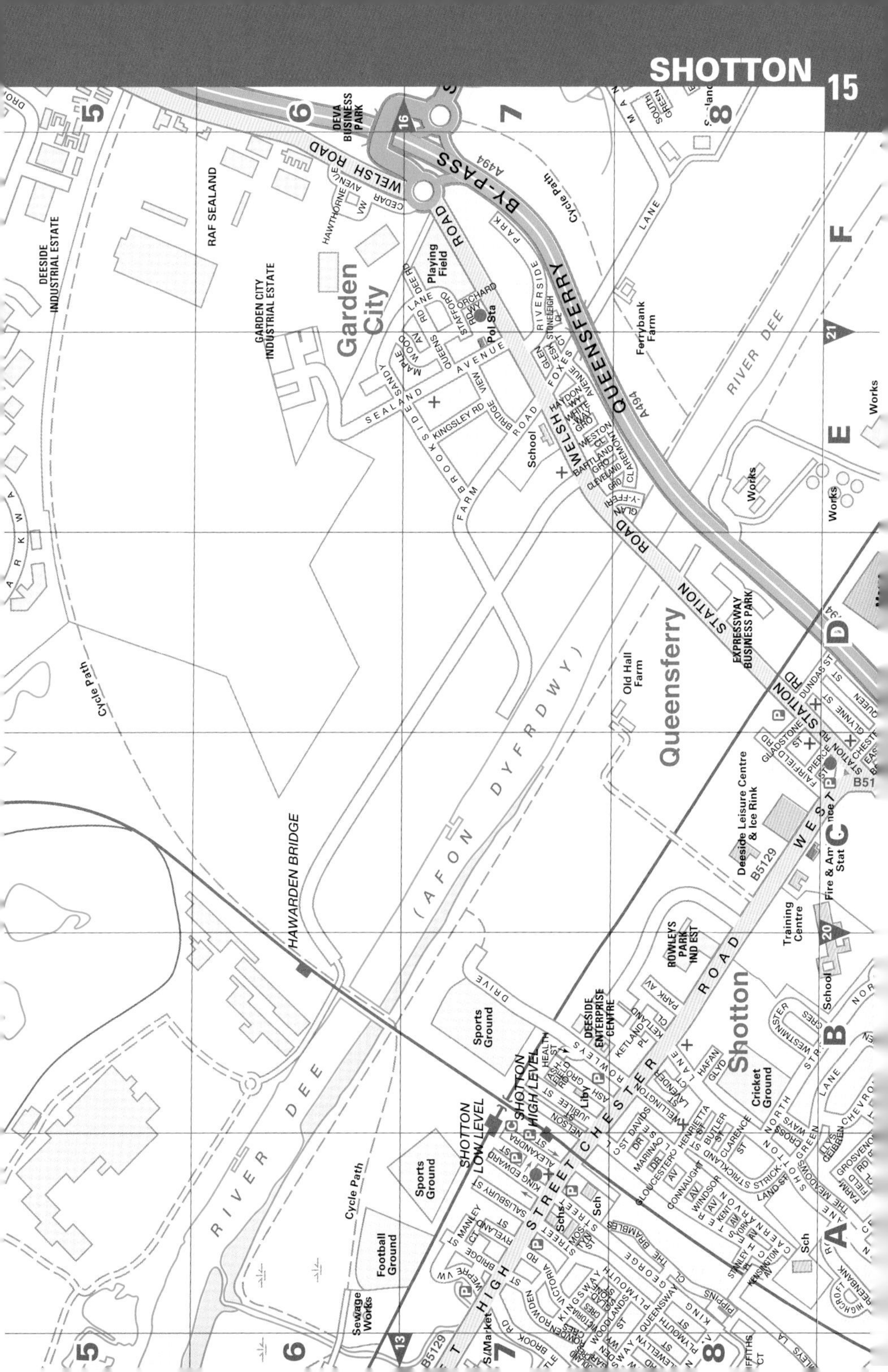
DEESIDE INDUSTRIAL ESTATE
RAF SEALAND
GARDEN CITY INDUSTRIAL ESTATE
DEVA BUSINESS PARK
WELSH ROAD
BY-PASS
A494
Cycle Path
Garden City
Playing Field
Pol Sta
School
QUEENSFERRY
Ferrybank Farm
RIVER DEE
Works
STATION ROAD
EXPRESSWAY BUSINESS PARK
Queensferry
Old Hall Farm
(AFON DYFRDWY)
HAWARDEN BRIDGE
Deeside Leisure Centre & Ice Rink
B5129
Fire & Amb Stat
Training Centre
ROWLEYS PARK IND EST
DEESIDE ENTERPRISE CENTRE
Sports Ground
Shotton
Cricket Ground
CHESTER ROAD
SHOTTON HIGH LEVEL
SHOTTON LOW LEVEL
Liby
HIGH STREET
Football Ground
Sewage Works
S/Market

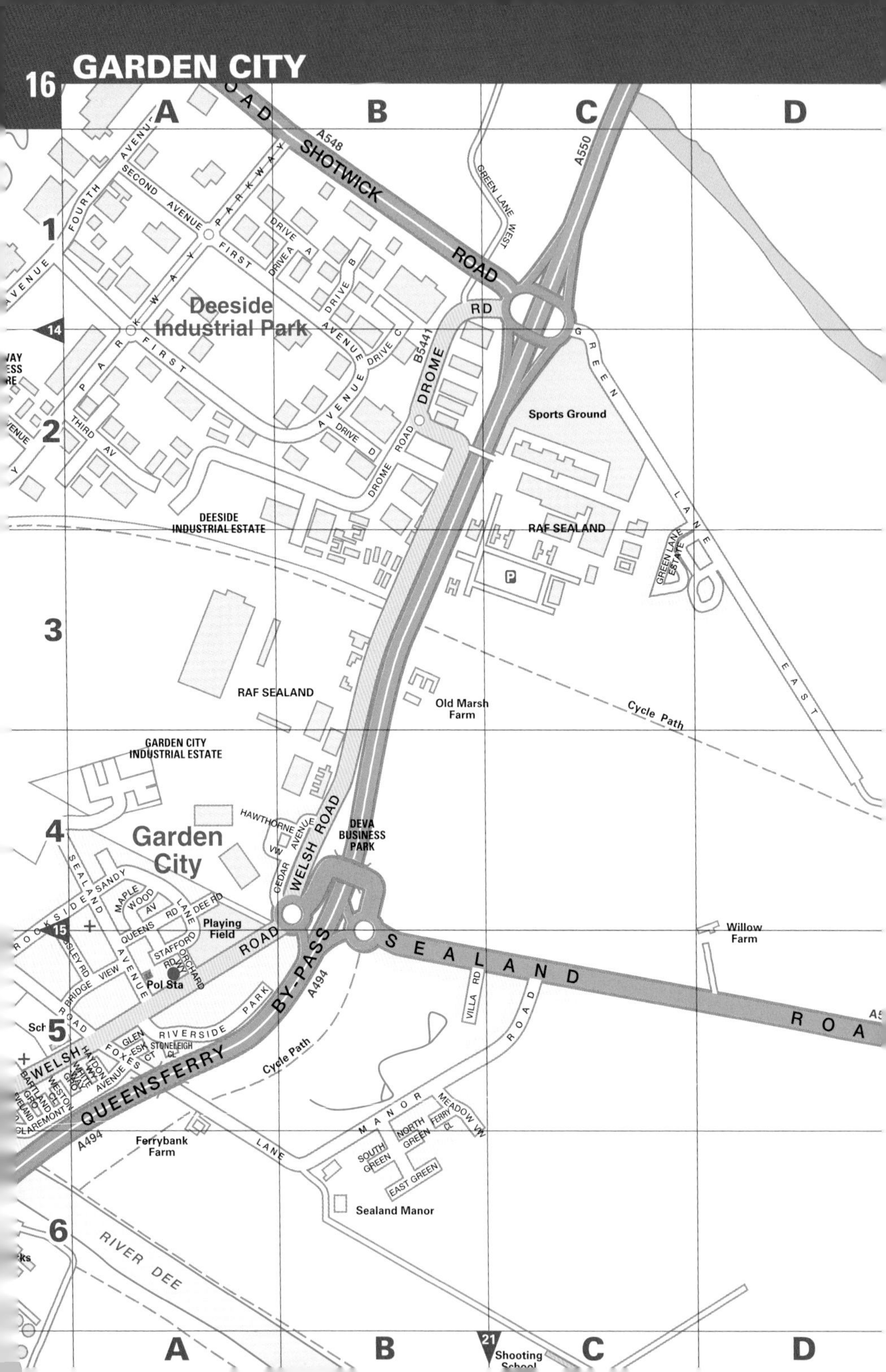

A
B
C
D
1
2
3
4
5
6
14
15
21
SHOTWICK ROAD
A548
A550
GREEN LANE WEST
FOURTH AVENUE
SECOND AVENUE
PARKWAY
FIRST AVENUE
DRIVE A
DRIVE B
DRIVE C
DRIVE D
AVENUE
Deeside Industrial Park
RD
B5441
DROME ROAD
GREEN LANE
Sports Ground
THIRD AV
DEESIDE INDUSTRIAL ESTATE
RAF SEALAND
P
GREEN LANE ESTATE
EAST
Old Marsh Farm
Cycle Path
GARDEN CITY INDUSTRIAL ESTATE
HAWTHORNE AVENUE
VW
CEDAR
WELSH ROAD
DEVA BUSINESS PARK
Garden City
SEALAND AVENUE
SANDY LANE
MAPLE WOOD AV
QUEENS RD
DEE RD
Playing Field
ROCKSIDE
STAFFORD RD
ORCHARD WY
Pol Sta
BRIDGE VIEW
ROAD
BY-PASS
A494
SEALAND ROAD
VILLA RD
Willow Farm
RIVERSIDE PARK
GLEN ESK CT
STONELEIGH CL
FOXES
WELSH
QUEENSFERRY
Cycle Path
WESTON GRO
CLAREMONT
BARTLAND
MANOR LANE
NORTH GREEN
FERRY CL
MEADOW VW
SOUTH GREEN
EAST GREEN
Ferrybank Farm
Sealand Manor
RIVER DEE
Shooting School

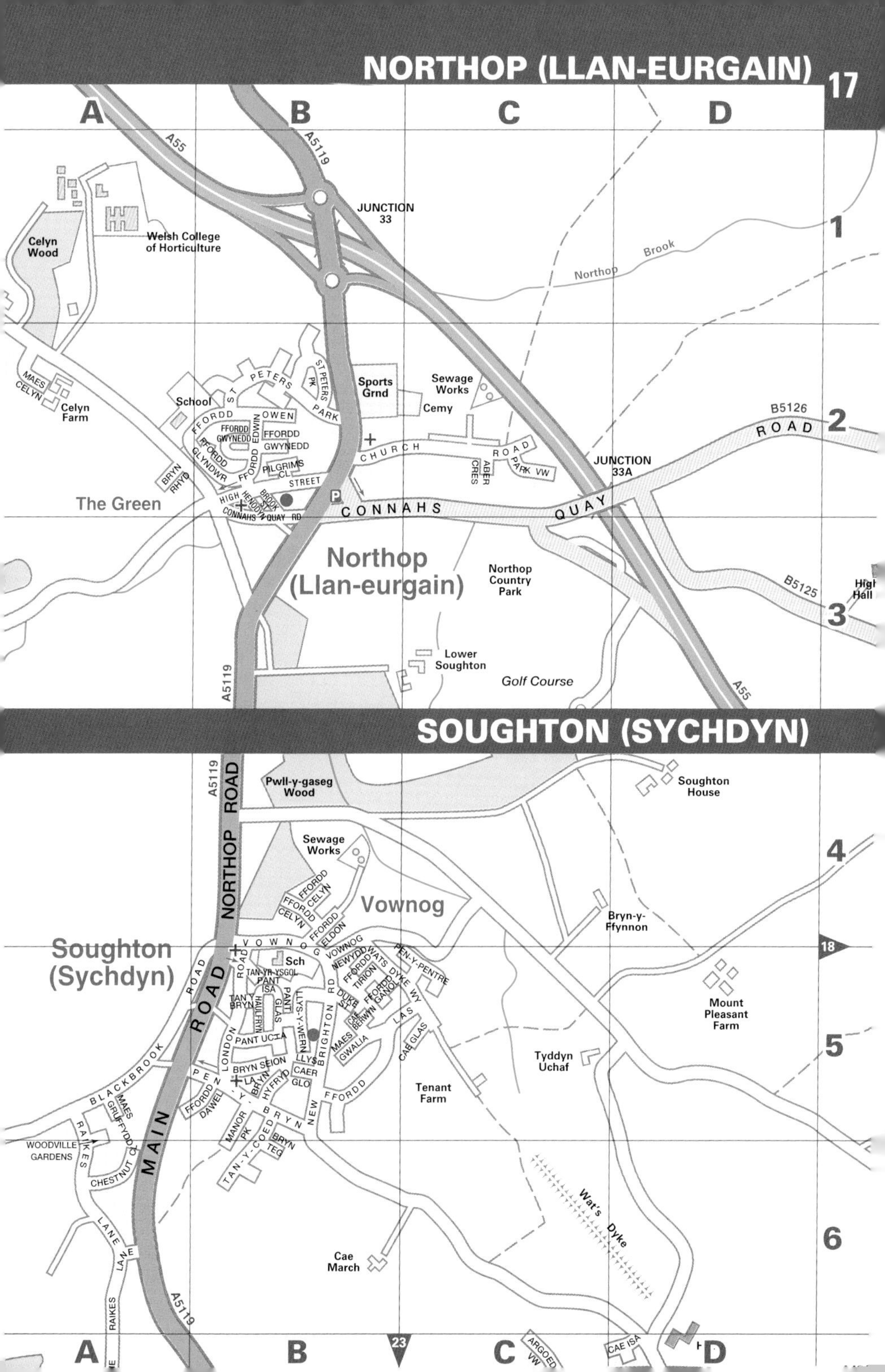

NORTHOP (LLAN-EURGAIN)
A
B
C
D
A55
A5119
JUNCTION 33
Celyn Wood
Welsh College of Horticulture
Northop Brook
MAES CELYN
Celyn Farm
School
ST PETERS
ST PETERS PK
PARK
Sports Grnd
Sewage Works
Cemy
FFORDD OWEN
FFORDD EDWIN
FFORDD GWYNEDD
FFORDD GLYNDWR
PILGRIMS CL
CHURCH ROAD
ABER CRES
PARK VW
B5126
ROAD
JUNCTION 33A
BRYN RHYD
The Green
HIGH STREET
HENDDWR
BROOK ST
CONNAHS QUAY RD
CONNAHS QUAY
Northop (Llan-eurgain)
Northop Country Park
B5125
High Hall
Lower Soughton
Golf Course
SOUGHTON (SYCHDYN)
NORTHOP ROAD
Pwll-y-gaseg Wood
Soughton House
Sewage Works
FFORDD CELYN
Vownog
Bryn-y-Ffynnon
Soughton (Sychdyn)
VOWNOG
Sch
TAN-YR-YSGOL
PANT ISA
PANT GLAS
TAN Y BRYN
HAULFRYN
LLYS-Y-WERN
BRIGHTON RD
NEWYDD
FFORDD TIRION
WATS DYKE WY
PEN-Y-PENTRE
FFORDD GANOL
CAE BERWYN
MAES GWALIA
CAE GLAS
LAS
Mount Pleasant Farm
18
PANT UCHA
LONDON ROAD
BRYN SEION
LLYS CAER GLO
BLACKBROOK
MAES GRUFFYDD
FFORDD DAWEL
PEN Y BRYN
HYFRYD
NEW BRYN
FFORDD
Tenant Farm
Tyddyn Uchaf
MAIN ROAD
WOODVILLE GARDENS
RAIKES
CHESTNUT
MANOR PK
TAN-Y-COED
BRYN TEG
Wat's Dyke
LANE
Cae March
A5119
RAIKES
23
ARGOED VW
CAE ISA

A
B
C
D
1
2
3
4
5
6
B5125
Galchog
Highfield Hall Hotel
Highfield Livery Stables
SMITHY LANE
Cricket Ground
THE RIDGEWAY
NEWTON CL
QUARRY CL
THE GROVE
ALUN CL
TUDOR CL
CHURCH CL
ST MARYS CL
School
LLYS BEN
GARDD
LLYS EITHIN
EITHIN
BRYN GWYN
TRUM-YR-HAF
HYDREF
CAE
GARDD-YR-
GWANWYN
LLYS Y
WENNOL
PRIMROSE CL
WEPRE LANE
17
A55
ELM
DR
ST MARYS DR
BROOKSIDE
BROOKSIDE CRES
YW DR
MOEL
WARED DR
Northop Hall
INSTITUTE LA
GOODWOOD GRO
WHITE OAKS DR
MONZA CL
DRIVE
DAYTONA
SEBRING AV
Wared Wood
Brook Park Farm
Hotel
EAST BOUND SERVICES
LANE
PINFOLD
MAGAZINE LA
Greenbank
Ewloe Wood House
PINFOLD LA
Workshop
A55 Westbound Services
Cobblers Wood
Warehouse
Cobblers Wood Farm
Depot
Alltami Brook
Stoneybeach Wood
EWLOE BARNS INDUSTRIAL ESTATE
Oaks Farm
Alltami
A494
Pinfold Workshops
23

Wepre Country Park
Visitor Centre
School
Golf Course
Wepre Wood
Wepre Inn
Ewloe Wood
Wepre Brook
STAMFORD WAY
Ewloe Castle (Remains of)
New Inn Brook
Castle Hill Farm
Stamford Way Farm
HOLYWELL ROAD
New Inn Bridge Farm
Aston Hill Farm
SHOTTON LANE
CHURCH LANE
Playing Field
Ewloe Green
LIVERPOOL ROAD
MOLD ROAD
OLD MOLD RD
School
Hotel
B5125 CHESTER RD
Redrow Offices
Offices
St Davids Park
A55 JUNCTION 34
LAKESIDE BUSINESS VILLAGE
Ewloe
Red Lion Inn
Ewloe Hall
B5127
A55
A494

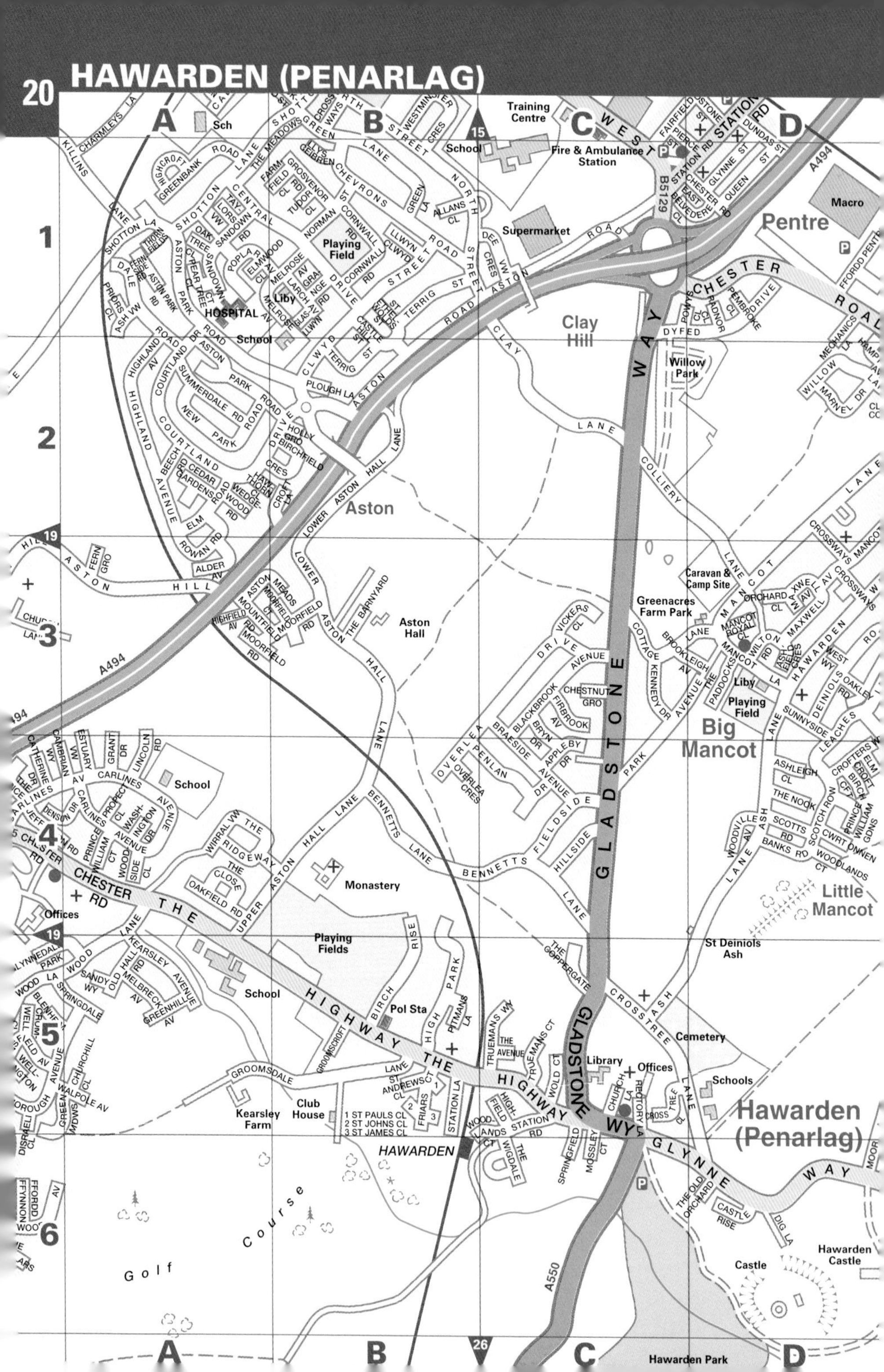
Training Centre
School
Fire & Ambulance Station
Supermarket
Macro
Pentre
Sch
HOSPITAL
School
Liby
Playing Field
Clay Hill
Willow Park
Aston
Aston Hall
Caravan & Camp Site
Greenacres Farm Park
Liby
Playing Field
Big Mancot
Little Mancot
School
Monastery
Offices
Playing Fields
School
Pol Sta
St Deiniols Ash
Cemetery
Library
Offices
Schools
Hawarden (Penarlag)
Kearsley Farm
Club House
HAWARDEN
Golf Course
Castle
Hawarden Castle
Hawarden Park
A494
A550
B5129
GLADSTONE WAY
CHESTER ROAD
THE HIGHWAY
GLYNNE WAY
ASTON HILL
LOWER ASTON HALL LANE
BENNETTS LANE
CROSS TREE
1 ST PAULS CL
2 ST JOHNS CL
3 ST JAMES CL
A
B
C
D
1
2
3
4
5
6
15
19
26

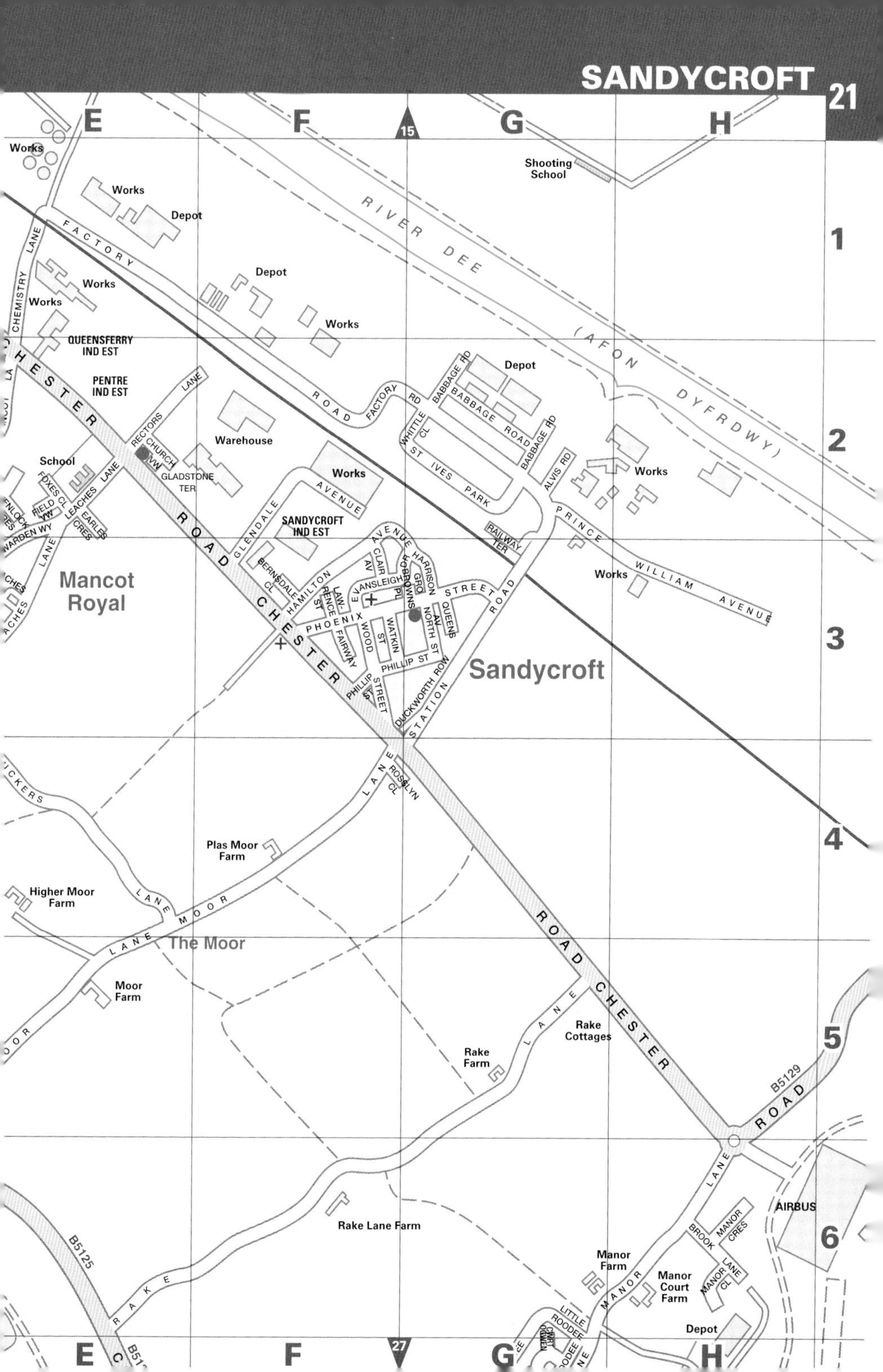
E
F
G
H
15
27
1
2
3
4
5
6
Works
Shooting School
Depot
RIVER DEE
(AFON DYFRDWY)
FACTORY ROAD
CHEMISTRY LANE
Depot
Works
QUEENSFERRY IND EST
PENTRE IND EST
CHESTER ROAD
Warehouse
Works
SANDYCROFT IND EST
Depot
BABBAGE RD
BABBAGE ROAD
WHITTLE CL
ST IVES PARK
ALVIS RD
PRINCE WILLIAM AVENUE
RAILWAY TER
School
RECTORS LANE
CHURCH VW
GLADSTONE TER
FOXES CL
LEACHES LANE
FIELD VW
EARLES CRES
WARDEN WY
GLENDALE AVENUE
BERNSDALE CL
HAMILTON
Mancot Royal
CLAIR AV
HARRISON GRO
EVANSLEIGH
BROWNS PL
STREET
LAWRENCE ST
PHOENIX
FAIRWAY
WOOD ST
WATKIN ST
NORTH AV
QUEENS
PHILLIP ST
PHILLIP STREET
DUCKWORTH ROW
STATION ROAD
Sandycroft
ROSSLYN CL
LANE
Plas Moor Farm
Higher Moor Farm
MOOR LANE
The Moor
Moor Farm
Rake Cottages
Rake Farm
LANE
B5129
ROAD
AIRBUS
Rake Lane Farm
B5125
RAKE
Manor Farm
Manor Court Farm
MANOR LANE
BROOK LANE
MANOR CRES
MANOR CL
LITTLE RODDEE
Depot

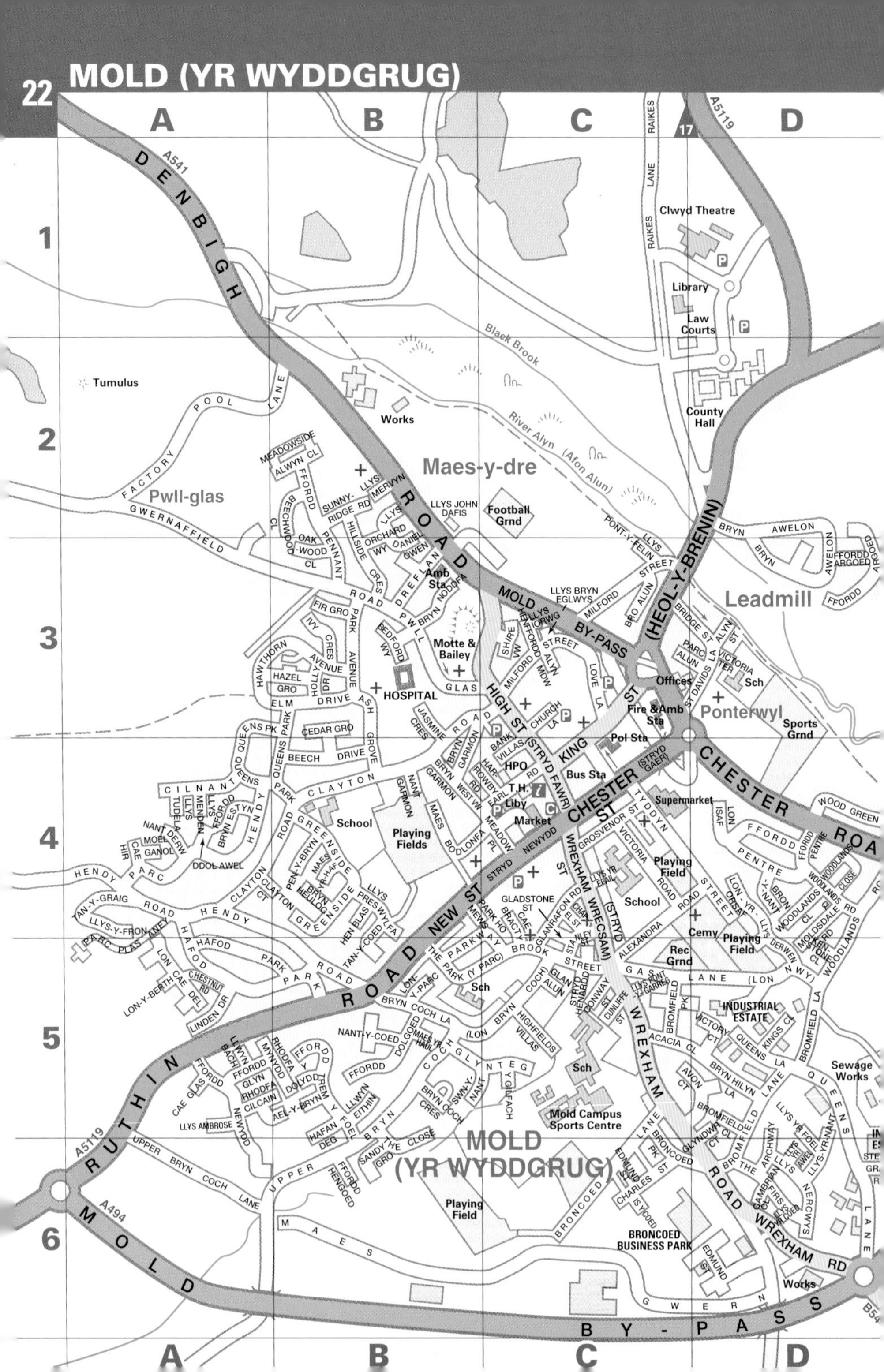
A
B
C
D
1
2
3
4
5
6
17
A541
A5119
A494
DENBIGH ROAD
Clwyd Theatre
Library
Law Courts
County Hall
RAIKES LANE
Black Brook
River Alyn (Afon Alun)
Tumulus
POOL LANE
FACTORY
Pwll-glas
GWERNAFFIELD
Works
Maes-y-dre
MEADOWSIDE
ALWYN CL
FFORDD BEECHWOOD
SUNNY-RIDGE RD
LLYS MERVYN
LLYS JOHN DAFIS
Football Grnd
PONT-Y-FELIN
LLYS
(HEOL-Y-BRENIN)
BRYN AWELON
FFORDD ARGOED
Leadmill
OAK-WOOD CL
PENNANT
HILLSIDE CRES
ORCHARD WY
LLYS DANIEL OWEN
DREFLAN
Amb Sta
NODDFA
MOLD BY-PASS
LLYS BRYN EGLWYS
MILFORD STREET
BRO ALUN
BRIDGE ST
ALYN ST
FIR GRO
IVY CRES
PARK AVENUE
PWLL
BRYN
BEDFORD WY
Motte & Bailey
SHIRE VW
HENFFORDD
LLYS IORWG
ALYN MDW
STREET
LOVE LA
Offices
PARC ALUN
VICTORIA TER
ST DAVIDS LA
Sch
HAWTHORN
AVENUE
HOLLY DR
HAZEL GRO
ELM DRIVE
ASH
HOSPITAL
GLAS
MILFORD
HIGH ST (STRYD FAWR)
CHURCH LA
Fire & Amb Sta
Ponterwyl
Sports Grnd
QUEENS PK
CEDAR GRO
BEECH DRIVE
GROVE
JASMINE CRES
ROAD
BRYN GARMON
BANK VILLAS
KING ST
Pol Sta
CHESTER ST (STRYD GAER)
CHESTER ROAD
HPO
Bus Sta
Supermarket
WOOD GREEN
CILNANT
TUDELA
LLYS MENDEN
LLYS FFOROD
BRYN ESTYN
QUEENS
HENDY
CLAYTON
School
Playing Fields
NANT GARMON
MAES BODLONFA
HARROWBY RD
WEST VW
EARL RD
T.H.
Liby
Market
TYDDYN
GROSVENOR ST
LON ISAF
FFORDD PENTRE
NANT DERW
MOEL
CAE GANOL
HIR
DDOL AWEL
HENDY PARC
GREENSIDE
PEN-Y-BRYN
MAES
BRYN HEULOG
MEADOW PL
NEWYDD
STRYD NEWYDD
WREXHAM ST
VICTORIA ROAD
Playing Field
WOODLANDS CLOSE
TAN-Y-GRAIG
LLYS-Y-FRON
PARC PLAS
ANEY
CLAYTON CT
LLYS PRESWYLFA
HEN BLAS
TAN-Y-COED
NEW ST
GLADSTONE ST
CAE BRACTY
PARK HO
MEWS
GLANRAFON RD
WRECSAM
(STRYD
School
STREET
LON-YR-LLYS
MOLDSDALE RD
HAFOD
LON CAE DEL
CHESTNUT RD
PARK
ROAD
THE PARK (Y PARC)
PARKWAY
BROOK STREET
ALEXANDRA
Rec Grnd
Cemy
Playing Field
DERWEN
GAS LANE (LON NWY)
LON-Y-BERTH
LINDEN DR
LLYS-Y-PARC
Sch
COCH
GLAN ALUN
CONWAY
CUNLIFFE ST
BROMFIELD PK
INDUSTRIAL ESTATE
VICTORY CT
QUEENS LA
KINGS CL
BROMFIELD LA
BRYN COCH LA
NANT-Y-COED
DOLGOED
(LON BRYN)
HIGHFIELDS
VILLAS
WREXHAM
ACACIA CL
AVON CT
BRYN HILYN LA
Sewage Works
RUTHIN
LLWYN BACH
FFORDD
MYNYDD
RHODFA
GLYN
CILCAIN
DOLYDD
FFORDD
GLYNTEG
Y GILFACH
Sch
Mold Campus Sports Centre
CAE GLAS
LLYS AMBROSE
NEWYDD
HAFAN DEG
BRYN COCH CRES
SWN-Y-NANT
MOLD (YR WYDDGRUG)
BRONCOED LANE PK
GLYNDWR CT
BROMFIELD CL
LLYS YR FOEL
LLYS-YR-NANT
UPPER BRYN COCH LANE
UPPER
FFORDD HENGOED
SANDY GRO
THE CLOSE
EDMUND ST
CHARLES ST
SYCOED
Playing Field
BRONCOED
BRONCOED BUSINESS PARK
WREXHAM RD
MOLD
MAES
GWERN
BY-PASS
Works
LANE
B54

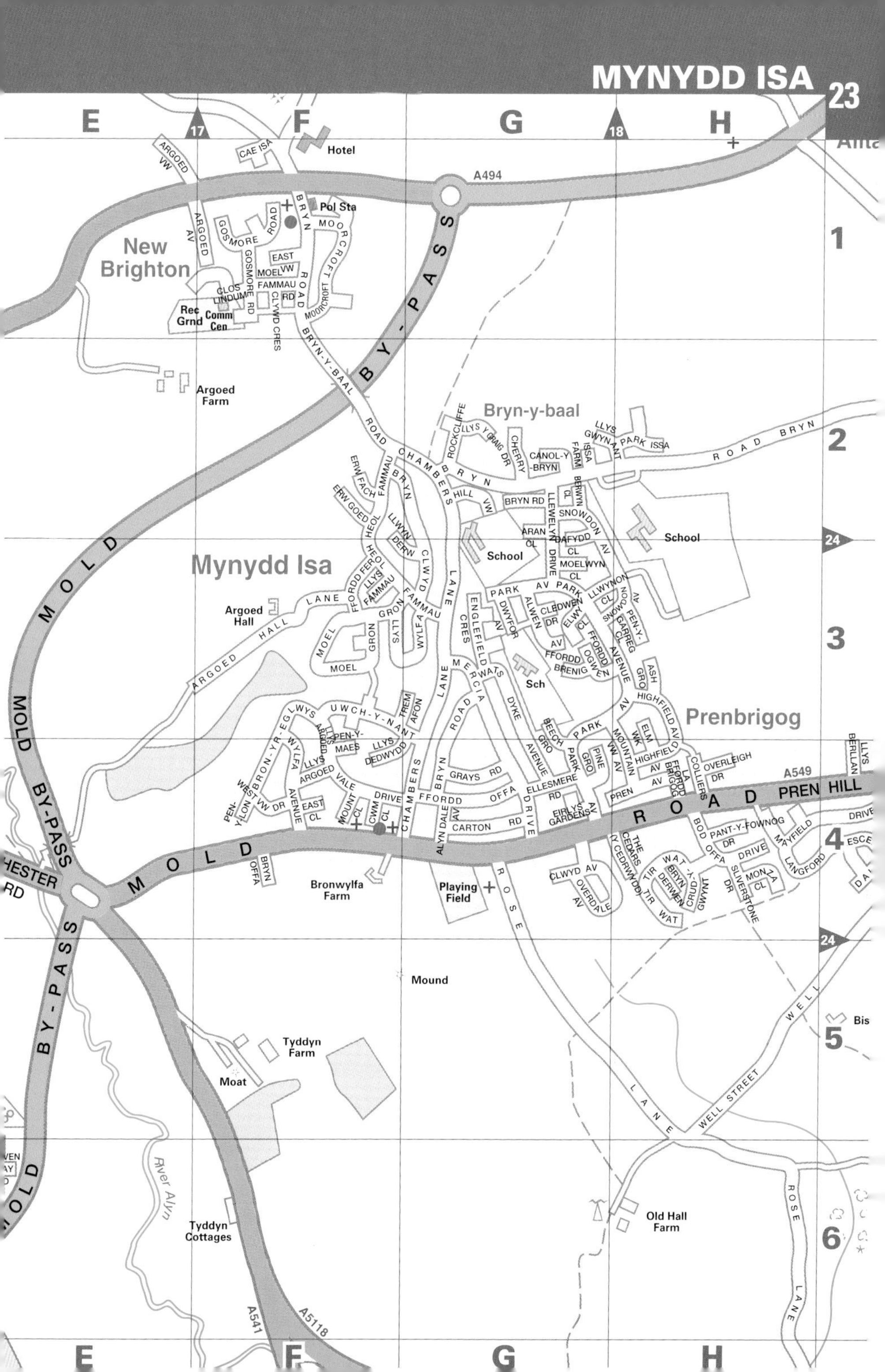
New Brighton
Mynydd Isa
Bryn-y-baal
Prenbrigog
Hotel
Pol Sta
Rec Grnd
Comm Cen
Argoed Farm
Argoed Hall
School
Sch
Bronwylfa Farm
Playing Field
Mound
Tyddyn Farm
Moat
Tyddyn Cottages
Old Hall Farm
River Alyn
A494
A549
A541
A5118
MOLD BY-PASS
MOLD ROAD
PREN HILL
ROAD BRYN
ARGOED HALL LANE
WELL STREET
ROSE LANE
CHAMBERS LANE
BRYN-Y-BAAL ROAD
MERCIA ROAD
ELLESMERE RD
CARTON RD
OFFA DRIVE
FFORDD

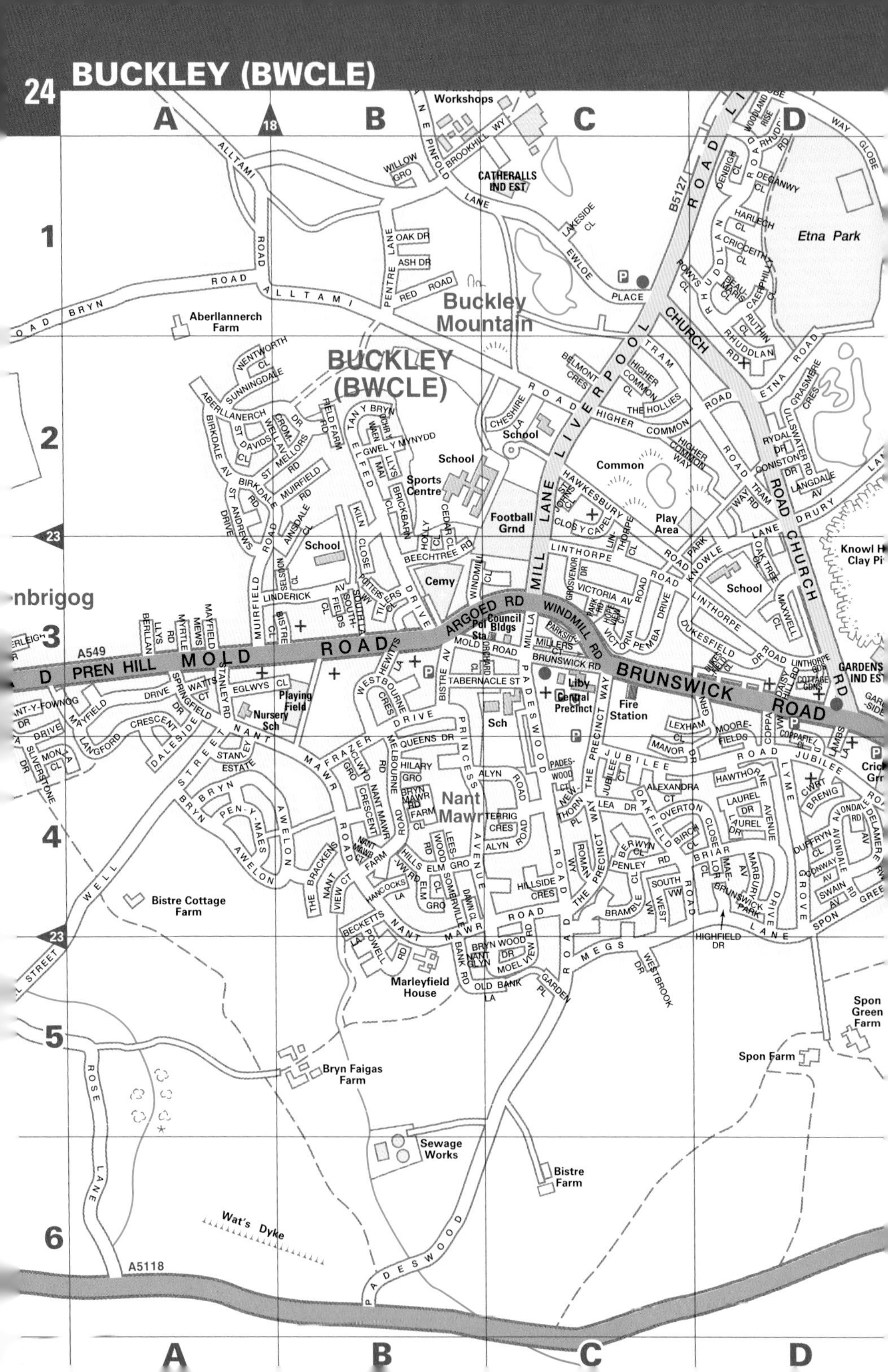
A
B
C
D
18
23
1
2
3
4
5
6
Workshops
WILLOW GRO
PINFOLD LANE
BROOKHILL WY
CATHERALLS IND EST
LAKESIDE CL
EWLOE PLACE
ALLTAMI ROAD
BRYN ROAD
OAK DR
ASH DR
PENTRE LANE
RED ROAD
Buckley Mountain
Aberllannerch Farm
B5127
LIVERPOOL ROAD
CHURCH ROAD
DENBIGH CL
WOODLAND RISE
RHUDDLAN RD
DEGANWY CL
HARLECH CL
CRICCIETH CL
BEAUMARIS CL
CAERPHILLY CL
POWYS CL
RUTHIN CL
Etna Park
ETNA ROAD
GLOBE WAY
BUCKLEY (BWCLE)
WENTWORTH CL
SUNNINGDALE
ABERLLANERCH DR
BIRKDALE AV
ST DAVIDS CL
ST MELLORS RD
MUIRFIELD RD
ST ANDREWS DRIVE
AINSDALE CL
FIELD FARM RD
TAN Y BRYN
GWEL Y MYNYDD
ELFED
School
Sports Centre
CHESHIRE LA
BELMONT CRES
HIGHER COMMON CL
THE HOLLIES
HIGHER COMMON ROAD
HIGHER COMMON WAY
Common
Play Area
TRAM ROAD
GRASMERE CRES
ULLSWATER RD
RYDAL DR
CONISTON DR
LANGDALE AV
DRURY LANE
HAWKESBURY
CLOS Y CAPEL
LINTHORPE CL
LINTHORPE ROAD
KNOWLE PARK ROAD
OAK TREE CL
Knowl Hill Clay Pit
KILN CLOSE
BRICKBARN CL
HOLLY CL
CEDAR CL
BEECHTREE RD
Football Grnd
Cemy
WINDMILL CL
MILL LANE
GROSVENOR DR
VICTORIA AV
VICTORIA RD
PEMBA DRIVE
MAXWELL CL
Ewlo Brigog
LINDERICK AV
POTTERS WY
TILERS CL
SOUTHFIELDS CL
DRIVE
ARGOED RD
WINDMILL RD
Pol Sta
Council Bldgs
MILLERS CT
PARKSIDE CT
DUKESFIELD DR
A549
PREN HILL
MOLD ROAD
BRUNSWICK ROAD
BRUNSWICK RD
MOLD ROAD
ORCHARD CL
TABERNACLE ST
PADESWOOD ROAD
Liby
Central Precinct
Fire Station
THE PRECINCT WAY
GARDENS IND EST
COTTAGE GDNS
DAISY HILL RD
BERLLAN
LLYS RD
MYRTLE MEWS
MAYFIELD
MUIRFIELD
BISTRE CL
HEWITTS LA
WESTBOURNE CRES
WESTBOURNE DRIVE
BISTRE AV
MAYFIELD
LANGFORD CRESCENT
DALESIDE
SPRINGFIELD DR
WATTS CT
EGLWYS CL
STANLEY RD
Playing Field
Nursery Sch
Sch
LEXHAM CL
MOOREFIELDS
MANOR DR
COPPAFIELD CL
LAMBS LA
JUBILEE ROAD
NANT STREET
STANLEY ESTATE
BRYN PEN-Y-MAES
AWELON
MAWR ROAD
FRAZER CL
CLWYD GRO
NANT MAWR CRESCENT
MELBOURNE RD
QUEENS DR
HILARY GRO
BRYN MAWR RD
FARM CL
PRINCESS AVENUE
Nant Mawr
ALYN ROAD
TERRIG CRES
ALYN RD
PADESWOOD CT
NEWTHORN PL
JUBILEE CT
ALEXANDRA CT
LEA DR
OAKFIELD RD
OVERTON
HAWTHORNE AVENUE
LAUREL DR
LYME GROVE
CWRT BRENIG
AVONDALE RD
DELAMERE AV
DUFFRYN CL
CONWAY AV
SWAIN RD
SPON GREEN
THE BRACKENS
NANT VIEW CT
HILLS VW
HANCOCKS LA
ELM GRO
WOOD RD
LEES-SOMERVILLE
HILLSIDE CRES
ROMAN WAY
BERWYN CL
PENLEY RD
SOUTH VW
WEST VW
BRAMBLE CL
BIRCH CL
BRIAR CLOSE
MAES LOR
MARBURY AV
BRUNSWICK PARK
HIGHFIELD DR
LANE
Bistre Cottage Farm
WELL STREET
BECKETTS LA
POWELL RD
NANT MAWR ROAD
BANK RD
BRYN WOOD DR
NANT GLYN
MOEL VIEW RD
OLD BANK LA
GARDEN PL
MEGS
WESTBROOK DR
Marleyfield House
Spon Green Farm
Spon Farm
ROSE LANE
Bryn Faigas Farm
Sewage Works
Bistre Farm
Wat's Dyke
A5118
PADESWOOD ROAD

E
F
G
H
1
2
3
4
5
6
19
26
26
28
SPENCER INDUSTRIAL ESTATE
Oaks Farm
Higher House
Burntwood Pentre
DRURY LANE IND EST
Knowl Hill
Drury
Sch
Lane End
Works
JUNCTION 35
Pentre
Playing Field
Dobs Hill
Bannel Farm
DOBSHILL HOSPITAL
Depot
BUCKLEY
Spon Green
Little Mountain
Bannel Bridge
Golf Driving Range
School
Waters Green
Ash Tree Farm
Sports Grnd
Bannel Dairy Farm
Works
A55
A550
A5118
A5104
CHESTER ROAD
DIRTY MILE
NEW ROAD
MOLD ROAD
BY-PASS
DRURY LANE
BANNEL LANE
PLEASANT ROAD
BURNTWOOD ROAD
PEN-Y-COED BANK LANE
SLACK LANE
LEDSHAM LANE
STATION ROAD
LITTLE MOUNTAIN ROAD
OLD HOPE ROAD
PADESWOOD DRIVE
CHESTER ROAD

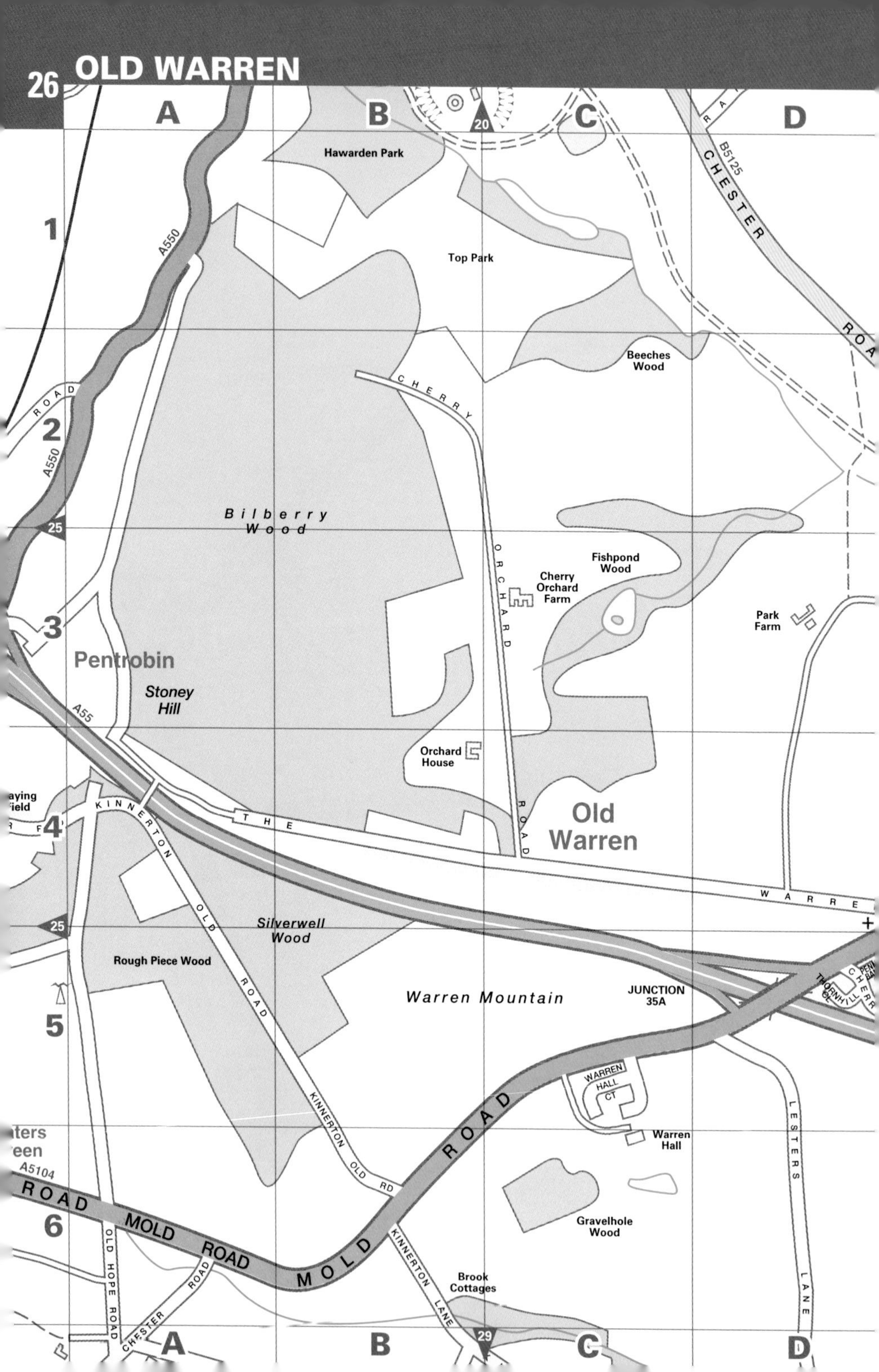
A
B
C
D
1
2
3
4
5
6
20
25
25
29
Hawarden Park
Top Park
Beeches Wood
CHESTER ROAD
B5125
A550
A550
ROAD
CHERRY ORCHARD ROAD
Bilberry Wood
Fishpond Wood
Cherry Orchard Farm
Park Farm
Pentrobin
Stoney Hill
A55
Orchard House
Old Warren
THE WARREN
KINNERTON OLD ROAD
Silverwell Wood
Rough Piece Wood
Warren Mountain
JUNCTION 35A
THORNHYLL CL
WARREN HALL CT
Warren Hall
LESTERS LANE
KINNERTON OLD RD
A5104
ROAD
MOLD ROAD
MOLD ROAD
OLD HOPE ROAD
CHESTER ROAD
KINNERTON LANE
Gravelhole Wood
Brook Cottages

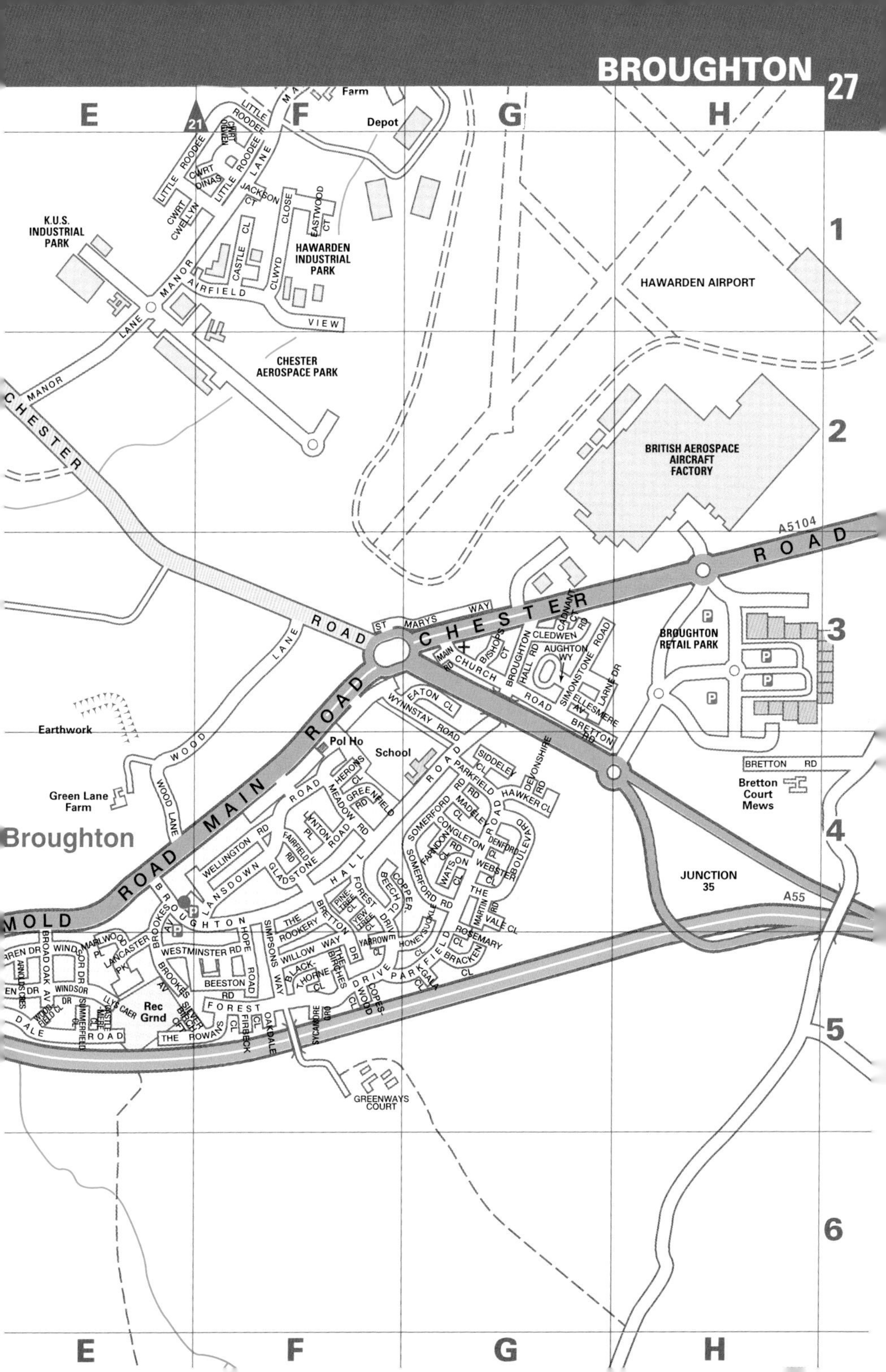
E
F
G
H
1
2
3
4
5
6
K.U.S.
INDUSTRIAL
PARK
HAWARDEN
INDUSTRIAL
PARK
CHESTER
AEROSPACE PARK
HAWARDEN AIRPORT
BRITISH AEROSPACE
AIRCRAFT
FACTORY
Depot
Farm
A5104
CHESTER ROAD
MAIN ROAD
MOLD ROAD
BROUGHTON
RETAIL PARK
Bretton
Court
Mews
BRETTON RD
JUNCTION
35
A55
Earthwork
Green Lane
Farm
Broughton
Pol Ho
School
Rec
Grnd
GREENWAYS
COURT
MANOR LANE
AIRFIELD VIEW
WOOD LANE
ST MARYS WAY
CHURCH ROAD
WYNNSTAY ROAD
EATON CL
BROUGHTON HALL RD
SIMONSTONE ROAD
CLEDWEN
AUGHTON WY
ELLESMERE AV
LARNE DR
BRETTON RD
PARKFIELD
SOMERFORD RD
CONGLETON
BOULEVARD
WELLINGTON RD
LANSDOWN
GLADSTONE
WESTMINSTER RD
BEESTON RD
HOPE ROAD
FOREST CL
THE ROWANS
OAKDALE
SYCAMORE GRO
WINDSOR DR
BROAD OAK AV
ROSEMARY CL
BRACKEN CL

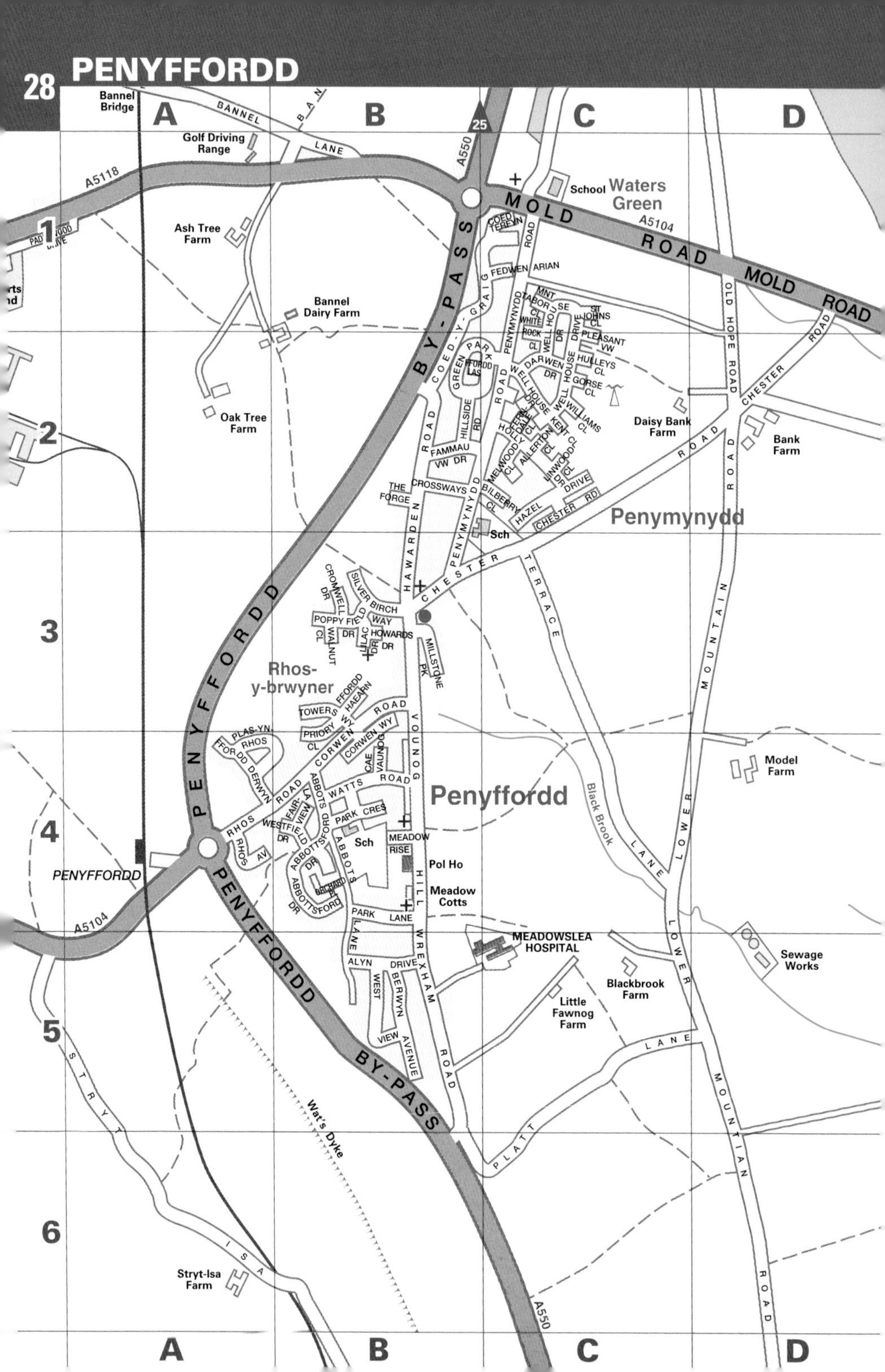

Bannel Bridge
BANNEL LANE
Golf Driving Range
A5118
A550
25
Ash Tree Farm
Bannel Dairy Farm
Oak Tree Farm
School
Waters Green
MOLD ROAD
A5104
MOLD ROAD
OLD HOPE ROAD
CHESTER ROAD
Daisy Bank Farm
Bank Farm
BY-PASS
COED-Y-GRAIG
FEDWEN ARIAN
PENYMYNYDD ROAD
HAWARDEN ROAD
THE FORGE
CROSSWAYS
Sch
Penymynydd
CHESTER ROAD
TERRACE
Rhos-y-brwyner
PENYFFORDD
Penyffordd
Black Brook
LOWER MOUNTAIN ROAD
Model Farm
RHOS ROAD
CORWEN ROAD
WATTS ROAD
VOUNOG HILL
PARK LANE
ALYN DRIVE
WREXHAM ROAD
Pol Ho
Meadow Cotts
MEADOWSLEA HOSPITAL
Blackbrook Farm
Little Fawnog Farm
Sewage Works
LANE
PLATT LANE
PENYFFORDD BY-PASS
Wat's Dyke
STRYT ISA
Stryt-Isa Farm
A5104
A550
PENYFFORDD
A
B
C
D
1
2
3
4
5
6

E
F
G
H
26
1
2
3
4
5
6
MOLD ROAD
KINNERTON OLD RD
WARREN HALL CT
Warren Hall
Gravelhole Wood
LESTERS LANE
KINNERTON LANE
Brook Cottages
Bramley Hall Farm
Warren Dingle
Mount Farm
LANE
The Covert
Kinnerton Lodge
ROAD
SPRINGFIELD CT
LLYS DERWEN
DEANSWAY
LATHE
The Grange
GREEN
Bramley Farm
BRAMLEY
Bramley Lane Farm
Crompton Hall Farm
THE CHASE
HUNTERS CROFT
FOXES WK
MAIN ROAD
Sch
OAK DR
SPRINGFIELD CL
GREENFIELD AV
PARK AV
CROMPTON CL
WILLOW CT
MYRTLE AV
Playing Field
MEADOWCROFT
PADDOCK WY
BLANTERN RD
BEESTON
Higher Kinnerton
KIRKETT AVENUE
BENNETTS LANE
KINNERTON HEIGHTS
ECCLESTON RD
SANDY LANE
Kinnerton Hall Farm
BURTON DR
HARTLEY CL
FAULKNERS CL
WAY
CANNON
GREEN LANE
Babylon
Cuckoo Hill
Sandy Lane Farm
Bradbrook Farm
Sand Pit
The Dale
Brad Brook
Kinnerton Bank Farm
SANDY

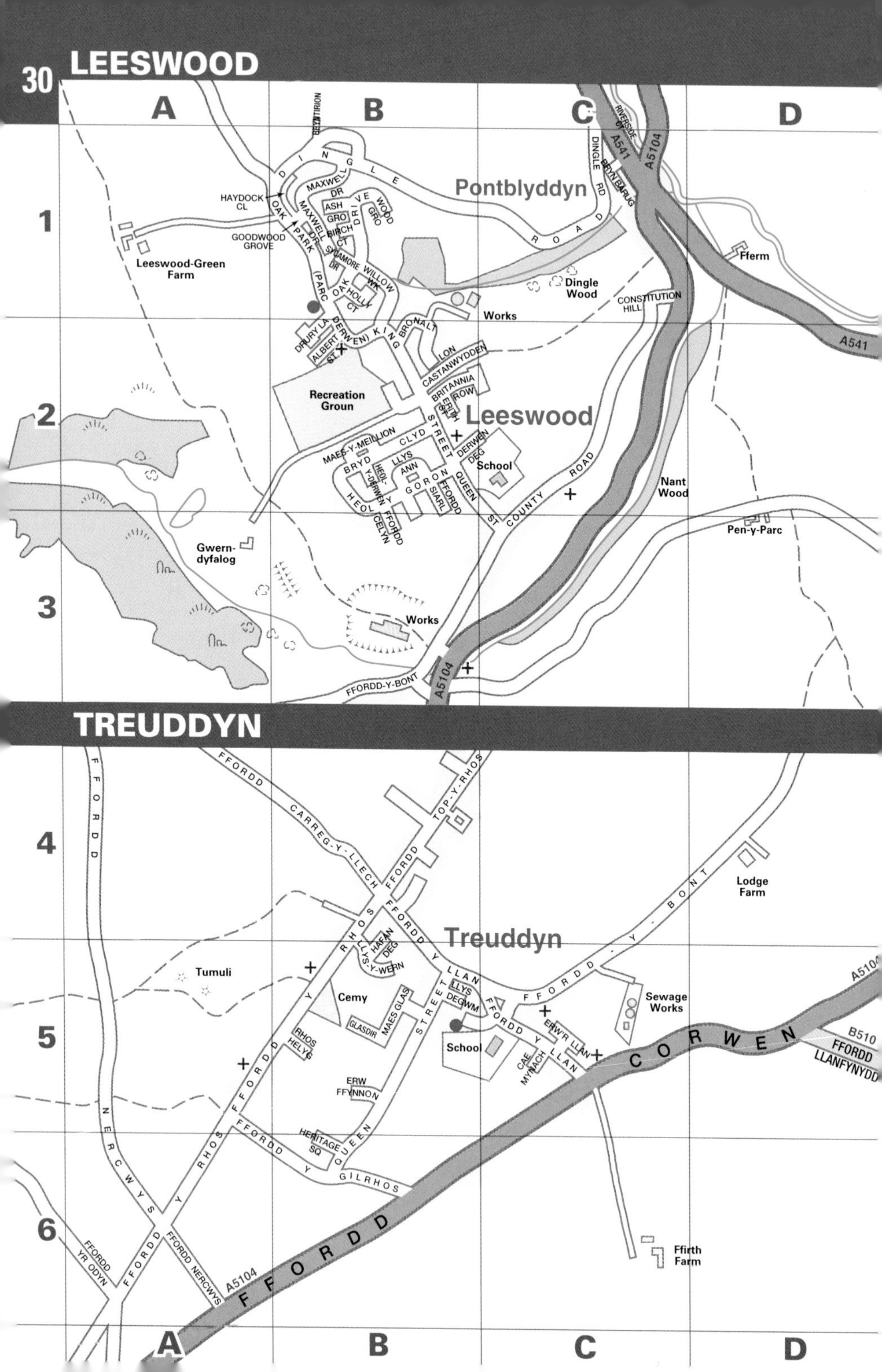
LEESWOOD
A
B
C
D
1
2
3
Pontblyddyn
DINGLE ROAD
MAXWELL DR
ASH GRO
BIRCH CT
SYCAMORE DR
DRIVE
WOOD GRO
HAYDOCK CL
GOODWOOD GROVE
OAK PARK
MAXWELL DR
(PARC DERWEN)
OAK HOLLY CT
WILLOW WK
Leeswood-Green Farm
DINGLE RD
BRYN BARUG
RIVERSIDE CT
A541
A5104
Fferm
Dingle Wood
Works
CONSTITUTION HILL
A541
DRURY LA
ALBERT ST
KING
BRONALT
LON CASTANWYDDEN
BRITANNIA ROW
ERITH ST
Recreation Groun
Leeswood
MAES-Y-MEILLION
CLYD
STREET
DERWEN DEG
School
BRYD
HEOL-Y-DERWEN
LLYS ANN
GORON
SIARL
FFORDD
QUEEN
ST
COUNTY ROAD
HEOL Y CELYN
FFORDD
Nant Wood
Pen-y-Parc
Gwern-dyfalog
Works
FFORDD-Y-BONT
A5104
TREUDDYN
FFORDD CARREG-Y-LLECH
TOP-Y-RHOS
FFORDD
4
Lodge Farm
Treuddyn
RHOS
LLYS HAFAN DEG
LLYS-Y-WERN
FFORDD Y LLAN
FFORDD-Y-BONT
Tumuli
Cemy
MAES GLAS
GLASDIR
STREET
LLYS DEGWM
FFORDD Y LLAN
Sewage Works
A5104
5
RHOS HELYG
School
CAE MYNACH
ERW'R LLAN
CORWEN
B510
FFORDD LLANFYNYDD
ERW FFYNNON
HERITAGE SQ
QUEEN
FFORDD Y GILRHOS
FFORDD NERCWYS
FFORDD Y RHOS
6
FFORDD YR ODYN
FFORDD
FFORDD NERCWYS
A5104
FFORDD
Ffirth Farm
A
B
C
D

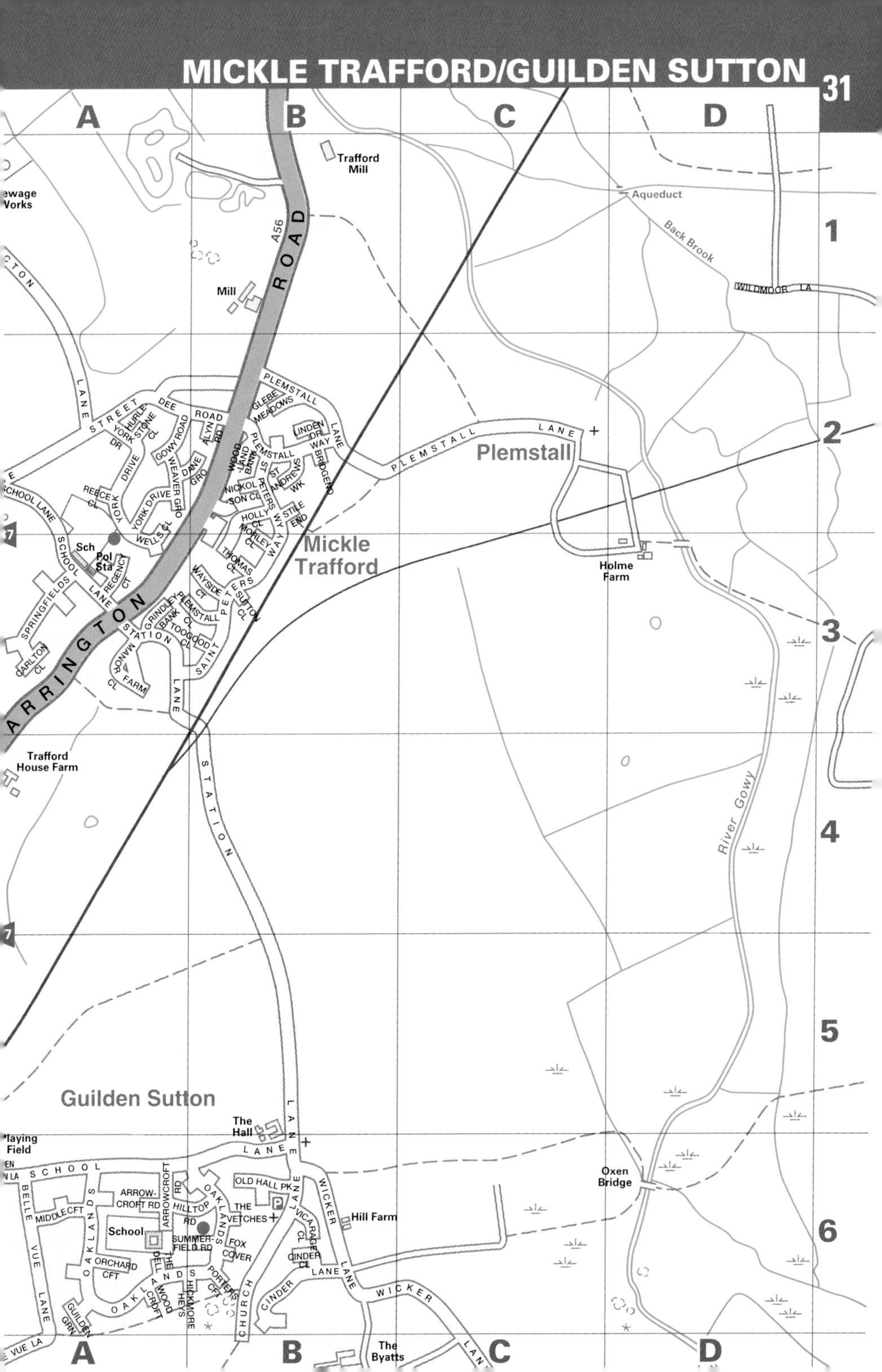
A
B
C
D
1
2
3
4
5
6
Trafford Mill
Aqueduct
Back Brook
WILDMOOR LA
Mill
A56
WARRINGTON ROAD
Plemstall
PLEMSTALL LANE
Mickle Trafford
Holme Farm
Trafford House Farm
STATION LANE
River Gowy
Guilden Sutton
The Hall
Playing Field
SCHOOL LANE
School
Hill Farm
Oxen Bridge
WICKER LANE
CHURCH LANE
The Byatts
Sch
Pol Sta
Sewage Works

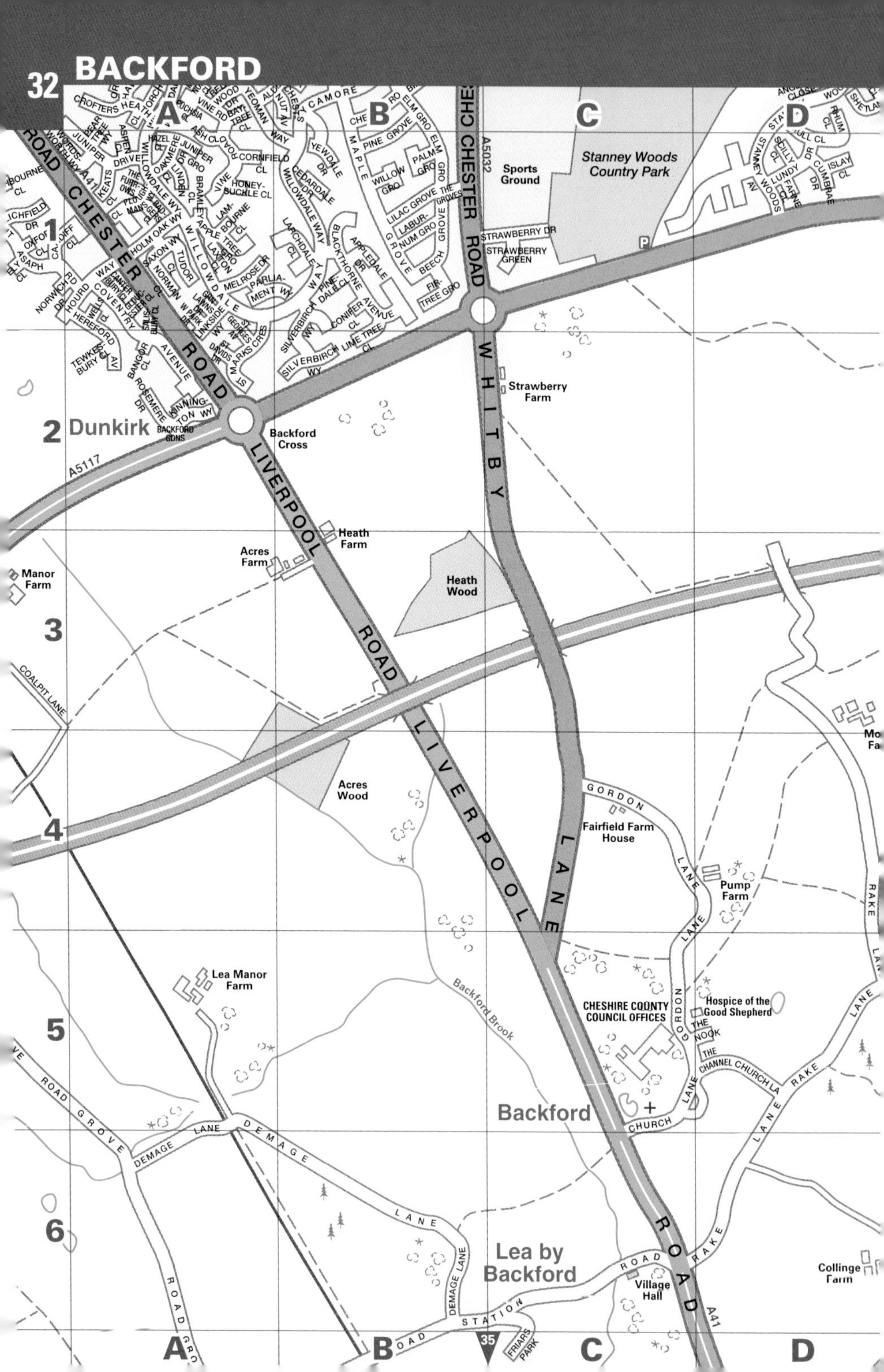
Stanney Woods Country Park
Sports Ground
STRAWBERRY DR
STRAWBERRY GREEN
CHESTER ROAD
A5032
WHITBY LANE
Strawberry Farm
Backford Cross
Dunkirk
A5117
LIVERPOOL ROAD
Heath Farm
Acres Farm
Manor Farm
Heath Wood
COALPIT LANE
Acres Wood
GORDON LANE
Fairfield Farm House
Pump Farm
Lea Manor Farm
Backford Brook
CHESHIRE COUNTY COUNCIL OFFICES
Hospice of the Good Shepherd
THE NOOK
THE CHANNEL
CHURCH LA
RAKE LANE
Backford
CHURCH LANE
DEMAGE LANE
GROVE ROAD
Lea by Backford
Village Hall
STATION ROAD
FRIARS PARK
A41
Collinge Farm
35
Dunkirk
BACKFORD GDNS
KINNINGTON WY
ROSEMERE DR
BANGOR CL
TEWKESBURY CL
HEREFORD AV
COVENTRY AV
NORWICH DR
SILVERBIRCH WY
LIME TREE CL
CONIFER CL
AVENUE
MELROSE DR
PARLIAMENT WY
YEWDALE DR
CEDARDALE DR
WILLOWDALE WAY
LARCHDALE CL
BLACKTHORNE AV
APPLEDALE DR
MAPLE GROVE
PINE GROVE
WILLOW GRO
PALM GRO
ELM GRO
LILAC GROVE
LABURNUM GROVE
BEECH GROVE
FIR-TREE GRO
THE GROVES
CORNFIELD CL
HONEYSUCKLE CL
JUNIPER DR
HOLM OAK WY
SAXON WY
TUDOR CL
NORMAN WY
A41
LUNDY DR
ISLAY CL
CUMBRAE DR
STANNEY WOODS AV

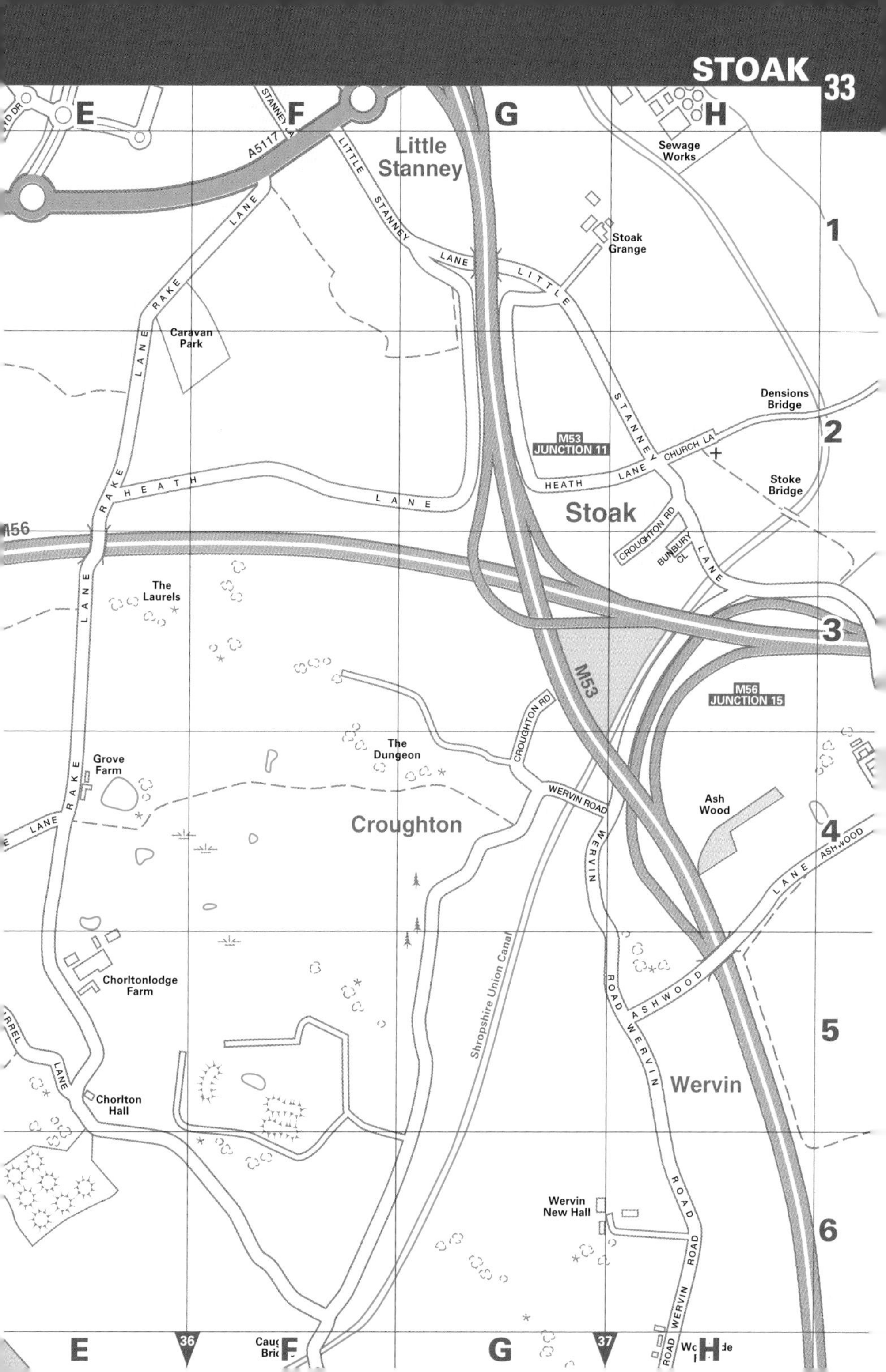
Little Stanney
A5117
LITTLE STANNEY LANE
RAKE LANE
Caravan Park
Sewage Works
Stoak Grange
LITTLE STANNEY LANE
M53 JUNCTION 11
HEATH LANE
CHURCH LA
Densions Bridge
Stoke Bridge
Stoak
CROUGHTON RD
BUNBURY CL
M56
The Laurels
M53
M56 JUNCTION 15
The Dungeon
Grove Farm
WERVIN ROAD
Ash Wood
Croughton
ASHWOOD LANE
Shropshire Union Canal
Chorltonlodge Farm
Chorlton Hall
Wervin
Wervin New Hall
E
F
G
H
1
2
3
4
5
6
36
37

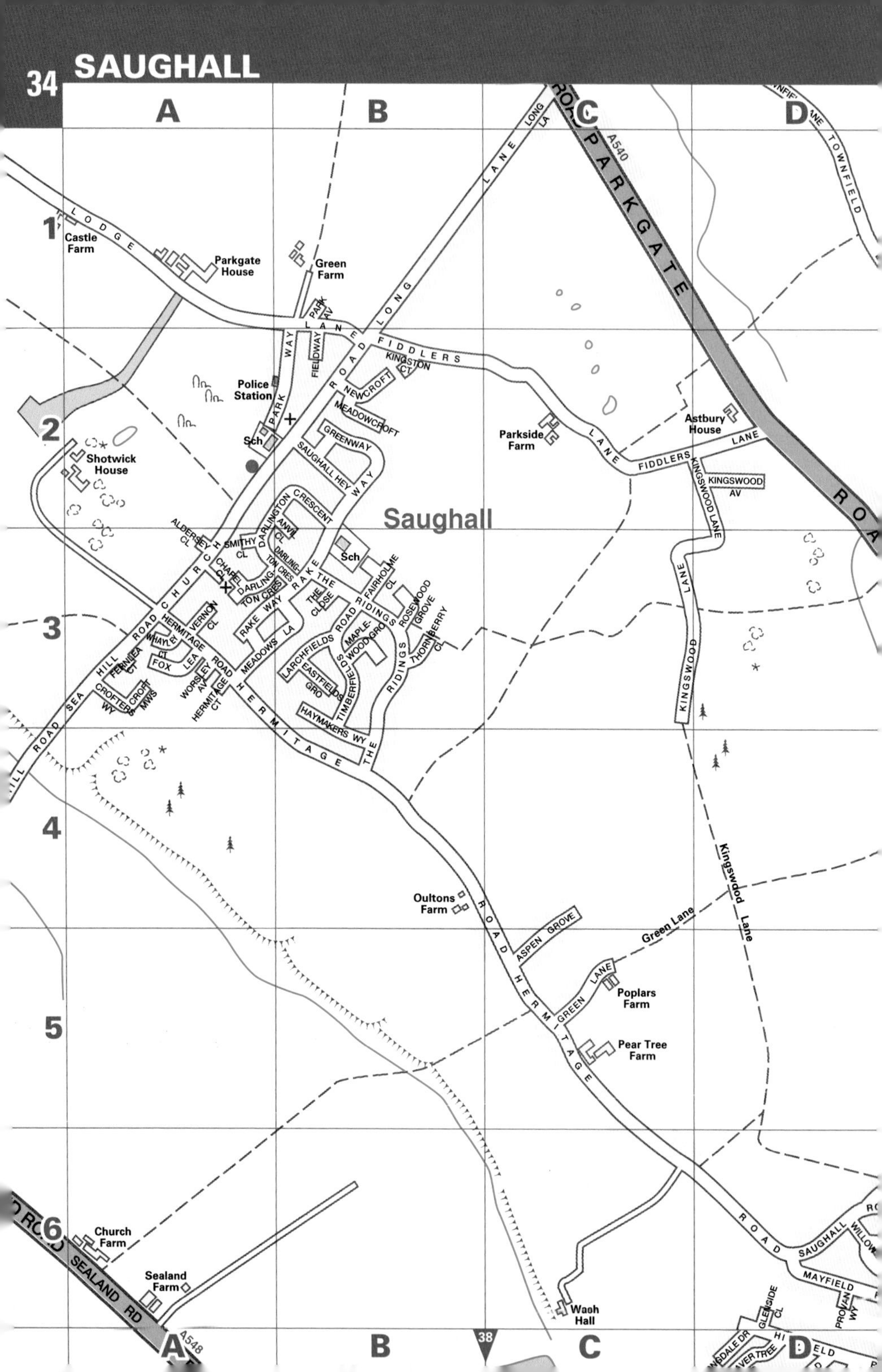

Saughall
Castle Farm
Parkgate House
Green Farm
Police Station
Sch
Shotwick House
Parkside Farm
Astbury House
Oultons Farm
Poplars Farm
Pear Tree Farm
Church Farm
Sealand Farm
Waoh Hall
LODGE LANE
LONG LANE
FIDDLERS LANE
PARKGATE ROAD
A540
KINGSWOOD LANE
KINGSWOOD AV
Kingswood Lane
Green Lane
GREEN LANE
ASPEN GROVE
HERMITAGE ROAD
SAUGHALL ROAD
MAYFIELD
SEALAND RD
A548
SEA HILL ROAD
CHURCH ROAD
PARK WAY
PARK AV
FIELDWAY
KINGSTON CT
NEWCROFT
MEADOWCROFT
GREENWAY
SAUGHALL HEY WAY
DARLINGTON CRESCENT
ANVIL CL
SMITHY CL
ALDERSEY CL
CHAPEL CL
DARLINGTON CRES
RAKE WAY
THE RAKE
THE CLOSE
FAIRHOLME CL
ROSEWOOD GROVE
THORNBERRY CL
THE RIDINGS
MAPLEWOOD GRO
LARCHFIELDS ROAD
EASTFIELDS GRO
TIMBERFIELDS
HAYMAKERS WY
MEADOWS LA
VERNON CL
HERMITAGE CT
WHAYLE CT
FERNLEA CT
FOX LEA
WORSLEY AV
CROFTERS WY
CROFT MWS
GLENSIDE CL
PROVAN WY
WILLOW
38

Mollington
Grove Farm
Sch
Lea Farm
Viaduct Wood
Backford Bridge
Moston Hall
Golf Course
Club House
Crabwell Hall
Hotel
Mollington Grange
Hotel
Knolls Bridge
Shropshire Union Canal
The Dale
COUNTESS OF CHESTER HOSPITAL
Playing Field
Playing Field
Divisional Police H.Q
PARKGATE ROAD
STATION ROAD
GROVE ROAD
TOWNFIELD LANE
WELL LANE
MOLLINGTON COURT
WILLOW LEA
FEILDEN CT
ALAMEIN ROAD
MALTA RD
PARSONS LANE
KIPLING ROAD
WORDSWORTH CRESCENT
BLACON AVENUE
STAMFORD ROAD
SHELLEY WAY
A540
A41
LIVERPOOL

A
B
C
D
32
33
35
40
1
2
3
4
5
6
Caughall Bridge
Collinge Wood
Shropshire Union Canal
A41
LIVERPOOL ROAD
Caughall Manor
BADGERS WALK
CAUGHALL ROAD
Butter Hill
Millennium Cycle Path
East Zoo
Reptiles
Giraffes
Main Entrance
Elephants
West Zoo
Rhinos
Monkey Island Sta
Monkeys
Dragons in Danger
Tigers
Lions
Jubilee Sq Sta
Deer
CHESTER ZOOLOGICAL GARDENS
Oakfield Ho
Oryx
Zebra's
WERVIN ROAD
Moston
Moston Hill Farm
MALTA ROAD
MALTA RD
Sports Ground
MOSTON RD
NORMANDY RD
PROSSER RD
THE DALE BARRACKS
SALERNO RD
CROOKEND RD
BRODIE CL
SIMPSON RD
CHARLES RD
DAUNCEY CL
HARRINGTON RD
PERCIVAL RD
NAPIER RD
MARTIN RD
MARTIN CL
HARDING RD
The Dale
PERCIVAL CLOSE
GREENFIELDS
GREENACRES CT
ACRES LANE
OAKFIELD AV
OAKFIELD DRIVE
ALWYN GDNS
Sch
FLAG LANE NORTH
ENDSLEIGH GDNS
ENDSLEIGH CL
ROSEDENE CL
THE ACORNS
Upton Heath
DALESIDE
ST CHRISTOPHERS CL
DEMAGE LANE
WILLOW CL
MEADOWS WAY
WHELDON CL
UPTON LANE
DULAS CT
BROOKE AV
LONG LANE
LONGFIELD AV
MALLARD CT
KINGS MEAD
PENFOLD HEY
WALNUT CL
Rec Ground
MARL HEYS
DUKESWAY
QUEENS CRES
THE OAKS DR
Club House
NIELD CT
GRANGESIDE
LAWN DR
EARLS OAK
CHURCH LANE
LINKSWAY
Golf Course
HEATH ROAD
Hall
MARINA DRIVE
SAINT JAMES AVENUE
GLASTONBURY AV
TEWKESBURY CL
COTEBROOK DRIVE
RUSHTON DRIVE
OULTON AV
WESTON GROVE
WOODLEA AVENUE
CORNWALL ROAD
ALDFORD ROAD
DORSET RD
WINDMILL RISE
GATESHEATH DR
ALPRAHAM CRESCENT
PECKFORTON WY
MARLOW AV
WOBURN DR
NEWHALL ROAD
DEVA LANE
WEALSTONE LANE
Golf Course
Upton
Sch
DORIN CT
Liby
MILL CLOSE
DEANS CL
CROSS GREEN
DORFOLD WY
HALTON RD
SHIPBROOK RD
BOLESWORTH RD
COTSWOLD CL
THE COURTYARD
THE ELMS
BEECHES
Upton Rec Cen
BEECH WAY
UPTON DRIVE
OLD MILL CT
DELVINE DR
UPTON PARK
Playing Field
DUNHAM WY
CHIRK CL
ARLEY CL
NEWTON MEWS
ULLSWATER
WINDERMERE AV
PINE GDNS
School
APPLETON RD
APPLETON ROAD
HANDFORD RD
TINTERN AV
AMBLESIDE
PLAS NEWTON
PEAR TREE WY
CONISTON
VALLEY DRIVE
BACHE AV
BACHE DRIVE
EGERTON
BIRCH RISE
ORCHARD CL
THE CROFT
GAYTON CL
ARRADON CT
BRETON CL
TIVERTON CL
NEWTON HO
NEWTON HALL CT
KENT RD
KENT GDNS
DEVON RD
ENNERDALE RD
DERWENT
MILL LANE
BACHE
Supermarket
BACHE HALL CT
STATION CL
ROSEWOOD AV
PENSBY AV
WHITBY AV
THORNTON DR
MOORHOUSE CL
DENHALL CL
SUTTON DRIVE
HORROCKS ROAD
WHITTON DR
MILBORNE CL
Playing Field
SOMERSET RD
SURREY ROAD
CALDY CL
BIDSTON CL
MENUHIN HO
DAWPOOL CL
GRASMERE RD
KIRBY
ELLESMERE AV
QUEENS WAY
NEWTON HALL DR
LANE

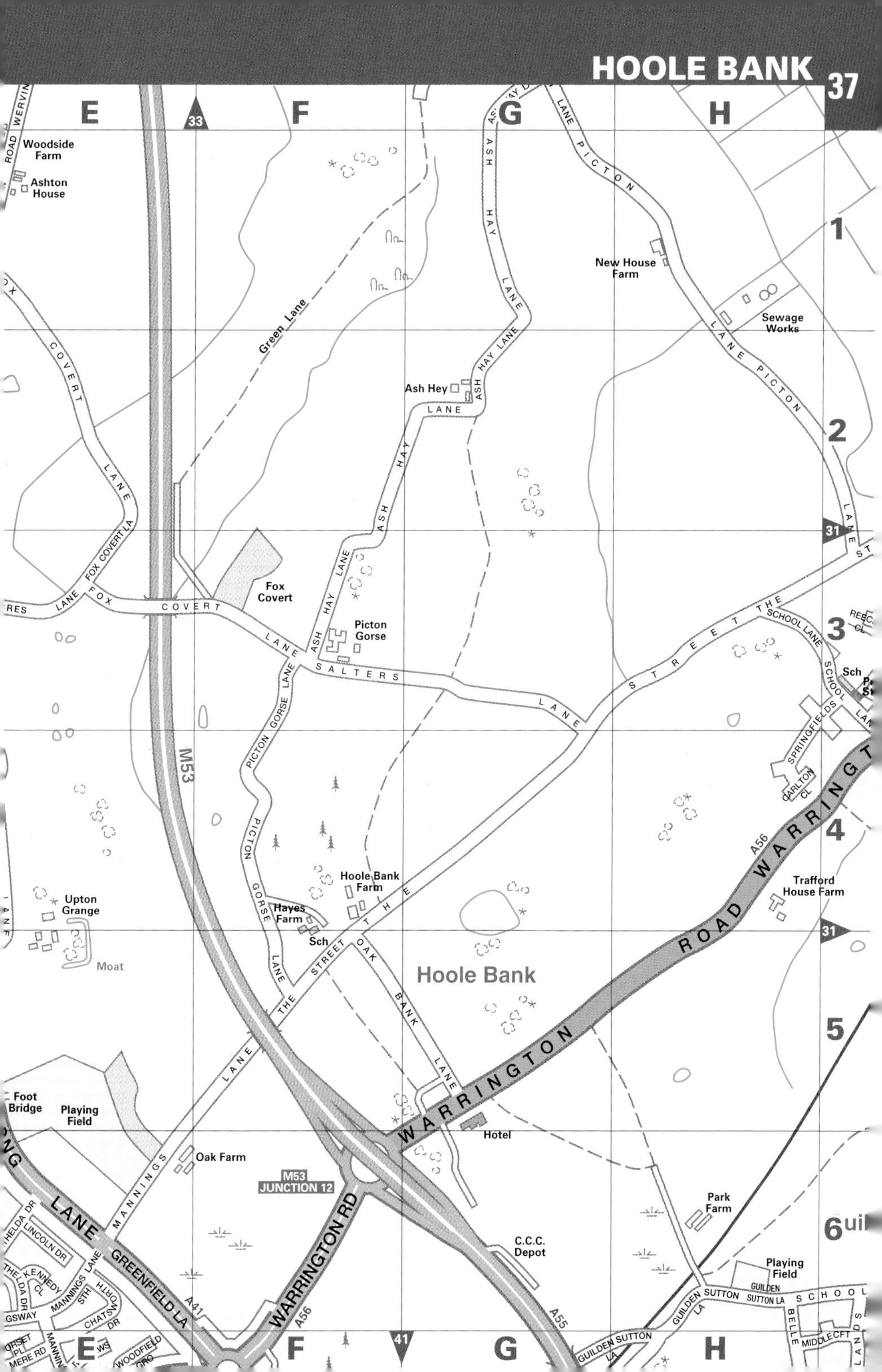

Woodside Farm
Ashton House
Green Lane
Fox Covert Lane
Fox Covert
Ash Hay Lane
Ash Hey
New House Farm
Sewage Works
Picton Lane
Picton Gorse
Salters Lane
Picton Gorse Lane
The Street
School Lane
Springfields
Carlton Cl
Sch
M53
Hoole Bank Farm
Hayes Farm
Upton Grange
Moat
Trafford House Farm
Hoole Bank
Oak Bank Lane
Warrington Road
A56
Mannings Lane
Foot Bridge
Playing Field
Oak Farm
Hotel
M53 JUNCTION 12
Warrington Rd
Greenfield Lane
Greenfield La
A41
A55
C.C.C. Depot
Park Farm
Guilden Sutton Lane
Guilden Sutton La
Lincoln Dr
Kennedy Cl
Chatsworth Dr
Woodfield Gro
Middlecroft
Belle
School

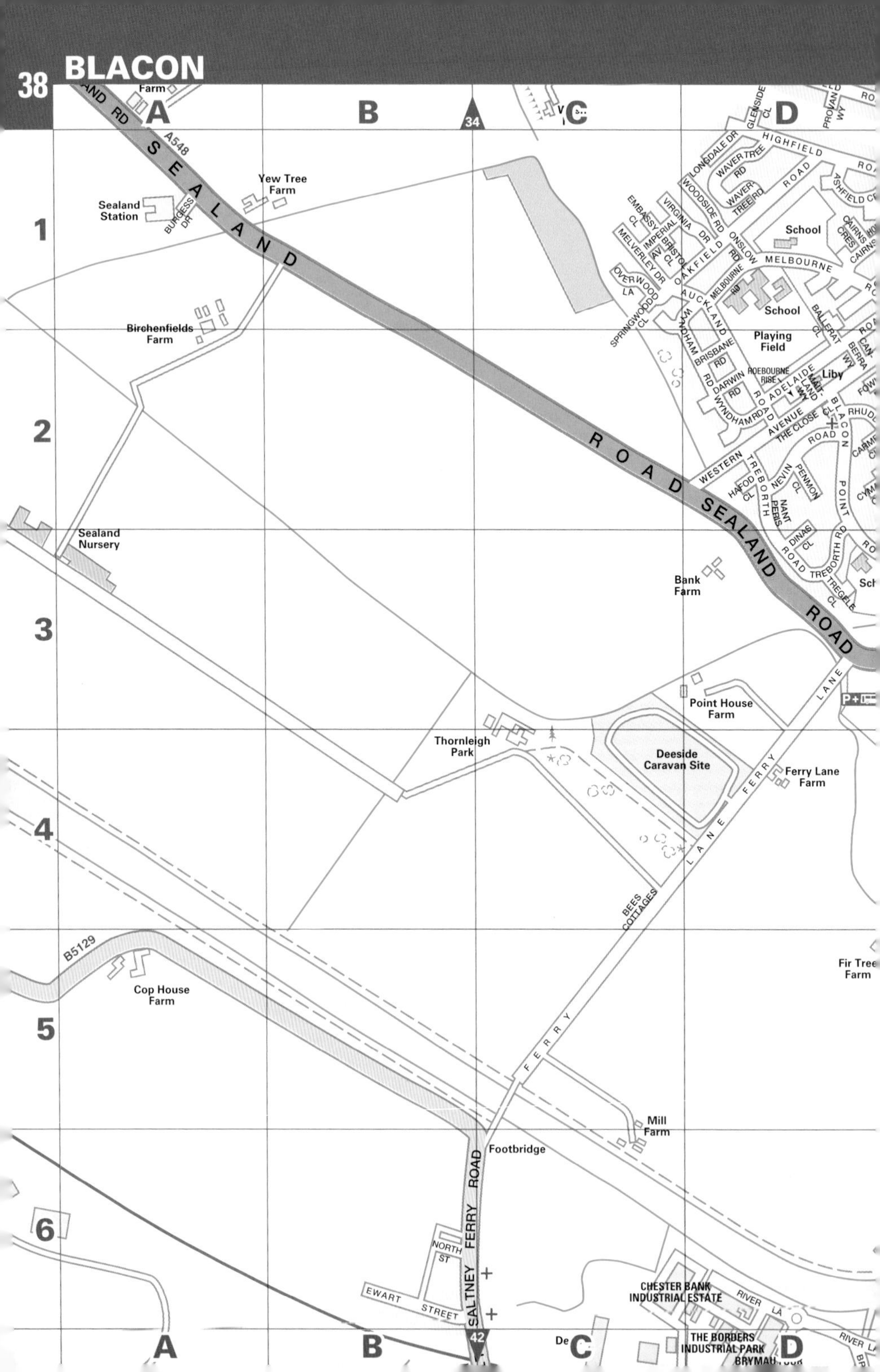
A
B
C
D
1
2
3
4
5
6
34
42
SEALAND ROAD
SEALAND RD
A548
B5129
Sealand Station
Burgess Dr
Yew Tree Farm
Birchenfields Farm
Sealand Nursery
Bank Farm
Point House Farm
Thornleigh Park
Deeside Caravan Site
Ferry Lane Farm
Ferry Lane
Bees Cottages
Cop House Farm
Fir Tree Farm
Mill Farm
Footbridge
Saltney Ferry Road
North St
Ewart Street
Chester Bank Industrial Estate
The Borders Industrial Park
River La
School
Playing Field
Liby
Highfield Road
Melbourne
Western Avenue
Blacon Point Road
Hafod Cl
Treborth Rd
Nevin Cl
Penmon Cl
Nant Peris
Dinas Cl
Tregele Cl
Springwood Cl
Overwood La
Melverley Dr
Embassy Cl
Imperial Av
Bristol Cl
Virginia Dr
Oakfield
Woodside Rd
Onslow
Longdale Dr
Waver Tree Rd
Glenside Cl
Ashfield
Auckland
Wyndham Rd
Brisbane Rd
Darwin Rd
Roebourne Rise
Adelaide Road
The Close
Ballerat Cl
Berra Wy

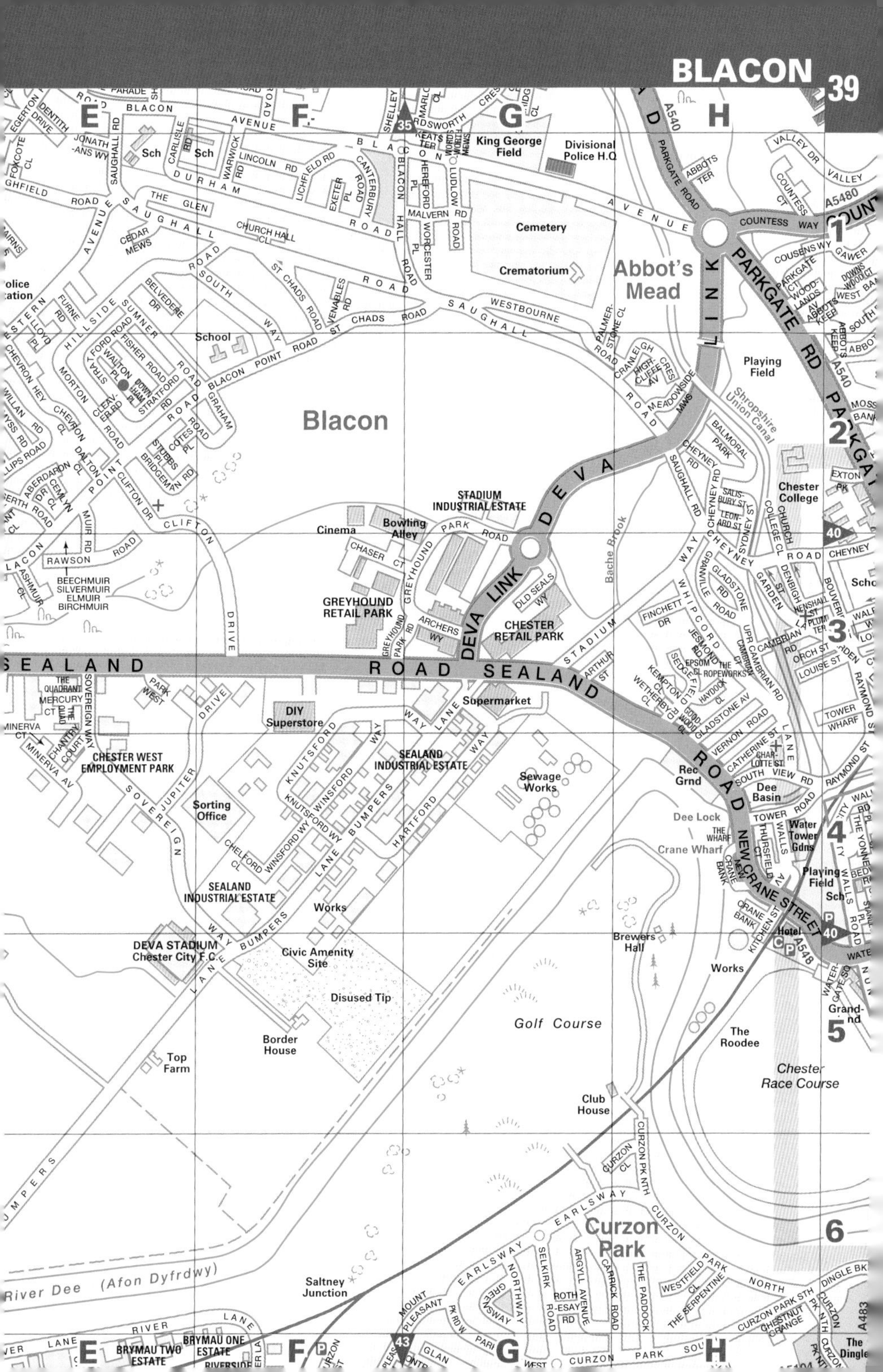
Blacon
Abbot's Mead
Curzon Park
King George Field
Divisional Police H.Q
Cemetery
Crematorium
School
Sch
Playing Field
Shropshire Union Canal
Chester College
STADIUM INDUSTRIAL ESTATE
Cinema
Bowling Alley
GREYHOUND RETAIL PARK
CHESTER RETAIL PARK
Supermarket
DIY Superstore
CHESTER WEST EMPLOYMENT PARK
SEALAND INDUSTRIAL ESTATE
Sorting Office
Sewage Works
Rec Grnd
Dee Basin
Dee Lock
Crane Wharf
Water Tower Gdns
DEVA STADIUM Chester City F.C.
Civic Amenity Site
Disused Tip
Border House
Top Farm
Works
Brewers Hall
Golf Course
The Roodee
Chester Race Course
Club House
Saltney Junction
River Dee (Afon Dyfrdwy)
BRYMAU TWO ESTATE
BRYMAU ONE ESTATE
Hotel
The Dingle
DEVA LINK
SEALAND ROAD
SAUGHALL ROAD
BLACON AVENUE
BLACON POINT ROAD
PARKGATE RD
NEW CRANE STREET
CURZON PARK NORTH
CURZON PARK SOUTH
EARLSWAY
BUMPERS LANE
SOVEREIGN WAY
CLIFTON DRIVE
A540
A5480
A548
A483
35
40
43
E
F
G
H
1
2
3
4
5
6

A
B
C
D
1
2
3
4
5
6
36
39
44
Supermarket
COUNTESS WAY
A5480
LIVERPOOL ROAD
PARKGATE RD
A540
Newton
Playing Field
School
Playground
Sports Ground
Sch
KINGSWAY
KINGSWAY WEST
NEWTON LANE
QUEENSWAY
WEALSTONE LANE
WELL LANE
SHEPHERDS AV
ELLESMERE AV
DICKSONS DRIVE
BROOK LANE
Newton Brook
WESTERN APP
WESTERN CT
WOODLANDS DRIVE
KILMOREY PK
HOOLE ROAD
Hotels
Liby
Hoole Alexandra Park
CANADIAN AV
Chester College
CHEYNEY RD
DENBIGH ST
BOUVERIE ST
GARDEN LANE
RAYMOND ST
TOWER WHARF
Northgate Arena
Fire Station
Amb Sta
ST OSWALDS WAY
HOOLE WY
BROOK ST BRIDGE
HOOLE
CHESTER ENTERPRISE CENTRE
STATION RD
Bus Depot
CHESTER
CITY RD
FRODSHAM ST
NORTHGATE ST
SAINT MARTINS WAY
GEORGE STREET
CANAL ST
Playing Field
UNION TER
LEADWORKS LA
BOUGHTON
Boughton
TARVIN RD
CHRISTLETON RD
Health Cen
THE BARS
FOREGATE ST
Abbey
Cathedral
Bus Sta
T.H.
Liby
EASTGATE ST
GROSVENOR PRECINCT
WATERGATE ST
NICHOLAS ST
VICARS LA
UNION ST
Grosvenor Park
PEPPER ST
Court
GROSVENOR ST
City Wall
Mus
Courts
The Castle
County Hall
Little Roodee
Grosvenor Bridge
GROSVENOR ROAD
Grandstand
Chester Race Course
River Dee
CHESTER
DEVA
Roman Legionary Fortress
Earl's Eye
Queens Park
Queens Park Bridge
Weir
Edgars Field
Playing Field
School
QUEENS PARK RD
VICTORIA CRESCENT
BOTTOMS LANE
Handbridge
Cemetery
A483
The Dingle
SANDY LANE
DEE BANKS
The Bishops Blue Coat High School
Liby & Rec C
Sch

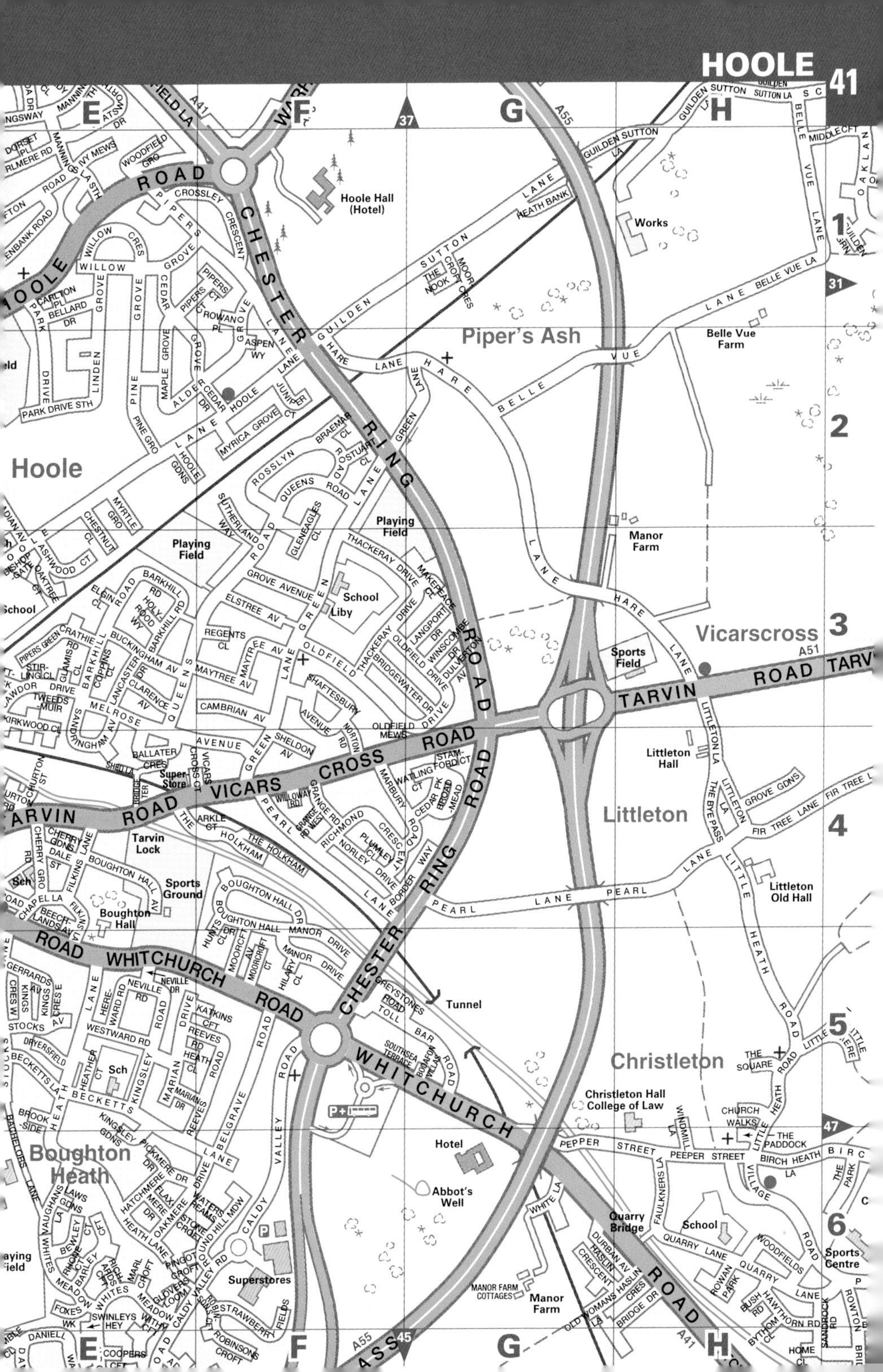
Hoole
Piper's Ash
Vicarscross
Littleton
Christleton
Boughton Heath
Hoole Hall (Hotel)
Works
Belle Vue Farm
Manor Farm
Sports Field
Littleton Hall
Littleton Old Hall
Playing Field
School
Liby
Tarvin Lock
Sports Ground
Boughton Hall
Tunnel
Hotel
Abbot's Well
Superstores
Christleton Hall College of Law
Quarry Bridge
Sports Centre
CHESTER RING ROAD
VICARS CROSS ROAD
TARVIN ROAD
WHITCHURCH ROAD
HOOLE ROAD
GUILDEN SUTTON LANE
HARE LANE
BELLE VUE LANE
PEARL LANE
LITTLE HEATH ROAD
PEPPER STREET
QUARRY LANE
A41
A51
A55

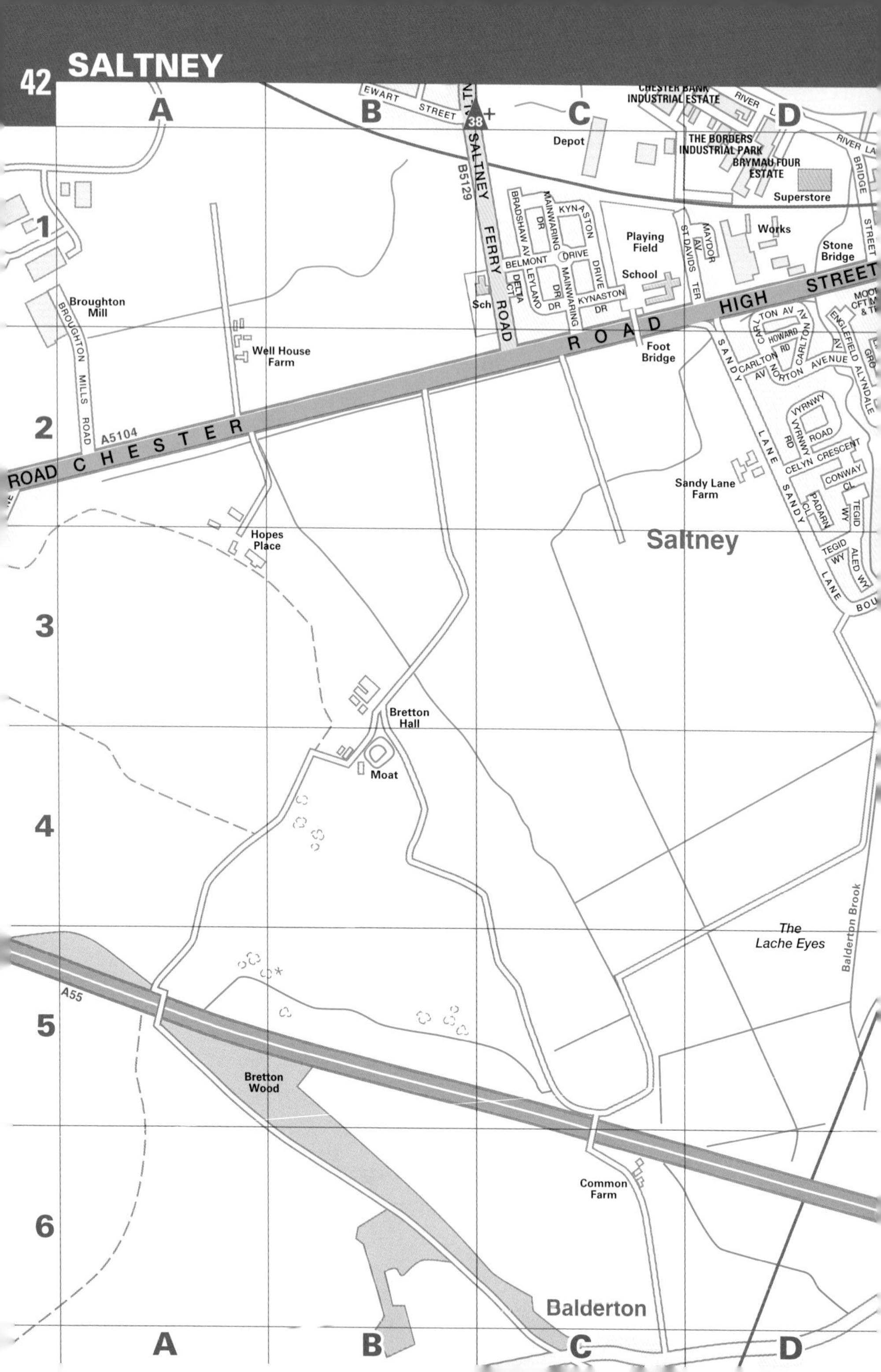

A
B
C
D
1
2
3
4
5
6
EWART STREET
SALTNEY
38
B5129
Depot
CHESTER BANK INDUSTRIAL ESTATE
RIVER
THE BORDERS INDUSTRIAL PARK
BRYMAU FOUR ESTATE
Superstore
RIVER LA
BRIDGE STREET
Works
Stone Bridge
Playing Field
School
ST DAVIDS TER
MAYDOR AV
BRADSHAW AV
MAINWARING DR
KYNASTON DRIVE
BELMONT DR
LEYLAND DR
MAINWARING DR
DELTA CT
KYNASTON DR
Sch
FERRY ROAD
ROAD HIGH STREET
Foot Bridge
CARLTON AV
HOWARD RD
NORTON AVENUE
ENGLEFIELD AV
ALYNDALE
VYRNWY ROAD
VYRNWY RD
CELYN CRESCENT
CONWAY CL
PADARN CL
TEGID WY
ALED WY
SANDY LANE
Sandy Lane Farm
Saltney
Broughton Mill
BROUGHTON MILLS ROAD
Well House Farm
A5104
ROAD CHESTER
Hopes Place
Bretton Hall
Moat
The Lache Eyes
Balderton Brook
A55
Bretton Wood
Common Farm
Balderton

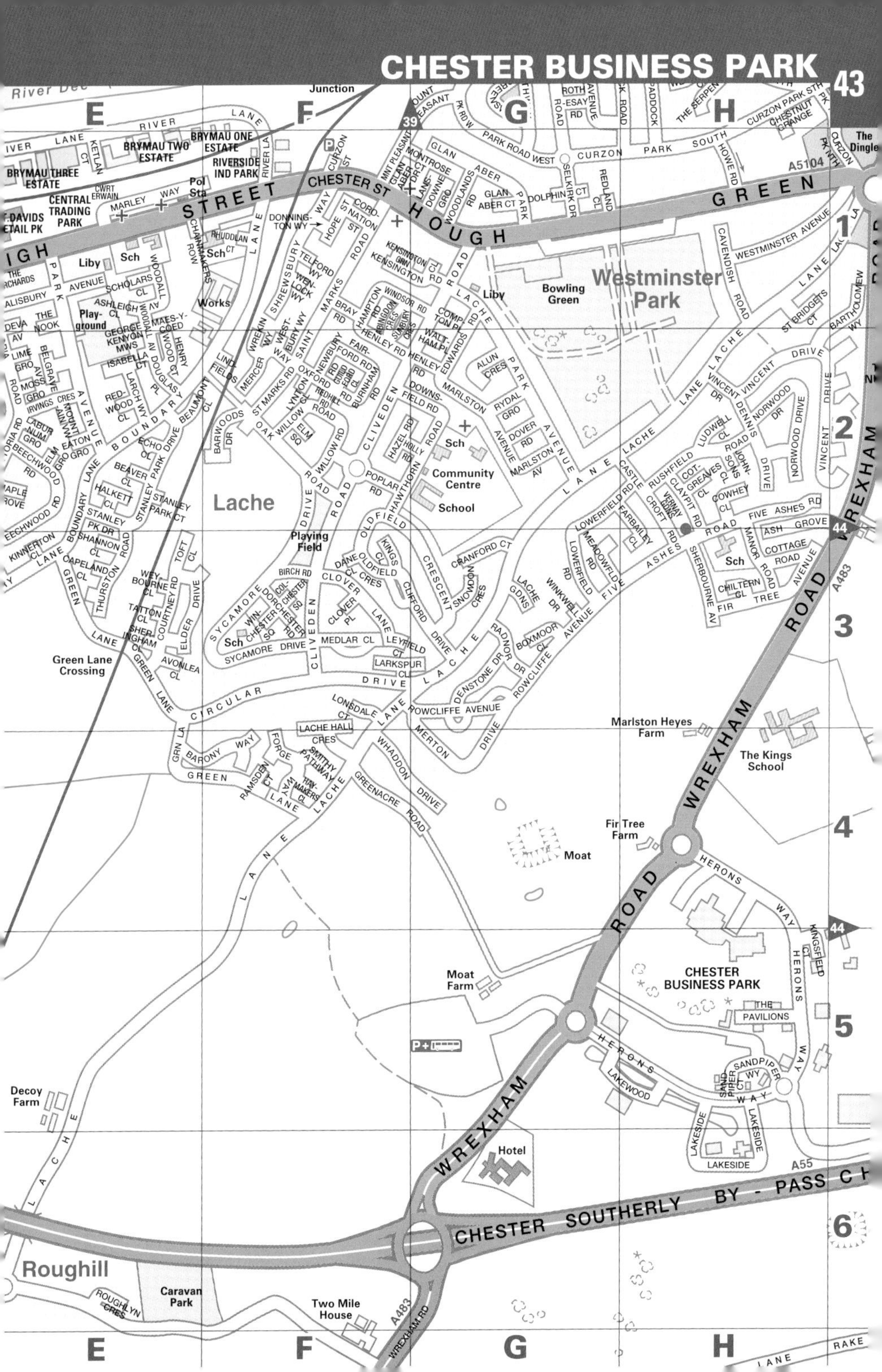
E
F
G
H
1
2
3
4
5
6
River Dee
Junction
RIVER LANE
BRYMAU TWO ESTATE
BRYMAU ONE ESTATE
BRYMAU THREE ESTATE
RIVERSIDE IND PARK
RIVER LA
KETLAN CT
CENTRAL TRADING PARK
CWRT ERWAIN
MARLEY WAY
Pol Sta
ST.DAVIDS RETAIL PK
CHESTER ST
STREET
HOUGH GREEN
CURZON PARK
CURZON PARK SOUTH
CURZON PARK STH
CHESTNUT GRANGE
The Dingle
A5104
PARK ROAD WEST
GLAN ABER PARK
GLAN ABER CT
DOLPHIN CT
SELKIRK DR
REDLAND CL
MONTROSE CT
DOWNE GRO
WOODLANDS RD
HOWE RD
CAVENDISH ROAD
WESTMINSTER AVENUE
Westminster Park
Bowling Green
Liby
Sch
Works
Lache
Playing Field
Community Centre
School
LACHE LANE
LACHE PARK AVENUE
FIVE ASHES RD
ASH GROVE
COTTAGE ROAD
CHILTERN CL
FIR TREE AV
MANOR ROAD
CASTLE DR
LOWERFIELD RD
WINKWELL DR
ROWCLIFFE AVENUE
CIRCULAR DRIVE
CLIVEDEN ROAD
SYCAMORE DRIVE
MEDLAR CL
LARKSPUR CL
LEYFIELD CT
CLIFFORD DRIVE
CRESCENT
SNOWDON CRES
CRANFORD CT
BOUNDARY LANE
GREEN LANE
Green Lane Crossing
BARONY WAY
FORGE
SMITHY PATHWAY
HAYMAKERS CL
RAMSDEN CT
LACHE HALL CRES
LONSDALE CT
MERTON
WHADDON DRIVE
GREENACRE ROAD
Marlston Heyes Farm
The Kings School
Fir Tree Farm
Moat
Moat Farm
P+
WREXHAM ROAD
A483
HERONS WAY
KINGSFIELD CT
CHESTER BUSINESS PARK
THE PAVILIONS
SANDPIPER WY
SANDPIPER CT
LAKEWOOD
LAKESIDE
A55
CHESTER SOUTHERLY BY-PASS
Hotel
Decoy Farm
Roughill
ROUGHLYN CRES
Caravan Park
Two Mile House
WREXHAM RD
RAKE LANE
39
44

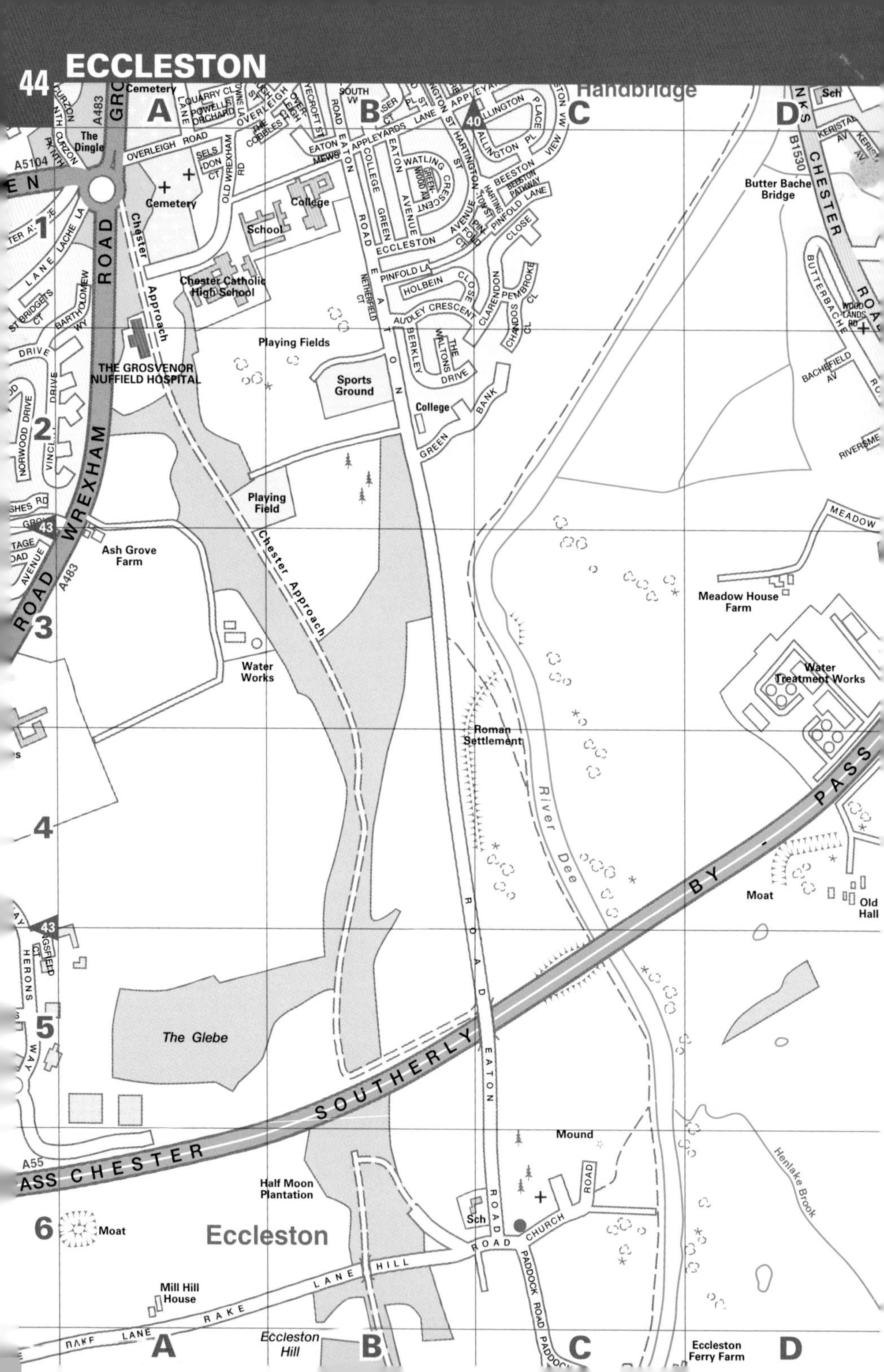
Handbridge
Cemetery
The Dingle
A5104
A483
OVERLEIGH ROAD
Chester Approach
College
School
Chester Catholic High School
THE GROSVENOR NUFFIELD HOSPITAL
Playing Fields
Sports Ground
College
Playing Field
WREXHAM ROAD
Ash Grove Farm
Water Works
EATON ROAD
Butter Bache Bridge
CHESTER ROAD
B1530
Meadow House Farm
Water Treatment Works
Roman Settlement
River Dee
Moat
Old Hall
CHESTER SOUTHERLY BY-PASS
The Glebe
A55
Half Moon Plantation
Eccleston
Mound
Sch
CHURCH ROAD
PADDOCK ROAD
Henlake Brook
Mill Hill House
RAKE LANE
Eccleston Hill
Eccleston Ferry Farm

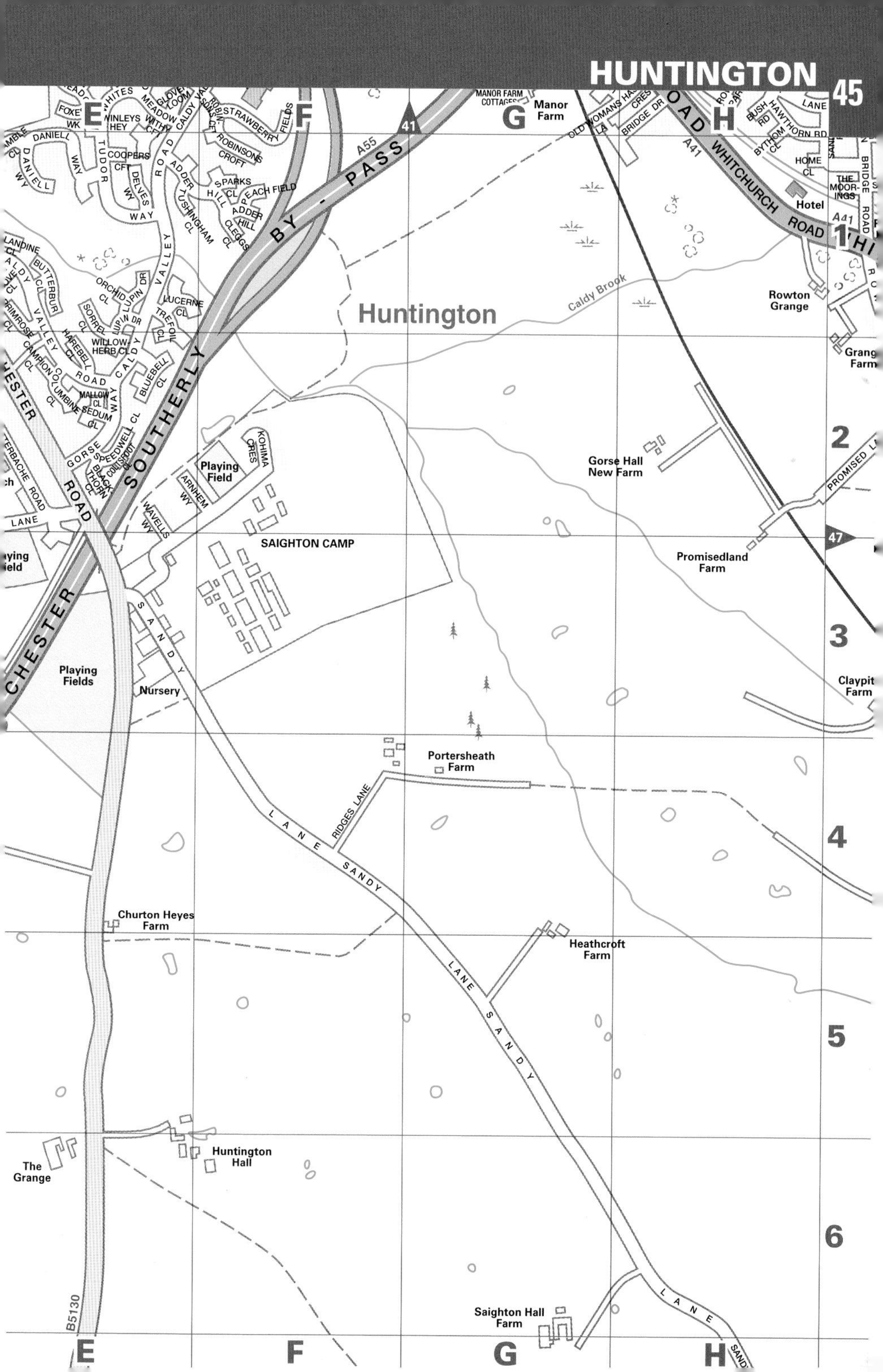
Huntington
SOUTHERLY BY - PASS
A55
41
CHESTER ROAD
WHITCHURCH ROAD
A41
Manor Farm
MANOR FARM COTTAGES
OLD WOMANS LA
BRIDGE DR
CRES
BUSH RD
HAWTHORN RD
BYTHOM CL
HOME CL
THE MOORINGS
Hotel
Rowton Grange
Grange Farm
Caldy Brook
STRAWBERRY FIELDS
ROBINSONS CROFT
SPARKS CL
PEACH FIELD
ADDER HILL
CLEGGS
TUSHINGHAM CL
DELVES WY
COOPERS CFT
TUDOR WAY
DANIELL WAY
WINLEYS HEY
WHITES MEADOW
GLOVERS LOOM
CALDY VALLEY ROAD
ORCHID CL
LUPIN DR
LUCERNE CL
TREFOIL CL
BUTTERBUR CL
SORREL CL
HAREBELL CL
WILLOW-HERB CL
BLUEBELL CL
CAMPION CL
COLUMBINE CL
MALLOW CL
SEDUM CL
PRIMROSE CL
GORSE WAY
SPEEDWELL CL
BLACKTHORN CL
LANE
Playing Field
KOHIMA CRES
ARNHEM WY
WAVELLS WY
SAIGHTON CAMP
Gorse Hall New Farm
PROMISED LA
47
Promisedland Farm
Playing Fields
Nursery
SANDY LANE
Claypit Farm
Portersheath Farm
RIDGES LANE
Churton Heyes Farm
Heathcroft Farm
Huntington Hall
The Grange
Saighton Hall Farm
B5130
E
F
G
H
1
2
3
4
5
6

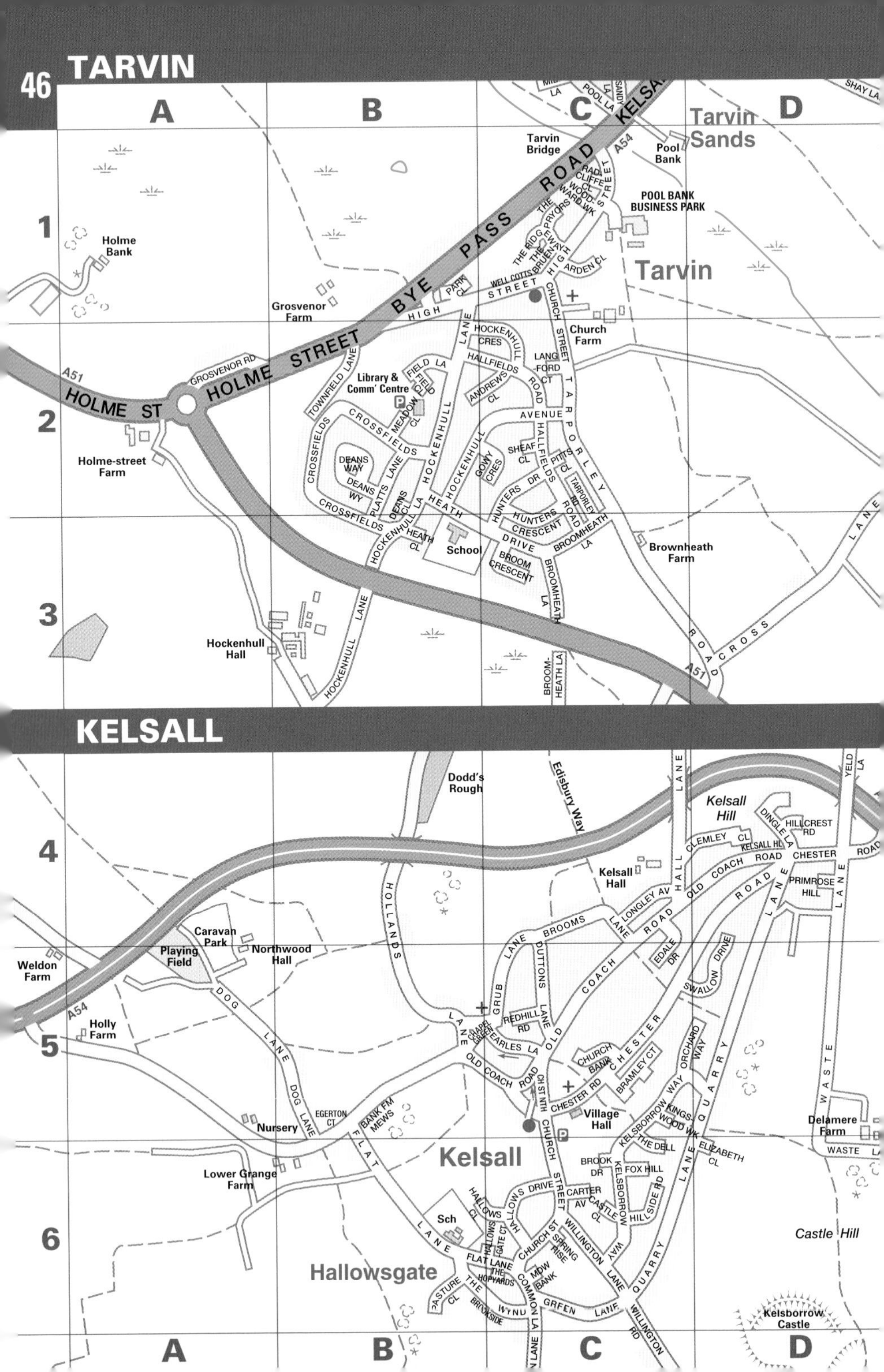
TARVIN
A
B
C
D
1
2
3
Tarvin Bridge
Tarvin Sands
Pool Bank
POOL BANK BUSINESS PARK
Tarvin
Holme Bank
Grosvenor Farm
BYE PASS ROAD
HIGH STREET
HOLME STREET
HOLME ST
A51
A54
GROSVENOR RD
Library & Comm' Centre
Church Farm
Holme-street Farm
TOWNFIELD LANE
CROSSFIELDS
DEANS WAY
DEANS WY
PLATTS LANE
DEANS CL
MEADOW CL
FIELD LA
FIELD CL
HOCKENHULL LANE
HOCKENHULL LA
HOCKENHULL CRES
HALLFIELDS ROAD
HALLFIELDS
ANDREWS CL
AVENUE
LANGFORD CT
TARPORLEY
TARPORLEY RD
PITTS CL
SHEAF CL
GOWY CRES
HUNTERS DR
HUNTERS CRESCENT
HEATH
HEATH CL
School
DRIVE
BROOM CRESCENT
BROOMHEATH LA
BROOMHEATH LANE
Brownheath Farm
CROSS ROAD
Hockenhull Hall
THE RIDGE
THE BRUEN
THE PRYORS
WOODWARD WK
RADCLIFFE CL
ARDEN CL
WELL COTTS
PARK CL
CHURCH STREET
STREET
KELSALL
Dodd's Rough
Edisbury Way
Kelsall Hill
DINGLE LA
HILLCREST RD
CLEMLEY CL
KELSALL HL
CHESTER ROAD
YELD LA
PRIMROSE HILL
Kelsall Hall
HOLLANDS LANE
HALL LANE
LONGLEY AV
OLD COACH ROAD
BROOMS LANE
EDALE DR
SWALLOW DRIVE
GRUB LANE
DUTTONS LANE
COACH ROAD
Caravan Park
Northwood Hall
Playing Field
Weldon Farm
Holly Farm
DOG LANE
REDHILL RD
CHAPEL GREEN
EARLES LA
OLD COACH ROAD
CHURCH BANK
CHESTER
BRAMLEY CT
ORCHARD WAY
QUARRY LANE
CHESTER RD
CH ST NTH
Village Hall
EGERTON CT
BANK FM MEWS
Nursery
FLAT LANE
KELSBORROW WAY
KINGSWOOD WK
THE DELL
ELIZABETH CL
Delamere Farm
WASTE LANE
Kelsall
Lower Grange Farm
BROOK DR
FOX HILL
HILLSIDE RD
HALLOWS DRIVE
HALLOWS CL
CARTER AV
CASTLE CL
Sch
HALLOWS GATE CT
CHURCH ST
SPRING RISE
WILLINGTON LANE
Castle Hill
Hallowsgate
THE HOPYARDS
MDW BANK
COMMON LA
PASTURE CL
THE BROOKSIDE
WYND
GREEN LANE
WILLINGTON RD
Kelsborrow Castle
4
5
6

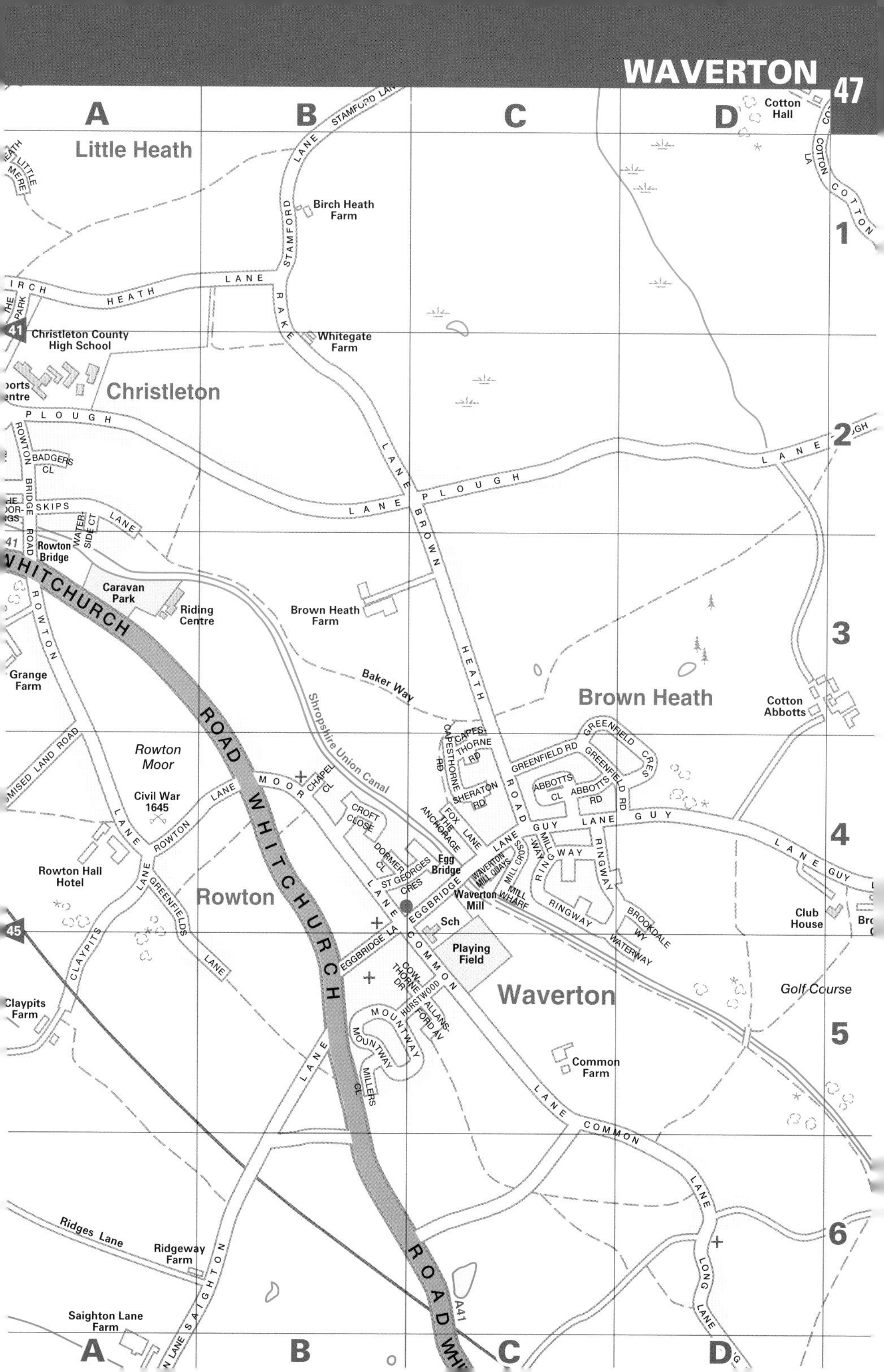
Little Heath
Birch Heath Farm
Stamford Lane
Heath Lane
Rake Lane
Christleton County High School
Whitegate Farm
Christleton
Cotton Hall
Cotton La
Plough Lane
Brown Heath Road
Rowton Bridge Road
Badgers Cl
Skips Lane
Waterside Ct
Rowton Bridge
Whitchurch Road
Caravan Park
Riding Centre
Brown Heath Farm
Baker Way
Shropshire Union Canal
Brown Heath
Cotton Abbotts
Grange Farm
Rowton Moor
Civil War 1645
Moor Lane
Chapel Cl
Croft Close
Capesthorne Rd
Sheraton Rd
Fox Lane
The Anchorage
Greenfield Rd
Greenfield Cres
Abbotts Cl
Abbotts Rd
Guy Lane
Ringway
Dormer Cl
St Georges Cres
Egg Bridge
Waverton Mill Quays
Mill Cross
Mill Wharf
Waverton Mill
Eggbridge Lane
Brookdale Wy
Waterway
Club House
Golf Course
Rowton Lane
Rowton Hall Hotel
Greenfields Lane
Rowton
Sch
Playing Field
Waverton
Common Lane
Cowthorne Dr
Hurstwood
Allansford Av
Mountway
Millers Cl
Claypits Lane
Claypits Farm
Common Farm
Long Lane
Ridges Lane
Ridgeway Farm
Saighton Lane
Saighton Lane Farm
A41
1 2 3 4 5 6
A B C D

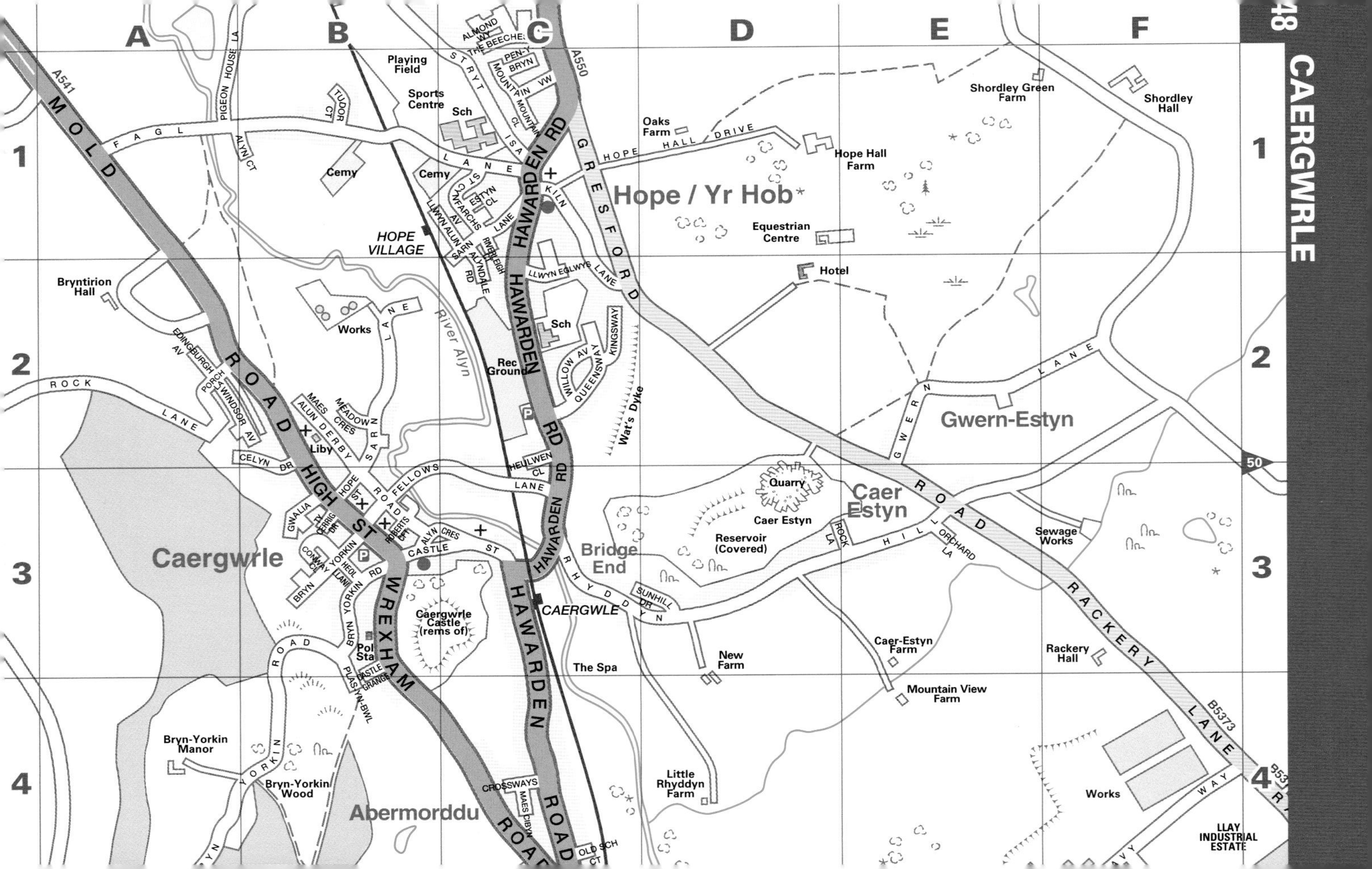

A B C D E F
1 2 3 4
Playing Field
Sports Centre
Sch
ALMOND WY
THE BEECHES
PEN-Y BRYN
MOUNTAIN VW
MOUNTAIN CL
STRYT ISA
A550
Oaks Farm
HOPE HALL DRIVE
Hope Hall Farm
Shordley Green Farm
Shordley Hall
MOLD ROAD
A541
PIGEON HOUSE LA
TUDOR CT
FAGL
ALYN CT
Cemy
Cemy
LANE
HAWARDEN RD
GRESFORD ROAD
KILN
Hope / Yr Hob
Equestrian Centre
Hotel
ST CYNFARCHS AV
ESTYN CL
LANE
LLWYN ALUN
SARN
RIVERLEIGH
ALYNDALE RD
HOPE VILLAGE
LLWYN EGLWYS LANE
Bryntirion Hall
Works
LANE
River Alyn
Sch
KINGSWAY
WILLOW AV
QUEENSWAY
Rec Ground
Wat's Dyke
EDINBURGH AV
PORCH
WINDSOR AV
ROCK LANE
MAES ALUN
DERBY
MEADOW CRES
SARN
Liby
CELYN DR
HIGH ST
HEULWEN CL
FELLOWS LANE
HOPE ST
ROAD
GWERN LANE
Gwern-Estyn
50
Quarry
Caer Estyn
Caer Estyn
Reservoir (Covered)
ROCK LA
HILL
ORCHARD LA
Sewage Works
GWALIA
TY CERRIG DR
ROBERTS CT
ALYN CRES
CASTLE ST
Caergwrle
CONWAY CL
YORKIN
HEOL LANI
RD
BRYN
WREXHAM
HAWARDEN ROAD
Bridge End
RHYDDYN
SUNHILL DR
CAERGWLE
Caergwrle Castle (rems of)
ROAD
BRYN YORKIN
Pol Sta
CASTLE GRANGE
PLAS-YN-BWL
The Spa
New Farm
Caer-Estyn Farm
Rackery Hall
RACKERY LANE
B5373
Mountain View Farm
Bryn-Yorkin Manor
YORKIN
Bryn-Yorkin Wood
Abermorddu
CROSSWAYS
MAES CIBYN
OLD SCH CT
Little Rhyddyn Farm
Works
WAY
LLAY INDUSTRIAL ESTATE

Cefn-y-bedd
CEFN-Y-BEDD
Gwastad Farm
Gwastad Hall
WREXHAM RD
WREXHAM ROAD
MOLD ROAD
A541
LLAY ROAD
B5102
Llay Hall Farm
Llay Bank
River Alyn
(Afon Alun)
RIVERSIDE BUSINESS PK
LLAY HALL IND EST
Works
OAK ALYN COURT
BRYN DERW
TAN-YR-ALLT
Sydallt
Sydallt Farm
Sydallt Wood
Windy Hill
FFRWD ROAD
FURNACE RD
ROAD
CAE-PEN-TY
GLYON LANE
Golf Course
MINERA ROAD
River Cegidog
Cymau
BRYN YORKIN ROAD
CYMAU
Plas Maen
PLAS MAEN DR
PETIT CLOSE
ALUNDALE RD
WYNDHAM DR
WYNDHAM
ROAD
MINERS ROAD
Works
Hall Wood
Visitor Centre
ALYN WATERS PARK (PARC DYFROEDD ALYN)
Old Hall Farm
Barn
50
A
B
C
D
E
F
5
6
7
8

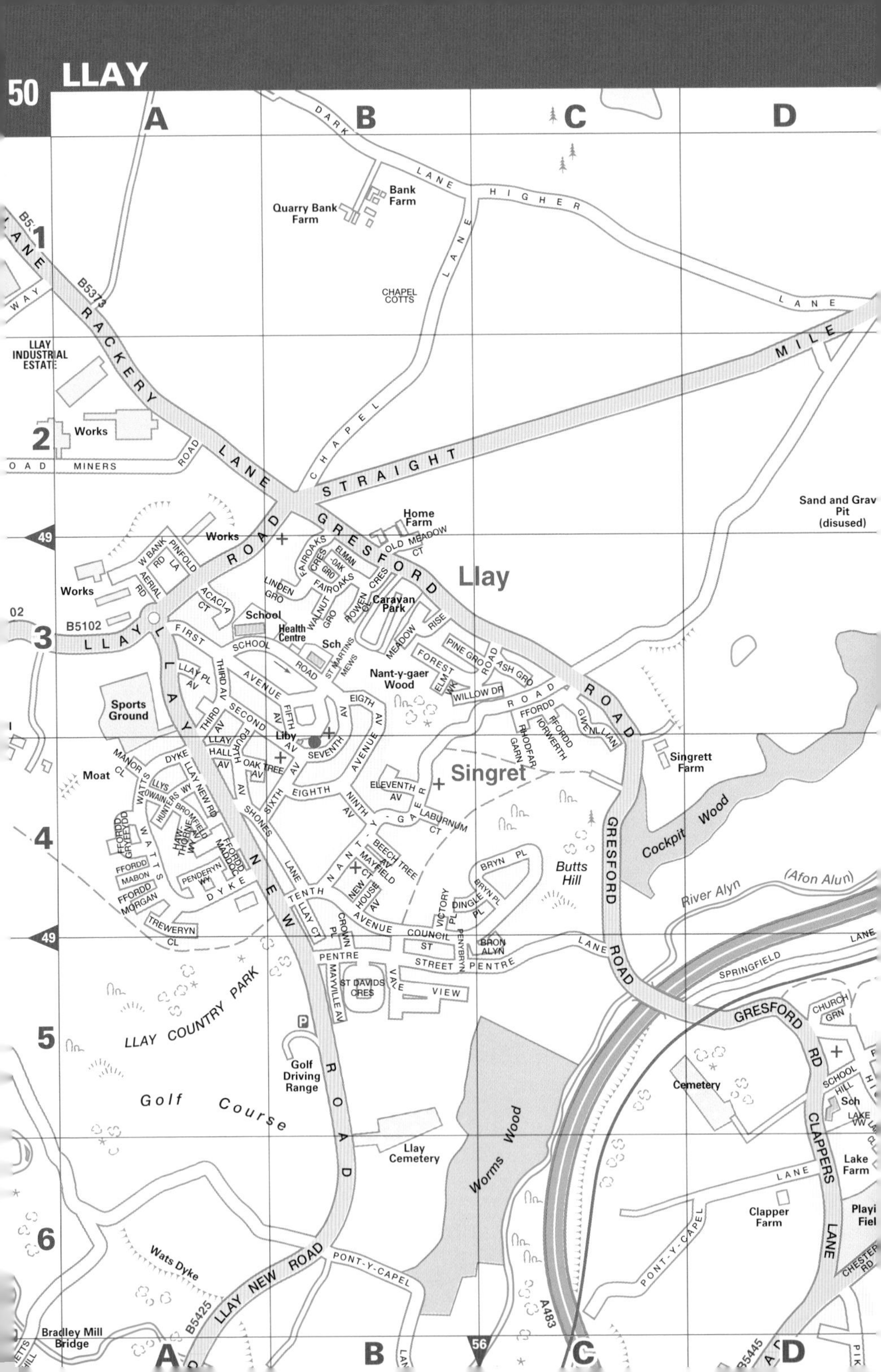

Quarry Bank Farm
Bank Farm
DARK LANE
HIGHER LANE
CHAPEL LANE
CHAPEL COTTS
STRAIGHT MILE
RACKERY LANE
LLAY INDUSTRIAL ESTATE
Works
MINERS ROAD
GRESFORD ROAD
Home Farm
OLD MEADOW CT
Llay
Sand and Grav Pit (disused)
School
Health Centre
Sch
Caravan Park
Nant-y-gaer Wood
Sports Ground
Liby
Moat
Singret
Singrett Farm
Cockpit Wood
Butts Hill
River Alyn
(Afon Alun)
LLAY NEW ROAD
LLAY COUNTRY PARK
Golf Course
Golf Driving Range
Llay Cemetery
Worms Wood
Wats Dyke
Bradley Mill Bridge
PONT-Y-CAPEL
Cemetery
Clapper Farm
Lake Farm
CLAPPERS LANE
GRESFORD RD
SPRINGFIELD LANE
B5102
B5373
B5425
B5445
A483

E
F
G
H
1
2
3
4
5
6
52
57
Burton
The Grange
Strathalyn
Cemy
Yew Tree Farm
B5102
CROESHOWELL HILL
CROESHOWELL LANE
LLAY ROAD
LLAY RD
A483
JUNCTION 7
Mill Race
Rossett Mill
Marford Mill
Trevalyn Hall
STATION ROAD
CHESTER ROAD
MANOR LANE
TREVALYN HOSPITAL
River Alyn
(Afon Alyn)
THE SPINNEY
MARFORD HEIGHTS
VILLAGE WALKS
MARFORD HILL
Marford
Marford Hall
Sewage Works
SPRINGFIELD LANE
Marford Wood
Pant
QUARRY BROW
TURNPIKE LA
WOODLANDS RD
SUNNYRIDGE AV
WOODRIDGE AV
HOSELEY LANE
Pistyll House Farm
COX LANE
PISTYLL HILL
WYNNSTAY LA
WYNNSTAY LANE
STANCLIFFE AV
Wineberry Gorse
Gresford Park
GRESFORD PK
THE CONIFERS
HOLLYFIELDS
SANDY LA
CHESTER ROAD
CAVENDISH CT
BELGRAVE CT
Sch
SANDROCK RD
MEADOWS VIEW
CLAYPIT
SYCAMORE DR
NARROW LANE
PANT
CHESTNUT CL
BEECH AV
LIME AV
ANNEFIELD PARK
NEWTOWN
Pol Sta
BURTON RISE
BODWYN CRES
NAYLAND AV
POPLAR DR
MAYFLOWER DR
MEREILIAN AV
Playing Field
HUDSONS HILL
HOSELEY PARK LANE
Hoseley House
Gresford
Trewythen Park
Trewythen Hall
VICARAGE LANE
Liby
OLD WREXHAM ROAD
Caravan Park
Gatehouse Farm

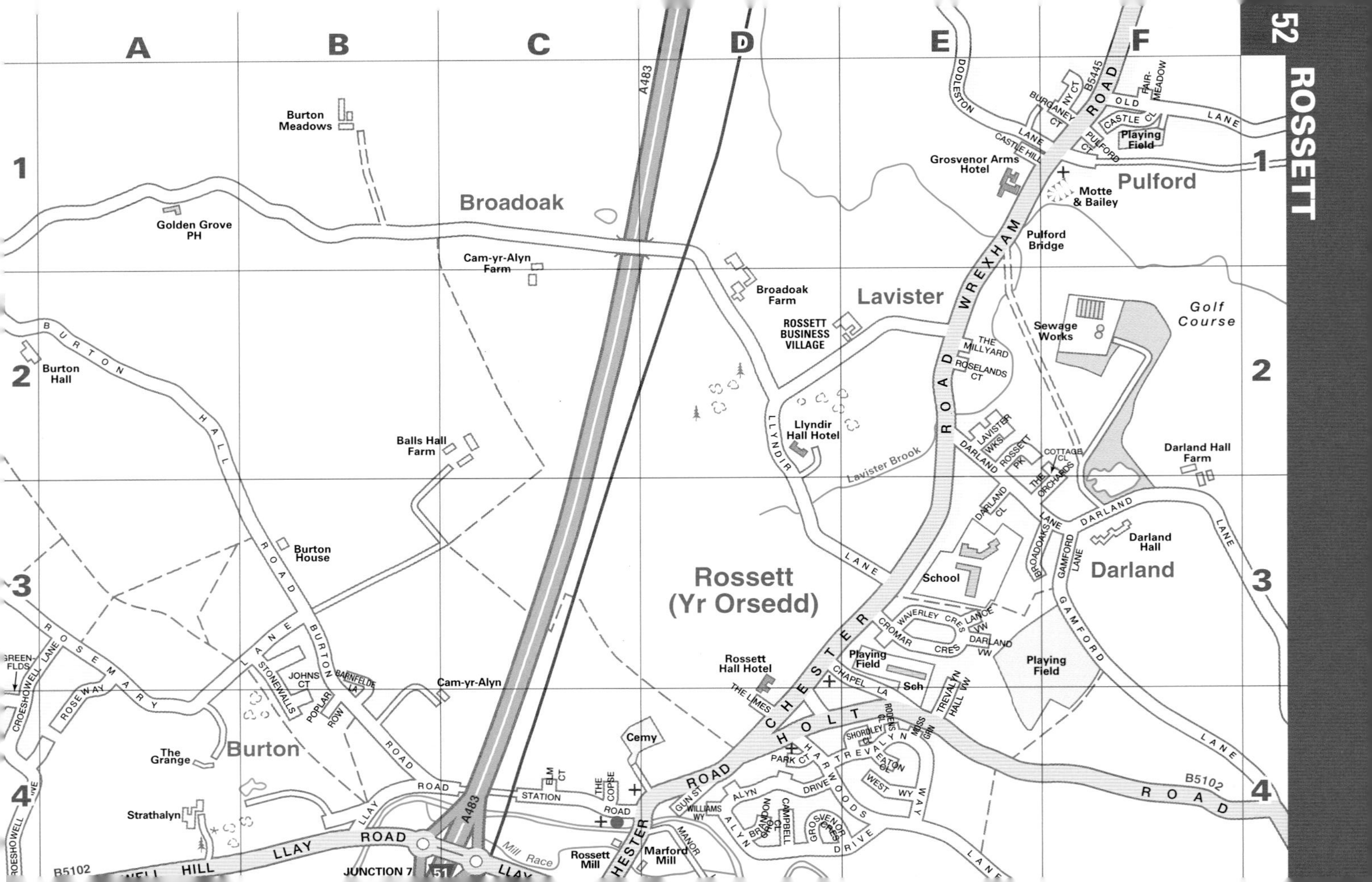
Burton Meadows
Broadoak
Golden Grove PH
Cam-yr-Alyn Farm
Broadoak Farm
Lavister
ROSSETT BUSINESS VILLAGE
Llyndir Hall Hotel
Lavister Brook
Grosvenor Arms Hotel
Pulford
Motte & Bailey
Pulford Bridge
Sewage Works
Golf Course
Playing Field
Darland Hall Farm
Darland Hall
Darland
School
Rossett (Yr Orsedd)
Rossett Hall Hotel
Burton Hall
BURTON HALL ROAD
Balls Hall Farm
Burton House
Cam-yr-Alyn
Burton
The Grange
Strathalyn
Cemy
Rossett Mill
Marford Mill
Mill Race
JUNCTION 7
LLAY ROAD
STATION ROAD
WREXHAM ROAD
CHESTER ROAD
HOLT ROAD
GAMFORD LANE
DODLESTON LANE
ROSEMARY LANE
B5102
B5445
A483

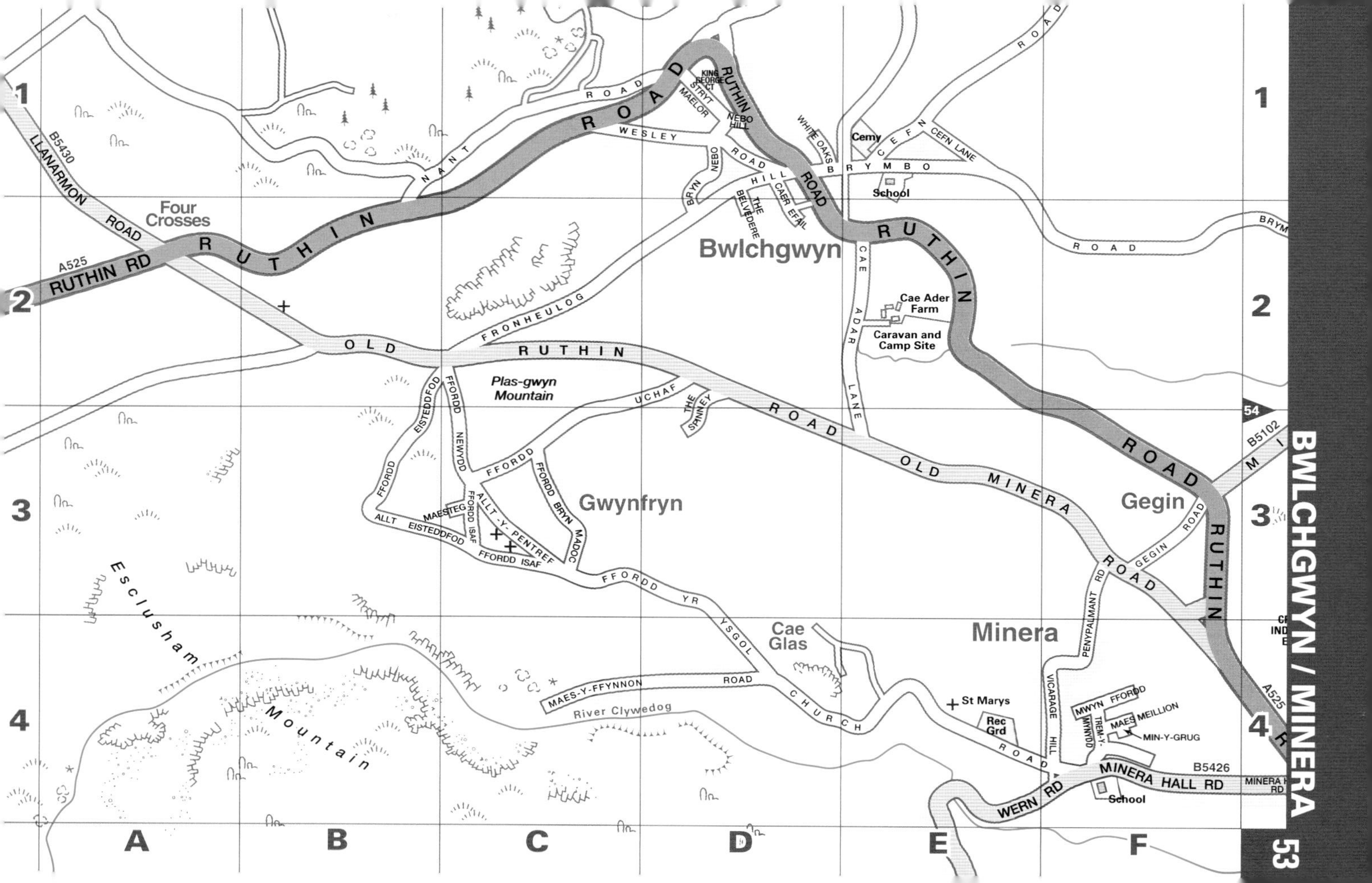

Bwlchgwyn
Minera
Gegin
Gwynfryn
Cae Glas
Four Crosses
Plas-gwyn Mountain
Esclusham Mountain
RUTHIN ROAD
RUTHIN RD
OLD RUTHIN ROAD
OLD MINERA ROAD
LLANARMON ROAD
B5430
A525
B5102
B5426
54
CAE ADAR LANE
Cae Ader Farm
Caravan and Camp Site
School
Cemy
CEFN LANE
BRYMBO ROAD
WHITE OAKS
CAER EFAIL
THE BELVEDERE
HILL
NEBO HILL
KING GEORGE CT
STRYT MAELOR
WESLEY ROAD
BRYN NEBO
FRONHEULOG
NANT ROAD
THE SPINNEY
UCHAF
FFORDD BRYN MADOC
FFORDD NEWYDD
FFORDD EISTEDDFOD
ALLT-Y-PENTREF
FFORDD ISAF
MAESTEG
ALLT EISTEDDFOD
FFORDD YR YSGOL
CHURCH ROAD
MAES-Y-FFYNNON ROAD
River Clywedog
St Marys
Rec Grd
VICARAGE HILL
PENYPALMANT RD
GEGIN ROAD
MINERA HALL RD
WERN RD
MWYN FFORDD
MAES MEILLION
MIN-Y-GRUG
TREM-Y-MYNYDD
A B C D E F
1 2 3 4

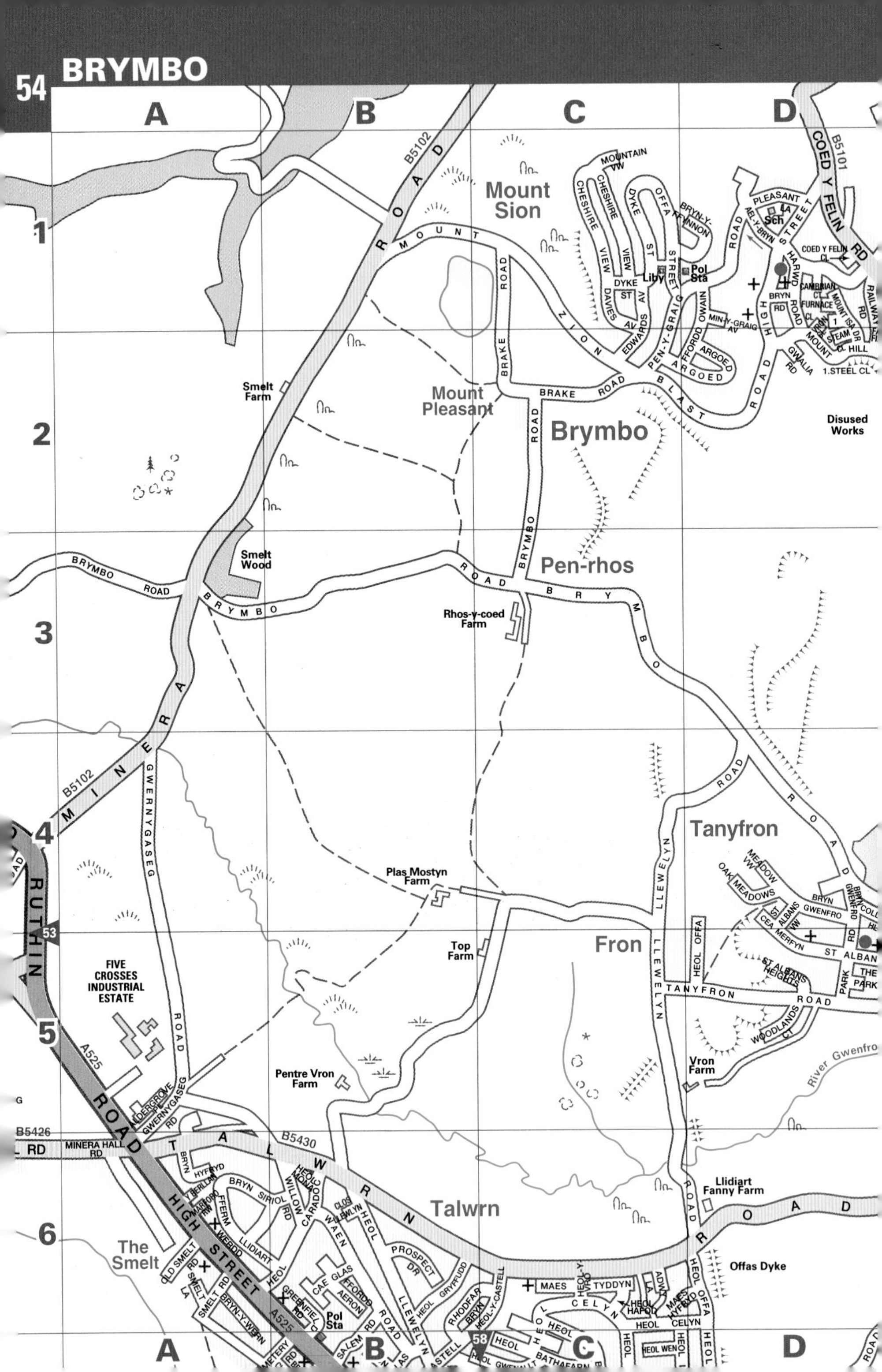
A
B
C
D
1
2
3
4
5
6
Mount Sion
Brymbo
Pen-rhos
Mount Pleasant
Tanyfron
Fron
Talwrn
The Smelt
Smelt Farm
Smelt Wood
Rhos-y-coed Farm
Plas Mostyn Farm
Top Farm
Pentre Vron Farm
Vron Farm
Llidiart Fanny Farm
Offas Dyke
Disused Works
FIVE CROSSES INDUSTRIAL ESTATE
River Gwenfro
MINERA ROAD
B5102
BRYMBO ROAD
MOUNT ZION
BRAKE ROAD
BLAST ROAD
COED Y FELIN RD
B5101
MOUNTAIN VW
CHESHIRE VIEW
DYKE ST
OFFA STREET
BRYN-Y-FFYNNON
DAVIES AV
EDWARDS AV
PEN-Y-GRAIG
FFORDD OWAIN
MIN-Y-GRAIG AV
ARGOED
PLEASANT LA
HIGH STREET
HARWD ROAD
COED Y FELIN CL
CAMBRIAN CT
FURNACE CL
GWALIA RD
1.STEEL CL
Liby
Pol Sta
Sch
GWERNYGASEG ROAD
RUTHIN ROAD
A525
B5426
B5430
MINERA HALL RD
ALDERGROVE
LLEWELYN ROAD
HEOL OFFA
TANYFRON ROAD
MEADOW VW
OAK MEADOWS
BRYN GWENFRO
ST ALBANS VW
CEA MERFYN
ST ALBANS HEIGHTS
WOODLANDS CT
PARK
THE PARK
HIGH STREET
BRYN SIRIOL
LLIDIART
FFERM
CLOS LLEWLYN
HEOL WAEN
PROSPECT DR
CAE GLAS
FFORDD AERON
GREENFIELD RD
SMELT RD
BRYN-Y-WERN
OLD SMELT RD
SMELT LA
HEOL GRYFFUDD
HEOL-Y-CASTELL
RHODFAR BRYN
MAES TYDDYN
HEOL HAFOD
HEOL CELYN
HEOL WEN
SALEM RD
58
53

E
F
G
H
1
2
3
4
5
6
Barn
Bryn Mally Farm
Brynmally Park
Golf Course
Club House
Moss
Pentre Broughton
Police Ho
Moss Quarry (dis)
Moss Wood
Golf Course
Moss Valley
Cefn
Liby
Playing Fields
Brynteg
Sch
Playing Field
Sch
Summerhill
Playing Field
Leisure Centre
Works
Depot
School
Sch
Works
GWERSYLLT
Sch
Gwersyllt Hill
Wks
Pol Ho
THE SYCAMORES
POUNTNEYS CORNER
Pool Mouth
Boating Lakes
Stansty Park
Cricket Ground
Sports Ground
Playing Field
Broughton Hall
Playing Field
Playing Field
Works
SOUTHSEA INDUSTRIAL ESTATE
Rec Grd
Southsea
Pol Sta
New Broughton
Sports Ground
Sch
Pendine Farm
Gatewen Hall
A541
MOLD ROAD
B5430
B5101
B5433
STATION ROAD
NEW KENT ROAD
HIGH STREET
HILL ST
WREXHAM ROAD
GATEWEN ROAD
CLAYTON ROAD
LONG LANE
BROUGHTON ROAD
SUMMERHILL ROAD
WHEATSHEAF LANE
POOLMOUTH RD
HIGHFIELDS ROAD
GRIFFITHS RD
SOUTHSEA RD
TANYFRON RD
BRYMBO ROAD
BERSE ROAD
SMITHY LANE
ROAD
WINDSOR RD
CORONATION ST
NEW RD
MILL FIELDS
ATLEE
HALL VW
56
59

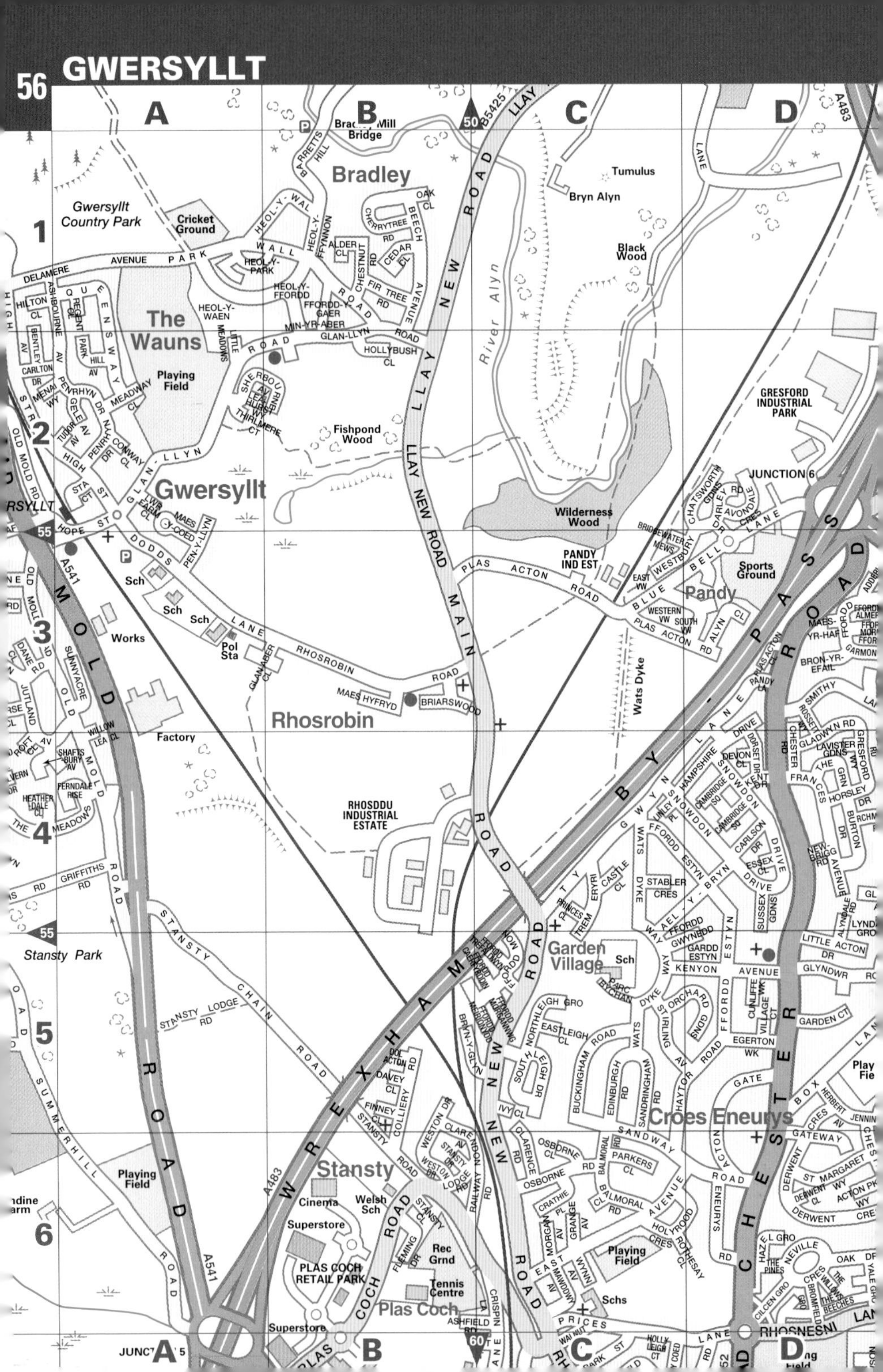
Gwersyllt Country Park
Cricket Ground
Bradley
Bradley Mill Bridge
Tumulus
Bryn Alyn
Black Wood
River Alyn
The Wauns
Playing Field
Fishpond Wood
Gwersyllt
Wilderness Wood
GRESFORD INDUSTRIAL PARK
JUNCTION 6
PANDY IND EST
Sports Ground
Pandy
Works
Pol Sta
Sch
Factory
Rhosrobin
Wats Dyke
RHOSDDU INDUSTRIAL ESTATE
Garden Village
Stansty Park
Croes Eneurys
Stansty
Cinema
Welsh Sch
Superstore
PLAS COCH RETAIL PARK
Rec Grnd
Tennis Centre
Plas Coch
Playing Field
Schs
RHOSNESNI
MOLD ROAD
WREXHAM BY-PASS
CHESTER ROAD
LLAY NEW ROAD
A541
A483
B5425

Caravan Park
51
Vicarage Lane
Carthagena Farm
Caia Farm
W.F.C Training Ground
B5445
A483
Pikey Lane
Old Wrexham Road
Wrexham Road
The Flash
Pant-yr-Ochain Farm
Pant-yr-Ochain Hotel
Pant-yr-Ochain Wood
F.b
Acton
Llan-y-Pwll
Borras Link
Barkers Lane
Borras Road
Borras Lane
Sand and Gravel Pit
Sand and Gravel Pit
Borras
Golf Course
Club House
Road
A5156
A534
Wrexham Rd
Holt Road
Tyn-twll Farm
Monument
Acton Park
Acton
Schools
Recreation Ground
Playing Field
Rhosnesni Lane
Jennings
Dean Road
Borras Road
61
Bryn Estyn Ct
E
F
G
H
1
2
3
4
5
6

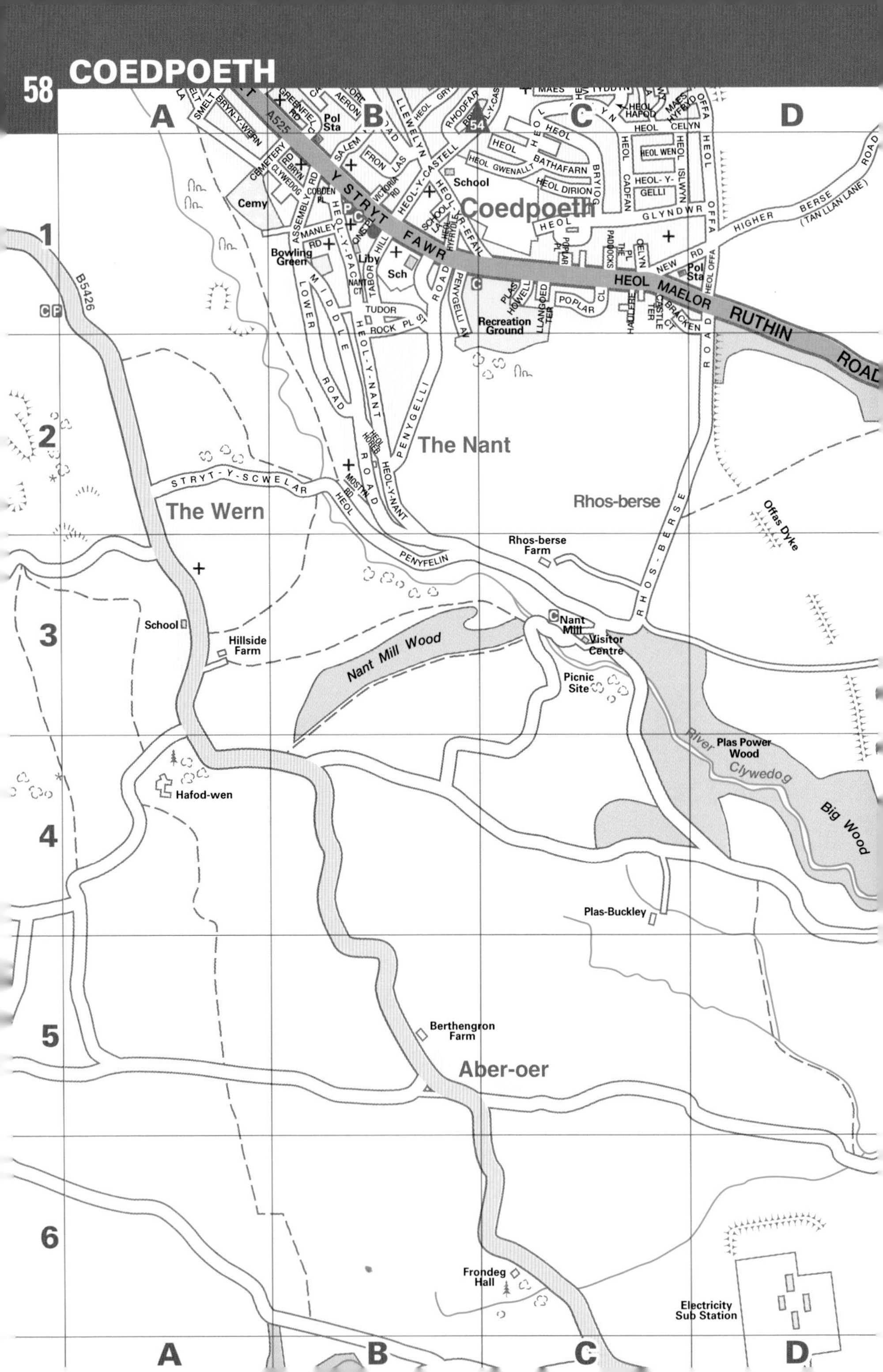

A
B
C
D
1
2
3
4
5
6
Coedpoeth
Y STRYT FAWR
A525
B5426
HEOL MAELOR
RUTHIN ROAD
Cemy
Pol Sta
School
Bowling Green
Liby
Sch
Recreation Ground
TUDOR
ROCK PL
LOWER ROAD
MIDDLE ROAD
HEOL-Y-NANT
PENYGELLI
PENYGELLI AV
The Nant
STRYT-Y-SCWELAR
The Wern
MOSTYN RD
HEOL PENYFELIN
Rhos-berse
Rhos-berse Farm
RHOS-BERSE
HIGHER BERSE (TAN LLAN LANE)
Offas Dyke
Nant Mill
Visitor Centre
Picnic Site
Nant Mill Wood
School
Hillside Farm
Hafod-wen
Plas Power Wood
River Clywedog
Big Wood
Plas-Buckley
Berthengron Farm
Aber-oer
Frondeg Hall
Electricity Sub Station

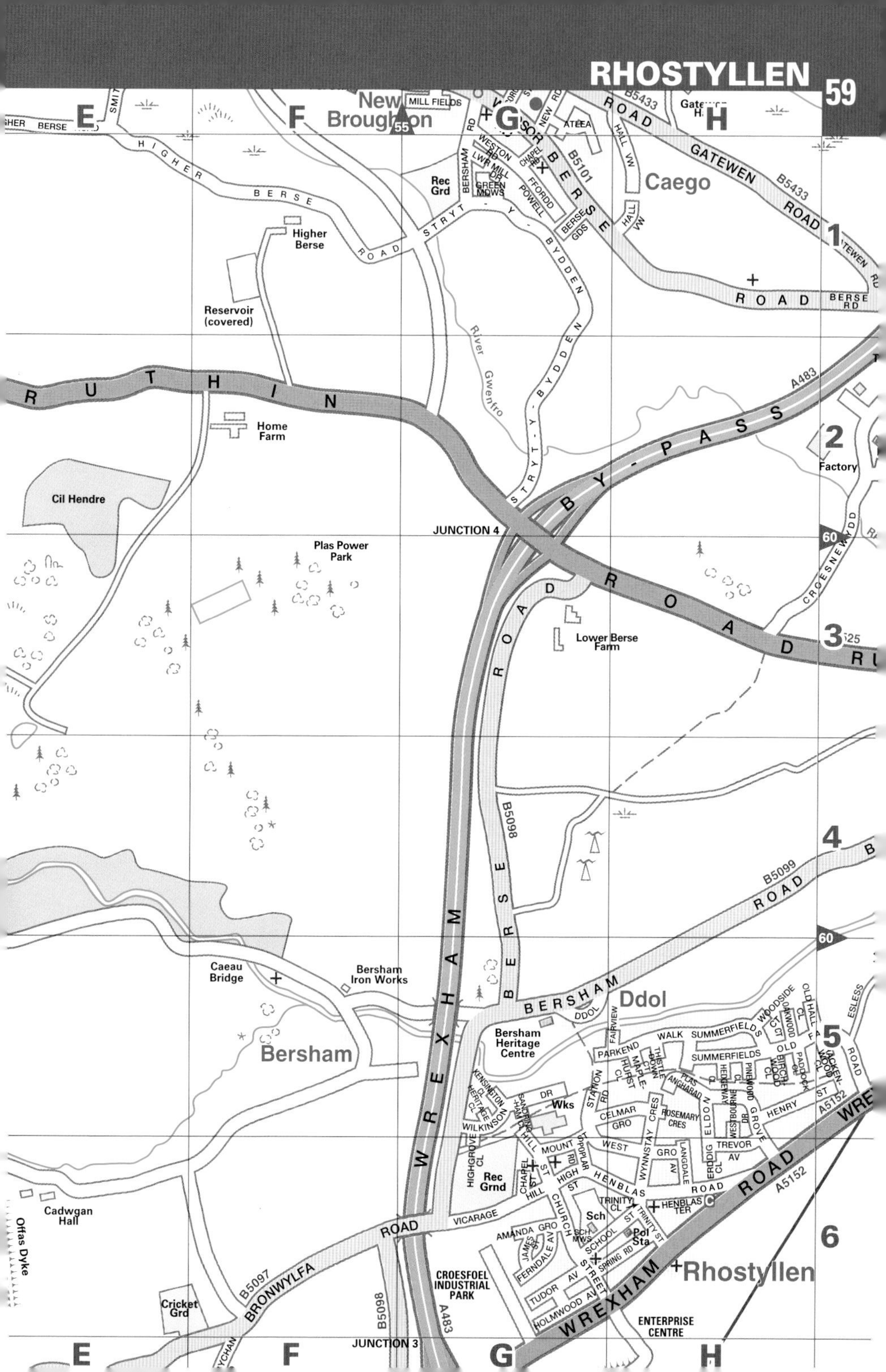
New Broughton
Caego
Higher Berse
Reservoir (covered)
Home Farm
Cil Hendre
Plas Power Park
JUNCTION 4
Lower Berse Farm
Factory
RUTHIN ROAD
BY-PASS
WREXHAM ROAD
BERSE ROAD
B5098
B5099
BERSHAM ROAD
Caeau Bridge
Bersham Iron Works
Bersham
Ddol
Bersham Heritage Centre
Rec Grnd
Cadwgan Hall
Offas Dyke
Cricket Grd
CROESFOEL INDUSTRIAL PARK
ENTERPRISE CENTRE
JUNCTION 3
Rhostyllen
B5097 BRONWYLFA ROAD
A5152
A483
Pol Sta
Sch
Wks

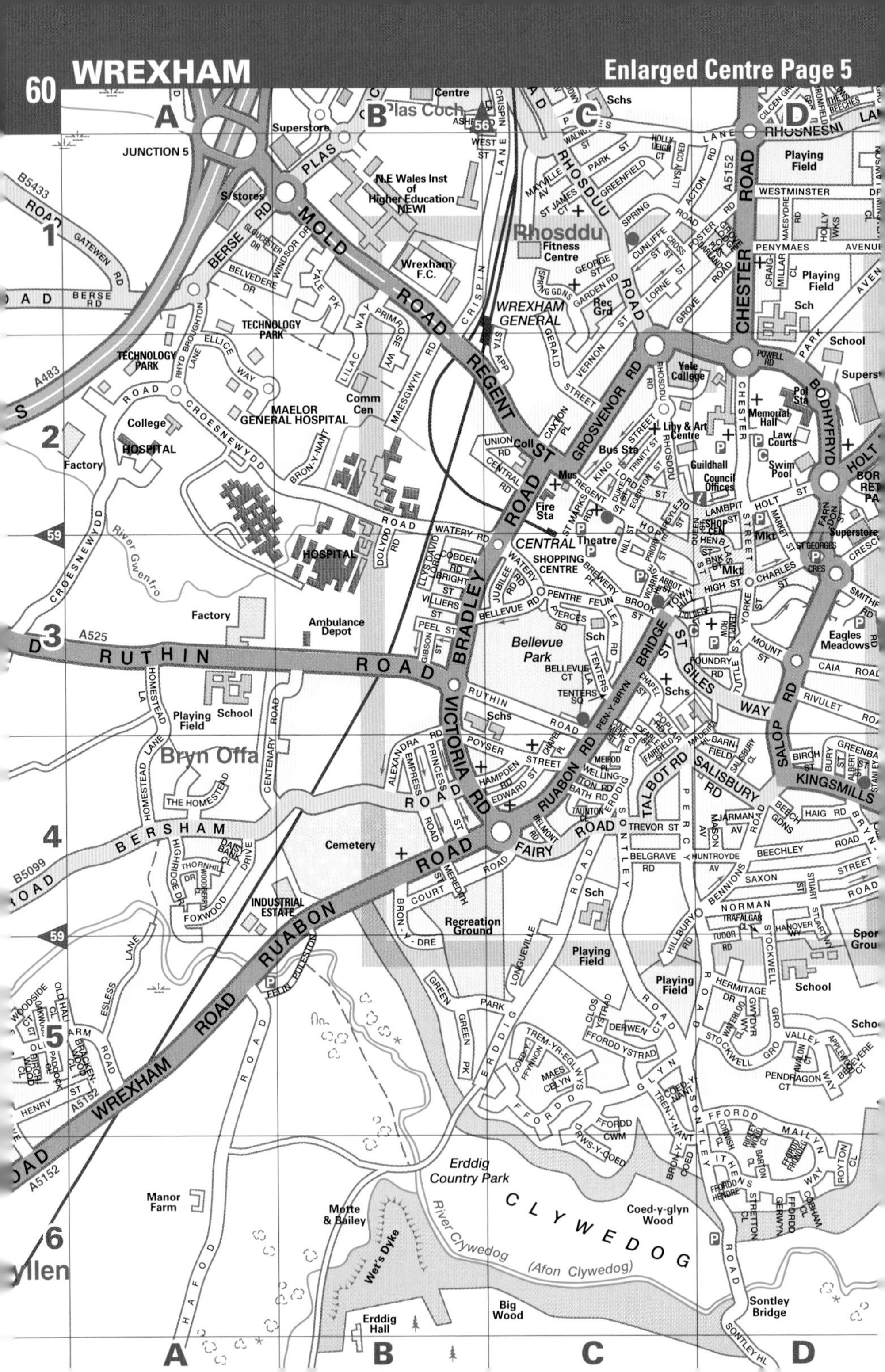
JUNCTION 5
TECHNOLOGY PARK
MAELOR GENERAL HOSPITAL
Wrexham F.C.
N.E Wales Inst of Higher Education NEWI
Rhosddu
WREXHAM GENERAL
CENTRAL
Bellevue Park
Bryn Offa
Cemetery
INDUSTRIAL ESTATE
Recreation Ground
Erddig Country Park
Erddig Hall
Wet's Dyke
Motte & Bailey
CLYWEDOG
River Clywedog
(Afon Clywedog)
Coed-y-glyn Wood
Big Wood
Sontley Bridge
Manor Farm
RUTHIN ROAD
MOLD ROAD
RUABON ROAD
WREXHAM ROAD
CHESTER ROAD
BERSHAM ROAD
KINGSMILLS

E
F
G
H
1
2
3
4
5
6
57
62
62
71
WREXHAM (WRECSAM)
Rhosnesni
Wrexham Rugby Club
Sports Ground
Fox Covert
Llwyn Knottia
Cottage Wood
Balloon Hill
Cefn Park
Llwyn Onn Hall
Mill Wood
Bryn-newydd
Bryn-y-grog Hall
Marchwes Res
Bryn-y-cabanau Wood
Kings Mills
Kings Mill Visitors Centre
Queensway Sports Complex
WHITEGATE LIGHT INDUSTRIAL ESTATE
Works
Wks
School
Sports Ground
Pol Sta
River Gwenfro
HOLT ROAD
A534
BRYNESTYN ROAD
BRYN ESTYN CT
HULLAH LANE
CEFN ROAD
QUEENSWAY
KINGSMILLS ROAD
BRYN-Y-GROG HILL
A525
ABENBURY RD
VALLEY
DEAN RD
BORRAS RD
CHARLES RD
PRINCE
CEFNDRE
CHURCHILL DRIVE
DEVA WAY
EATON DR
CONWAY DR
CEIRIOG RD
HAVARD WAY
TAN-Y-BRYN
BALA RD
ARENIG RD
COED ABEN
GLAN GORS
GWENFRO
Y WERN
PONT WEN ROAD
RUBERY WY
MILLBANK RISE
WINDRUSH CL
GOODWOOD
EPSOM WY
NEWPORT CL
PENTRE GWYN ROAD
TAN-Y-COED
SEDGEFIELD
BRAESIDE
GREENWAYS
BROOK CL
NEWMARKET
CHEPSTOW
KEMPTON
TAUNTON
BENJAMIN RD
MONTGOMERY
WYNNSTAY AV
MOORLAND
CHESHIRE VW
TREVENNA WY
ST GILES CRES
ST DAVIDS CRES
MEADOW LEA
CAMBERLEY DRIVE
ST ANDREWS CRES
AUGUSTA DR
LYTHAM CT
PINES
THORNHILL

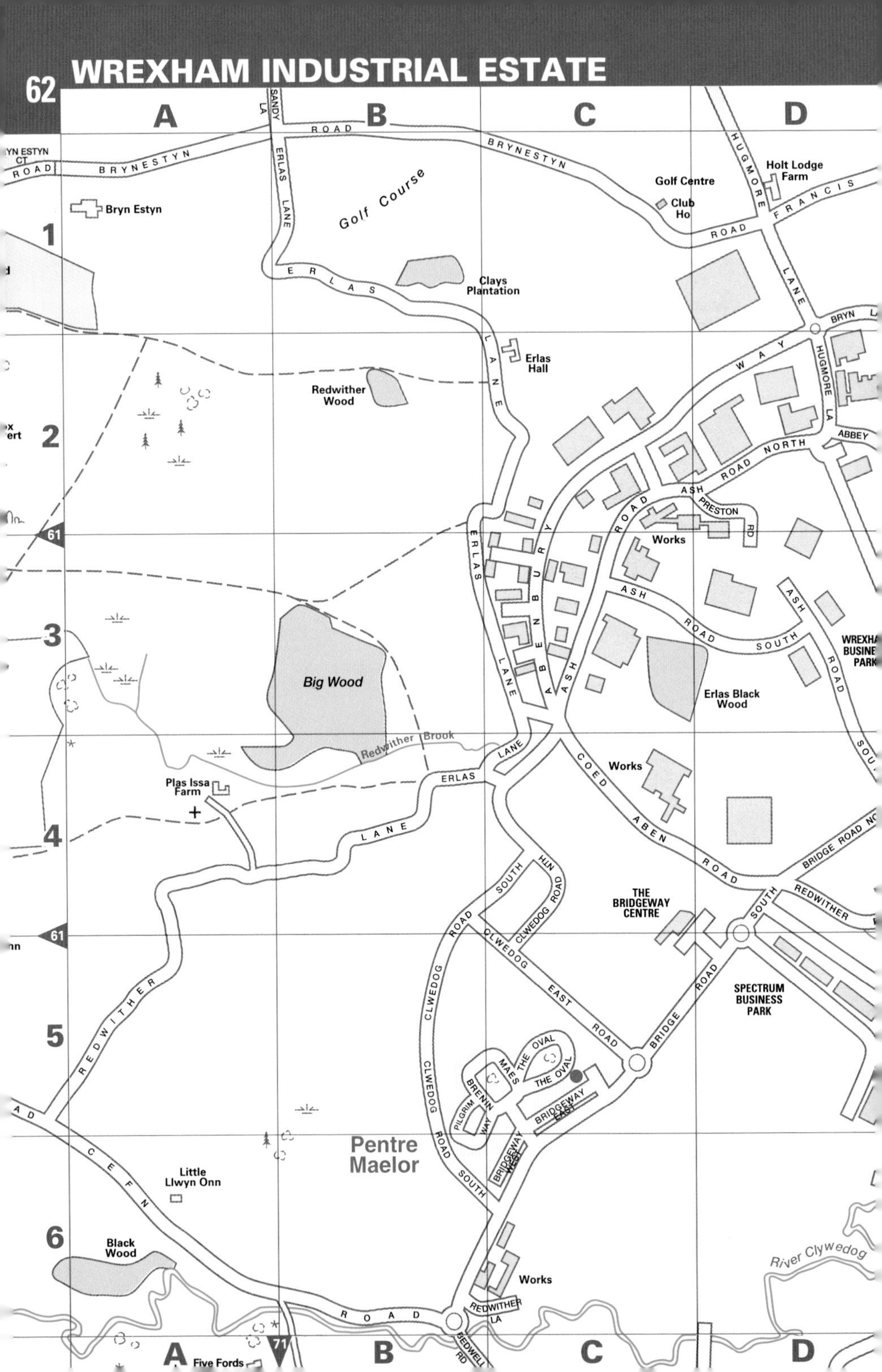

Golf Course
Bryn Estyn
Clays Plantation
Erlas Hall
Redwither Wood
Golf Centre
Club Ho
Holt Lodge Farm
Works
Big Wood
Redwither Brook
Plas Issa Farm
Erlas Black Wood
WREXHAM BUSINESS PARK
THE BRIDGEWAY CENTRE
SPECTRUM BUSINESS PARK
Pentre Maelor
Little Llwyn Onn
Black Wood
Five Fords
River Clywedog
BRYNESTYN ROAD
ERLAS LANE
HUGMORE LANE
FRANCIS ROAD
ASH ROAD NORTH
ASH ROAD SOUTH
PRESTON RD
ABENBURY WAY
COED ABEN ROAD
CLWEDOG ROAD SOUTH
CLWEDOG ROAD NTH
CLWEDOG EAST ROAD
BRIDGE ROAD
BRIDGE ROAD NORTH
BRIDGE ROAD SOUTH
REDWITHER ROAD
CEFN ROAD
THE OVAL
MAES BRENNIN
PILGRIM WAY
BRIDGEWAY EAST
BRIDGEWAY WEST
REDWITHER LA
BEDWELL RD
SANDY LA

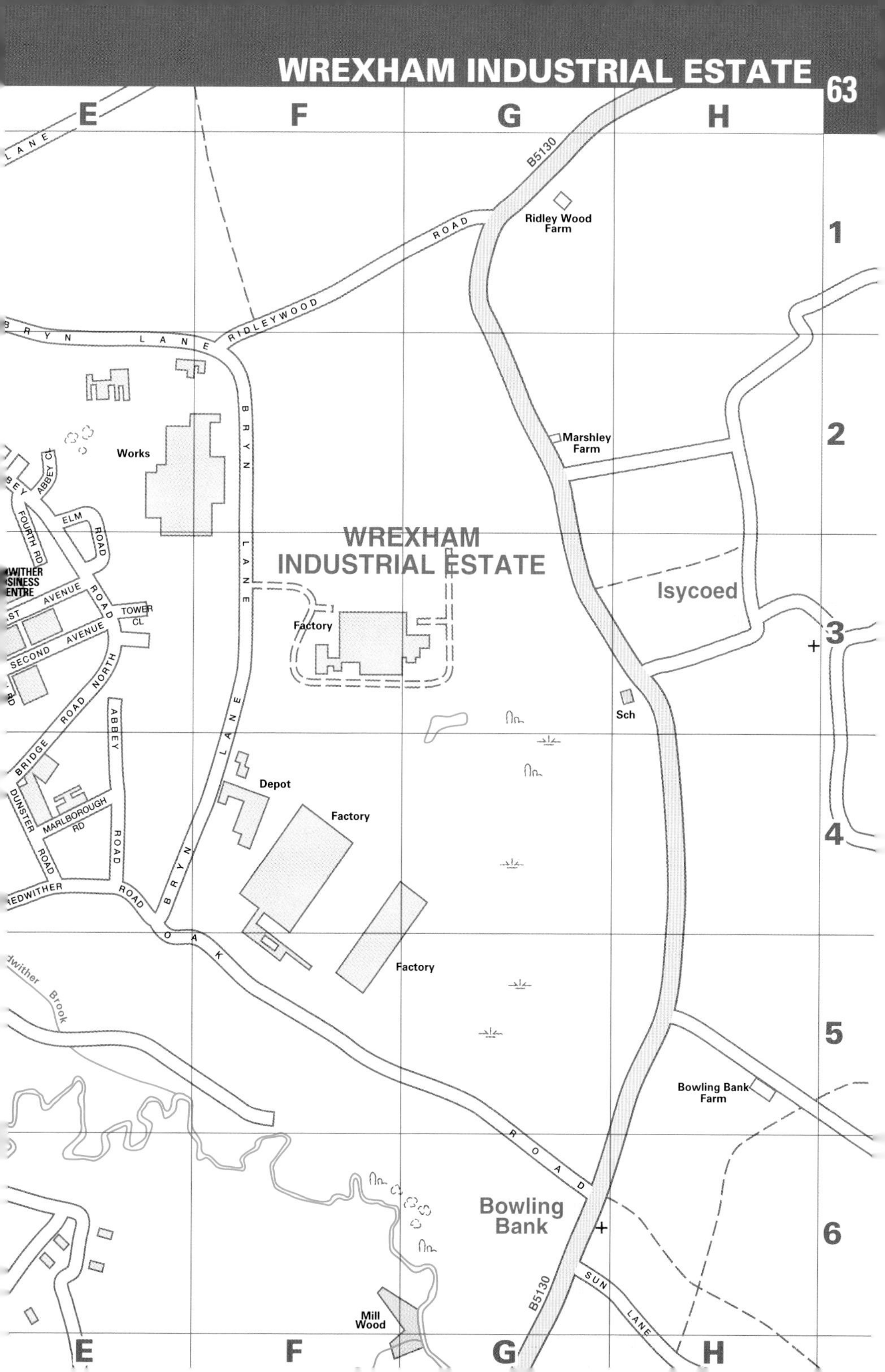
E
F
G
H
1
2
3
4
5
6
WREXHAM INDUSTRIAL ESTATE
Isycoed
Bowling Bank
Ridley Wood Farm
Marshley Farm
Bowling Bank Farm
B5130
RIDLEYWOOD ROAD
BRYN LANE
BRYN LANE
OAK ROAD
SUN LANE
Works
Factory
Depot
Factory
Factory
Sch
Mill Wood
ABBEY CL
FOURTH RD
ELM ROAD
AVENUE ROAD
TOWER CL
SECOND AVENUE
BRIDGE ROAD NORTH
ABBEY ROAD
DUNSTER ROAD
MARLBOROUGH RD
REDWITHER ROAD
Brook

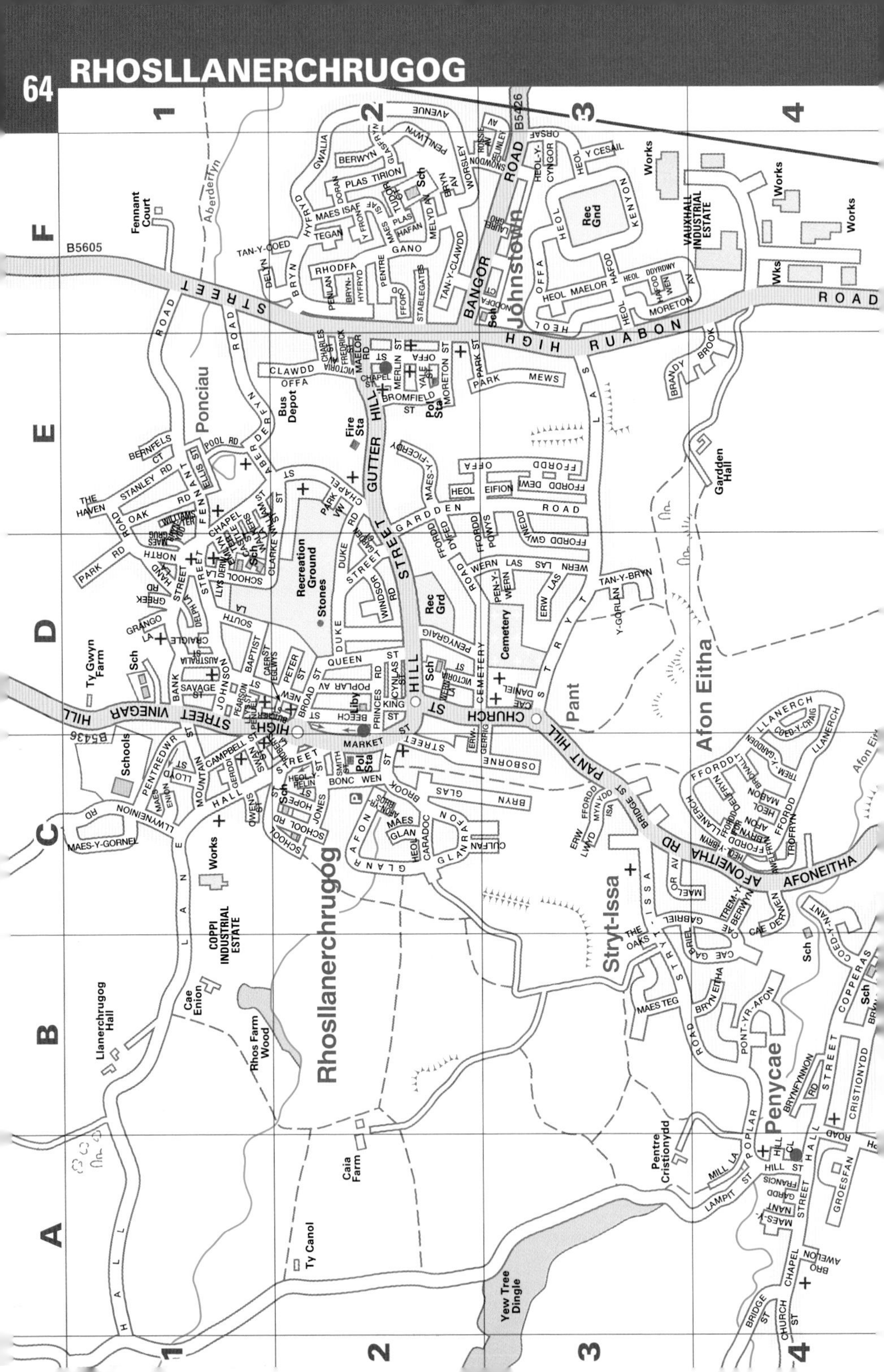
1
2
3
4
F
E
D
C
B
A
B5605
B5426
B5436
Fennant Court
Aberderfyn
TAN-Y-COED
GWALIA
BERWYN
PLAS TIRION
MAES ISAF
TEGAN
RHODFA
PENLAN
BRYN-HYFRYD
GANO
PENTRE
STABLEGATES
TAN-Y-CLAWDD
AVENUE
PENLLWYN
WORSLEY
SNOWDON
BANGOR
ROAD
Johnstown
HEOL-Y-CYNGOR
Y CESAIL
Rec Gnd
KENYON
HAFOD
OFFA
HEOL MAELOR
MORETON
VAUXHALL INDUSTRIAL ESTATE
Works
Wks
ROAD
HIGH STREET
RUABON
STREET
Ponciau
CLAWDD OFFA
CHARLES
FREDERICK
MAELOR RD
VICTORIA
CHAPEL ST
MERLIN ST
YALE ST
MORETON ST
PARK ST
PARK MEWS
BROMFIELD ST
Pol Sta
Bus Depot
Fire Sta
GUTTER HILL
BRANDY BROOK
Gardden Hall
BERNFELS CT
STANLEY RD
POOL RD
ELLIS ST
FENNANT RD
THE HAVEN
OAK
WILLIAMS TER
PARK RD
NORTH
CHAPEL
Sch
SCHOOL
CLARKE
Recreation Ground
Stones
MAES-Y-FICERDY
FFORDD OFFA
FFORDD DEWI
HEOL EIFION
GARDDEN ROAD
FFORDD GWYNEDD
FFORDD DYFED
FFORDD POWYS
WERN LAS
PEN-Y-WERN
ERW LAS
TAN-Y-BRYN
Y-GORLAN
DUKE STREET
WINDSOR RD
Rec Grd
HAND
GREEK RD
SOUTH LA
DELPHI
GRANGO LA
CRAIGLE
Ty Gwyn Farm
AUSTRALIA ST
SAVAGE ST
BANK
JOHNSON
BAPTIST
PEARSON
PETER ST
QUEEN ST
POPLAR AV
CYNLAS ST
PENYGRAIG
Cemetery
CEMETERY
VICTORIA ST
DANIEL
CAE
Pant
Afon Eitha
VINEGAR HILL
HIGH STREET
BROAD ST
BEECH ST
PRINCES RD
KING ST
HILL ST
CHURCH
Liby
MARKET ST
Schools
PENTREDWR
LLOYD ST
MOUNTAIN
CAMPBELL
HALL
OWENS ST
HOPE ST
JONES
SCHOOL RD
STREET
BONC WEN
BROOK
BRYN GLAS
OSBORNE
ERW-GERRIG
PANT HILL
LLWYNENION RD
MAES-Y-GORNEL
Works
COPPI INDUSTRIAL ESTATE
MAES GLAN
CARADOC
GLAN AFON
CULFAN
Rhosllanerchrugog
FFORDD MYNYDD ISA
ERW LWYD
BRIDGE ST
AFONEITHA RD
LLANERCH
COED-Y-GRAIG
TREM-Y-GARDDEN
FFORDD BRONALLT
HEOL MABON
FFORDD TROFRYN
Stryt-Issa
THE OAKS
GABRIEL
CAE GABRIEL
TREM-Y-BERWYN
CAE DERWEN
AFONEITHA
Afon Eitha
COED-Y-NANT
COPPERAS
BRYN EITHA
MAES TEG
PONT-YR-AFON
Penycae
BRYNFFYNNON RD
STREET
CRISTIONYDD
Cae Enion
Llanerchrugog Hall
Rhos Farm Wood
Caia Farm
Pentre Cristionydd
POPLAR
HILL ST
MILL LA
LAMPIT ST
FRANCIS
GARDD
NANT
MAES-Y-
HALL
GROESFAN
ROAD
BRO AWELON
CHAPEL
BRIDGE ST
CHURCH ST
Ty Canol
Yew Tree Dingle
HALL
LANE

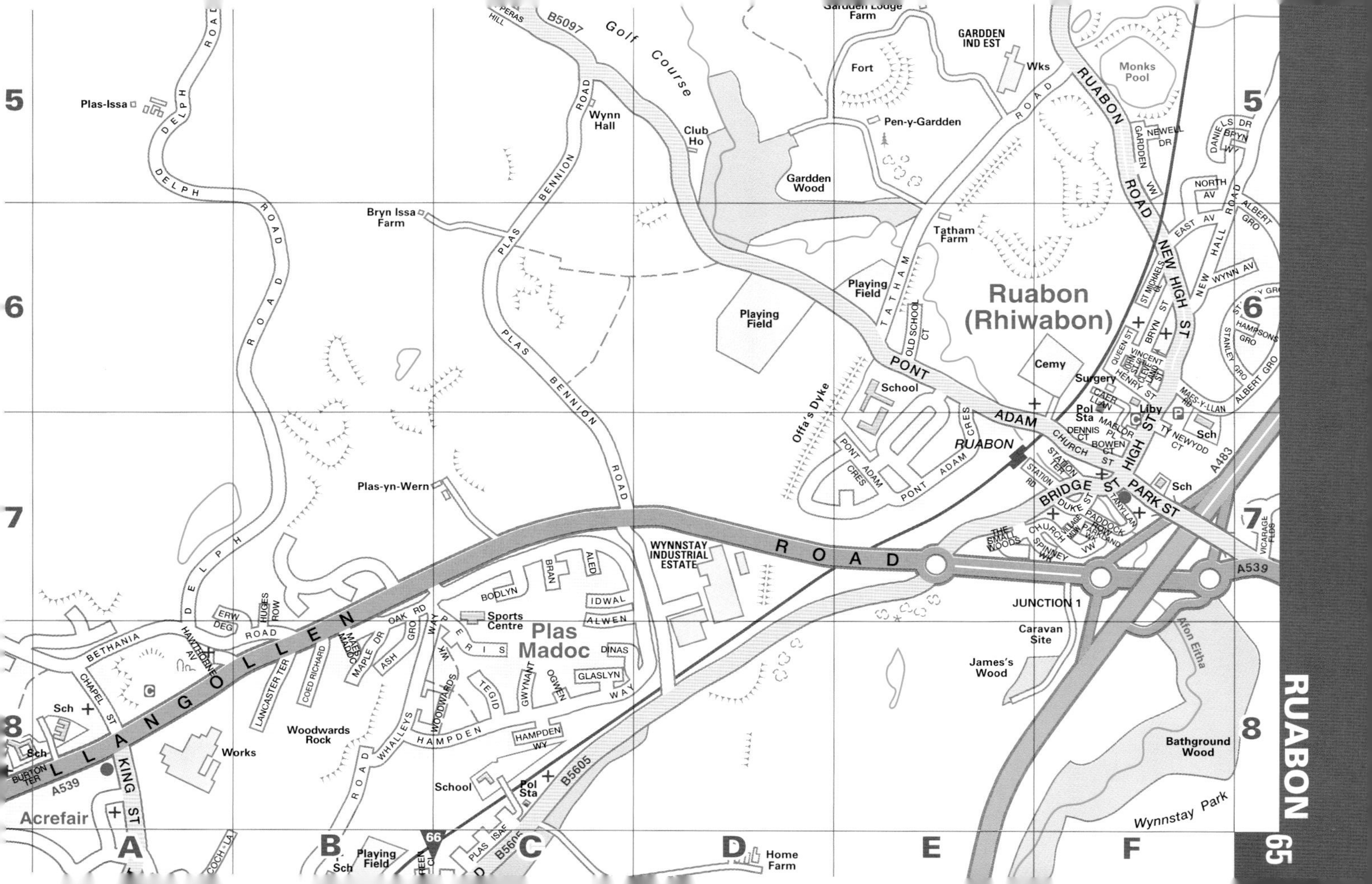
Ruabon
(Rhiwabon)
Plas Madoc
Acrefair
Wynnstay Park
Bathground Wood
Afon Eitha
James's Wood
Caravan Site
JUNCTION 1
A539
A483
B5605
B5097
RUABON ROAD
NEW HIGH ST
HIGH ST
PARK ST
BRIDGE ST
CHURCH ST
STATION RD
STATION TER
ADAM ST
PONT ADAM CRES
OLD SCHOOL CT
TATHAM RD
GARDDEN VW
NEWELL DR
NEW HALL ROAD
ALBERT GRO
STANLEY GRO
HAMPSONS GRO
WYNN AV
EAST AV
NORTH AV
DANIELS DR
BRYN WY
BRYN ST
QUEEN ST
HENRY ST
ST MICHAELS CL
VINCENT CL
MAELOR CT
DENNIS PL
BOWEN CT
CAER LLAN
TY NEWYDD CT
MAES-Y-LLAN RD
TANYLLAN
PADDOCK ROW
VICARAGE FLDS
SPINNEY WK
DUKE ST
THE SMALL WOODS
Monks Pool
GARDDEN IND EST
Wks
Pen-y-Gardden
Tatham Farm
Fort
Gardden Wood
Gardden Lodge Farm
Playing Field
Cemy
Surgery
Liby
Pol Sta
Sch
School
Offa's Dyke
RUABON
Golf Course
Club Ho
Wynn Hall
PLAS BENNION ROAD
PERAS HILL
Bryn Issa Farm
Plas-yn-Wern
Plas-Issa
DELPH ROAD
WYNNSTAY INDUSTRIAL ESTATE
Home Farm
ALED
IDWAL
ALWEN
DINAS
GLASLYN
WAY
BRAN
OGWEN
GWYNANT
HAMPDEN WY
BODLYN
Sports Centre
TEGID
PERIS WAY
WOODWARDS WK
HAMPDEN
WHALLEYS ROAD
OAK RD
ASH GRO
MAPLE DR
MAES MADOC
COED RICHARD
LANCASTER TER
HUGES ROW
ERW DEG
ROAD
HAWTHORNE AV
BETHANIA
Woodwards Rock
Works
CHAPEL ST
KING ST
LLANGOLLEN ROAD
BURTON TER
PLAS ISAF
COCH LA
66
A
B
C
D
E
F
5
6
7
8

Cefn-mawr
Rhosymedre
Newbridge
Acrefair
Pont-Cysyllte
Cefn-bychan
Trevor
Rhos-y-coed
Froncysyllte
Pen-y-graig
Plas-yn-pentre
Pentre
VALE OF LLANGOLLEN
LLANGOLLEN ROAD
NEWBRIDGE ROAD
PARK ROAD
GATE ROAD
STATION RD
NEW ROAD
HIGH STREET
WELL STREET
KING STREET
CRANE ST
Hopyard Wood
Cross Keys Wood
Rhosymedre Wood
Cefn Wood
Waterloo Tower Wood
Gelli Wood
Tan-y-Cut Wood
Jeffrey's Wood
Dee Farm
Dolydd Farm
Bridge End Farm
Ty-Isa Farm
TY MAWR COUNTRY PARK
Visitors Centre
River Dee (Afon Dyfrdwy)
Shropshire Union Canal (Llangollen Branch)
Aqueduct
Viaduct
Community Centre
Playing Field
Rec Grd
IND EST
Works
Cemy
Pol Sta
Sch
Liby
Reservoir
New Bridge
Pen-y-bont
A539
A5
B5605
65
68

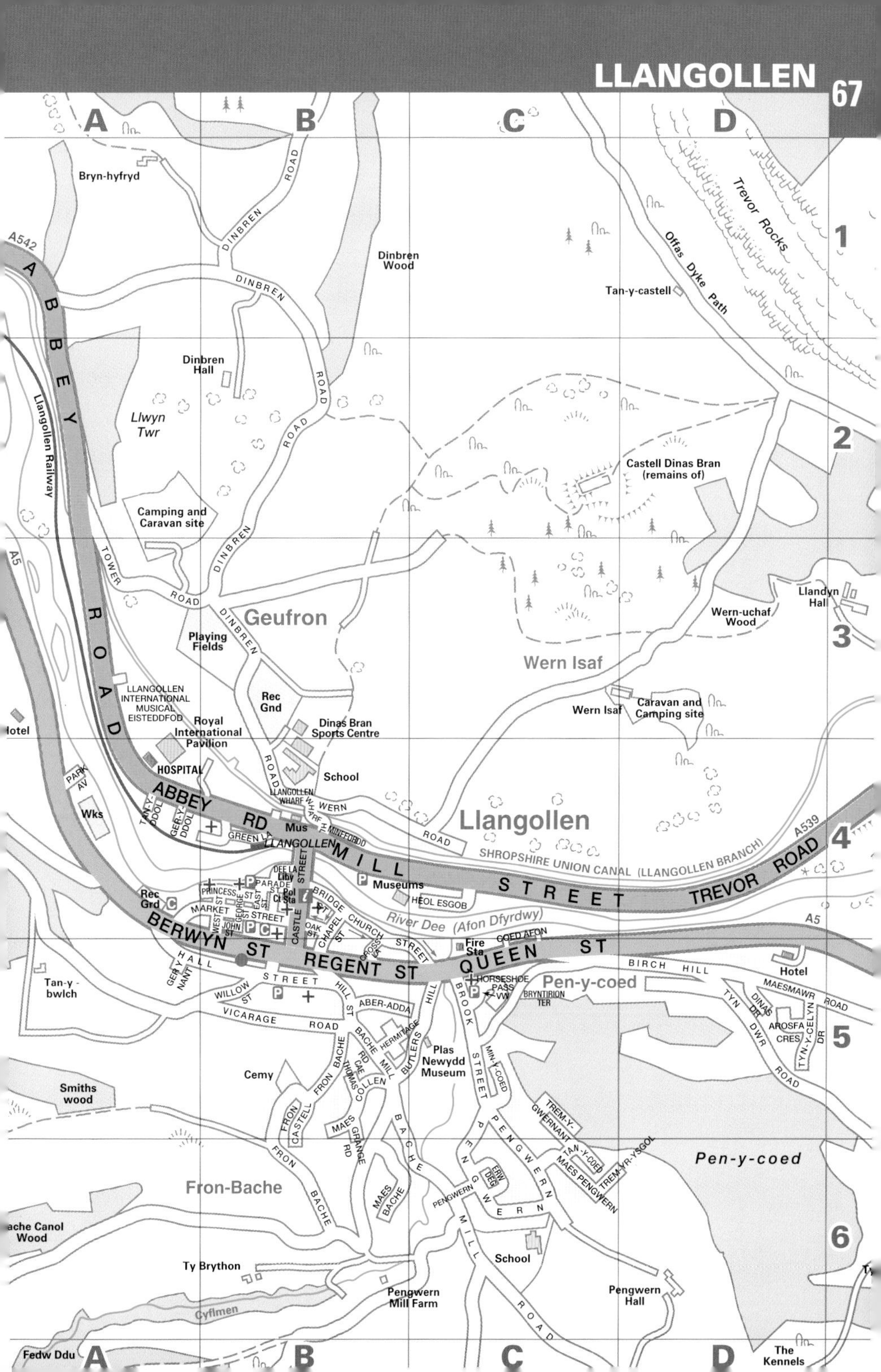
A
B
C
D
1
2
3
4
5
6
Bryn-hyfryd
DINBREN ROAD
A542
ABBEY ROAD
Dinbren Wood
Trevor Rocks
Offas Dyke Path
Tan-y-castell
Dinbren Hall
Llwyn Twr
Llangollen Railway
Castell Dinas Bran (remains of)
Camping and Caravan site
A5
TOWER ROAD
Geufron
Llandyn Hall
Wern-uchaf Wood
Playing Fields
Wern Isaf
Rec Gnd
LLANGOLLEN INTERNATIONAL MUSICAL EISTEDDFOD
Royal International Pavilion
Dinas Bran Sports Centre
Caravan and Camping site
Hotel
HOSPITAL
School
PARK AV
Wks
TAN-Y-DDOL
GER-Y-DDOL
LLANGOLLEN WHARF
WERN ROAD
Llangollen
ABBEY RD
Mus
MINFFORDD
GREEN LA
LLANGOLLEN
MILL STREET
SHROPSHIRE UNION CANAL (LLANGOLLEN BRANCH)
A539
TREVOR ROAD
DEE LA
Liby
Pol Sta
Museums
PRINCESS ST
PARADE ST
Rec Grd
MARKET ST
EAST ST
GEORGE ST
BRIDGE ST
HEOL ESGOB
River Dee (Afon Dyfrdwy)
WEST ST
JOHN ST
OAK ST
CASTLE STREET
CHAPEL ST
CHURCH STREET
BERWYN ST
CROSS LA
Fire Sta
COED AFON
QUEEN ST
REGENT ST
HALL STREET
GER-Y-NANT
BIRCH HILL
Hotel
Tan-y-bwlch
HORSESHOE PASS
Pen-y-coed
MAESMAWR ROAD
WILLOW ST
HILL ST
BROOK STREET
VW
BRYNTIRION TER
DINAS DR
ABER-ADDA
ARDSFA CRES
TYN-Y-CELYN DR
TYN DWR ROAD
VICARAGE ROAD
BACHE MILL
HERMITAGE
BUTLERS HILL
Plas Newydd Museum
Cemy
FRON BACHE
CAE THOMAS RD
COLLEN
MIN-Y-COED
Smiths wood
FRON CASTELL
MAES GRANGE RD
TREM-Y-GWERNANT
TAN-Y-COED
TREM-YR-YSGOL
MAES PENGWERN
Pen-y-coed
FRON BACHE
Fron-Bache
MAES BACHE
ERW DEG
PENGWERN
ache Canol Wood
School
Ty Brython
Pengwern Mill Farm
Pengwern Hall
Cyflmen
ROAD
Fedw Ddu
The Kennels

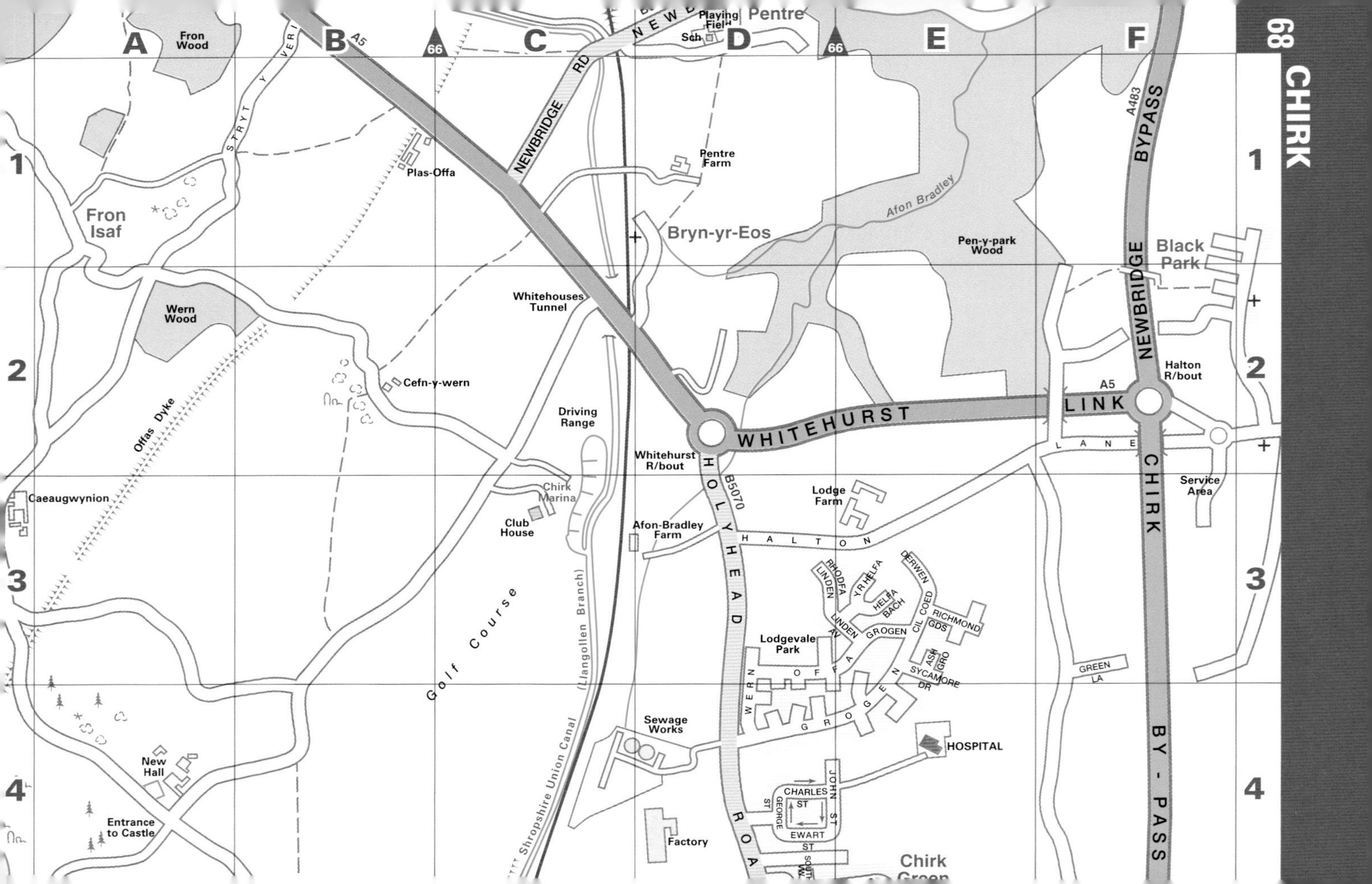

Fron Wood
Fron Isaf
STRYT Y VERI
A5
NEWBRIDGE RD
Plas-Offa
Playing Field
Sch
Pentre
Pentre Farm
Bryn-yr-Eos
Afon Bradley
Pen-y-park Wood
A483
NEWBRIDGE BYPASS
Black Park
Halton R/bout
LINK
WHITEHURST
LANE
CHIRK BY - PASS
Service Area
Wern Wood
Whitehouses Tunnel
Cefn-y-wern
Offas Dyke
Driving Range
Whitehurst R/bout
B5070
HOLYHEAD ROA
Chirk Marina
Club House
Caeaugwynion
Afon-Bradley Farm
Lodge Farm
HALTON
RHODFA LINDEN
YR HELFA
HELFA BACH
DERWEN
CIL COED
RICHMOND GDS
LINDEN AV
GROGEN
Lodgevale Park
OFFA GROVE
WERN
ASH GRO
SYCAMORE DR
GREEN LA
Golf Course
(Llangollen Branch)
Shropshire Union Canal
Sewage Works
HOSPITAL
JOHN ST
CHARLES ST
GEORGE ST
EWART ST
SOUTH VW
Factory
Chirk Green
New Hall
Entrance to Castle
A B C D E F
66
1 2 3 4

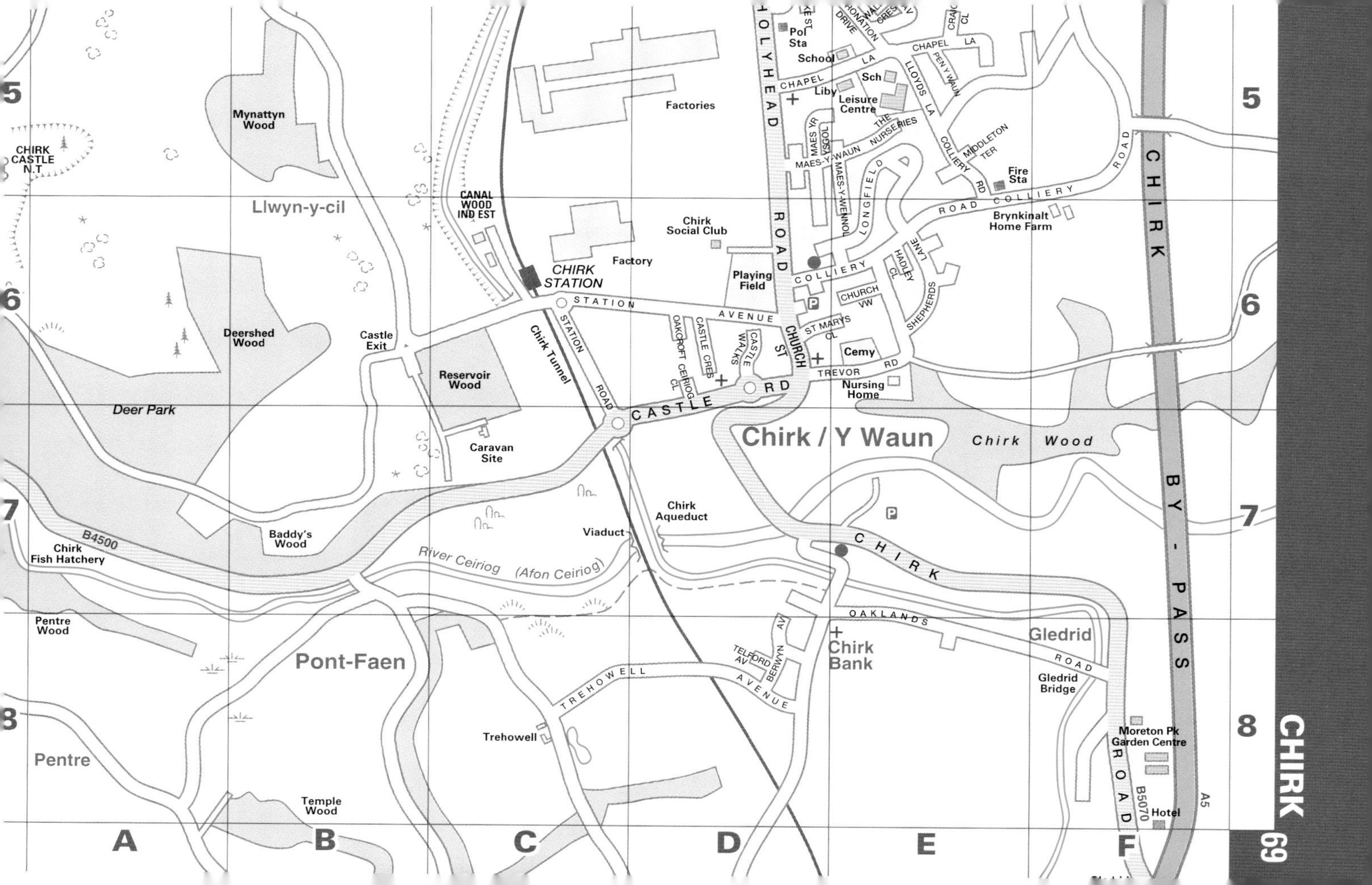

CHIRK BY-PASS
A5
B5070
ROAD
Moreton Pk Garden Centre
Hotel
Gledrid
Gledrid Bridge
ROAD
Chirk Wood
Brynkinalt Home Farm
Fire Sta
COLLIERY ROAD
COLLIERY RD
MIDDLETON TER
CHAPEL LA
PEN Y WAUN
LLOYDS LA
CORONATION DRIVE
SHEPHERDS LANE
HADLEY CL
LONGFIELD
THE NURSERIES
Sch
Leisure Centre
School
Liby
MAES-Y-WENNOL
MAES-Y-WAUN
MAES YR YSGOL
Pol Sta
CHAPEL
HOLYHEAD ROAD
COLLIERY
CHURCH VW
ST MARYS CL
Cemy
TREVOR RD
Nursing Home
CHURCH ST
Chirk / Y Waun
CHIRK
OAKLANDS
Chirk Bank
Playing Field
STATION AVENUE
CASTLE WALKS
CASTLE RD
CASTLE CRES
OAKCROFT
CEIRIOG CL
BERWYN AV
TELFORD AV
TREHOWELL AVENUE
Chirk Aqueduct
Chirk Social Club
Factories
Factory
STATION ROAD
CHIRK STATION
Chirk Tunnel
Viaduct
River Ceiriog (Afon Ceiriog)
Trehowell
CANAL WOOD IND EST
Reservoir Wood
Caravan Site
Castle Exit
Llwyn-y-cil
Pont-Faen
Mynattyn Wood
Deershed Wood
Baddy's Wood
Temple Wood
Deer Park
B4500
Chirk Fish Hatchery
Pentre Wood
Pentre
CHIRK CASTLE N.T.
5
6
7
8
A
B
C
D
E
F

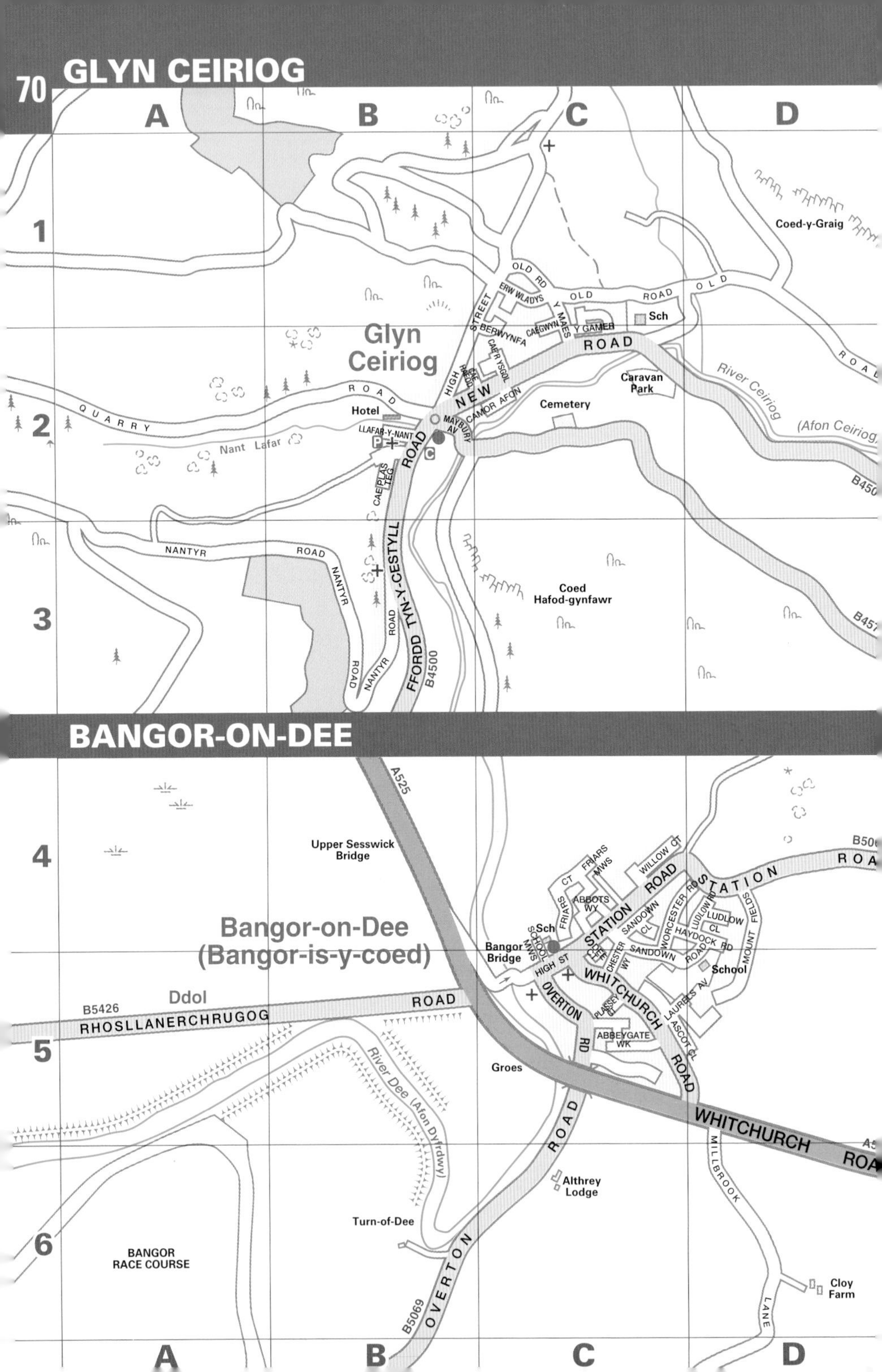

A
B
C
D
1
2
3
Coed-y-Graig
OLD RD
ERW WLADYS
Y MAES
OLD
ROAD
OLD
Sch
HIGH STREET
BERWYNFA
CAEGWYN
Y GAMER
ROAD
Glyn Ceiriog
CAE'R YSGOL
NEW
Caravan Park
River Ceiriog
(Afon Ceiriog)
ROAD
QUARRY
ROAD
Hotel
MAYBURY AV
CAMOR AFON
Cemetery
LLAFAR-Y-NANT
Nant Lafar
ROAD
CAE PLAS TEG
B450
NANTYR
ROAD
NANTYR
TYN-Y-CESTYLL
FFORDD
ROAD
NANTYR
ROAD
B4500
Coed Hafod-gynfawr
B457
BANGOR-ON-DEE
A525
4
5
6
Upper Sesswick Bridge
Bangor-on-Dee
(Bangor-is-y-coed)
FRIARS MWS
WILLOW CT
CT
ABBOTS WY
FRIARS
STATION
ROAD
STATION
ROAD
B506
Sch
SCHOOL MWS
SANDOWN CL
WORCESTER RD
LUDLOW RD
LUDLOW CL
MOUNT FIELDS
HAYDOCK RD
Bangor Bridge
HIGH ST
CHESTER WY
SANDOWN
ROAD
School
WHITCHURCH
LAURELS AV
B5426
Ddol
ROAD
RHOSLLANERCHRUGOG
OVERTON
PLASSEY CT
ASCOT CL
RD
ABBEYGATE WK
ROAD
Groes
River Dee (Afon Dyfrdwy)
WHITCHURCH
ROAD
A5
ROAD
MILLBROOK
Althrey Lodge
Turn-of-Dee
BANGOR RACE COURSE
OVERTON
B5069
LANE
Cloy Farm

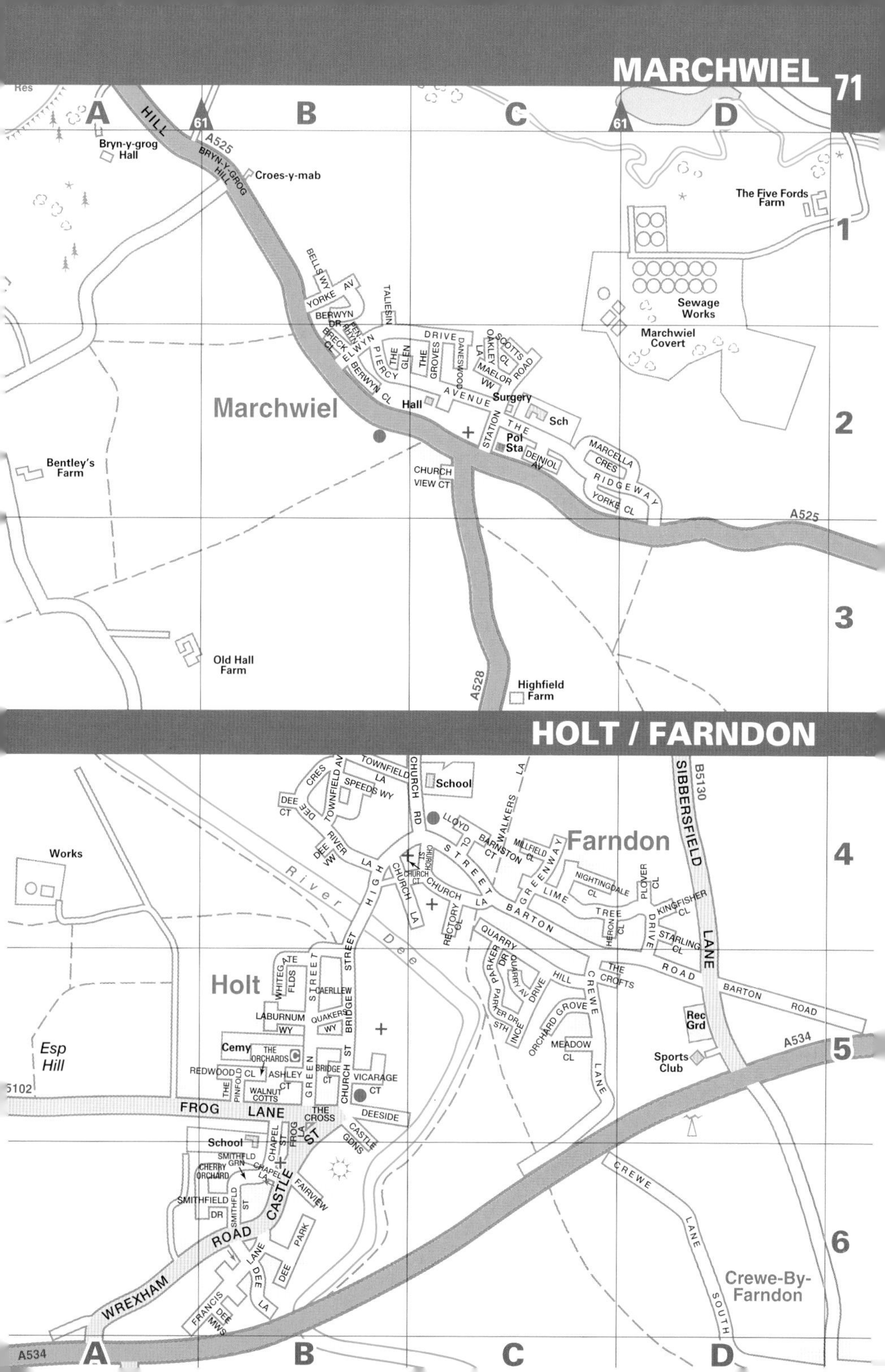
Bryn-y-grog Hall
Croes-y-mab
The Five Fords Farm
Sewage Works
Marchwiel Covert
Marchwiel
Hall
Surgery
Sch
Pol Sta
Bentley's Farm
Old Hall Farm
Highfield Farm
A525
A528
HOLT / FARNDON
School
Farndon
Works
River Dee
Holt
Esp Hill
Cemy
Rec Grd
Sports Club
Crewe-By-Farndon
A534
B5130
SIBBERSFIELD LANE
FROG LANE
WREXHAM ROAD
CASTLE ST
BARTON ROAD

INDEX TO STREETS

with Postcodes

The Index includes some names for which there is insufficient space on the maps. These names are indicated by an * and are followed by the nearest adjoining thoroughfare.

Aarons Rd LL11 55 G4
Abbey Cl LL13 63 E2
Abbey Gateway CH1 4 B3
Abbey Grn CH1 4 B3
Abbey Rd, Llangollen LL20 67 A1
Abbey Rd, Wrexham LL13 62 D2
Abbey Sq CH1 4 B3
Abbey St CH1 4 B3
Abbeydale Cl LL13 57 H6
Abbeygate Walk LL13 70 C5
Abbot St LL11 5 C4
Abbots Cl CH6 8 B6
Abbots Ct CH2 40 A1
Abbots Dr CH1 40 A1
Abbots Grange CH1 4 A1
Abbots Keep CH1 39 H1
Abbots La CH4 28 B4
Abbots Nook CH2 4 B1
Abbots Pk CH1 40 A2
Abbots Ter CH1 39 H1
Abbots Walk CH8 7 C6
Abbots Way LL13 70 C4
Abbotts Cl CH3 47 C4
Abbotts Rd CH3 47 C4
Abbottsford Dr CH4 28 B4
Abenbury Rd LL13 61 F5
Abenbury Way LL13 62 C3
Aber Adda LL20 67 B5
Aber Cres CH7 17 C2
Aber Las CH6 10 D4
Aber Pk Ind Est CH6 10 B1
Aber Rd CH6 10 B1
Aber Vw CH5 13 C6
Aberdaron Dr CH1 39 E2
Aberderfyn Rd LL14 64 E1
Aberllanerch Dr CH7 24 A2
Abingdon Cres CH4 43 F2
Acacia Cl CH7 22 C5
Acacia Ct LL12 50 A3
Acres La CH2 36 C3
Acton Gate LL11 56 D6
Acton Gdns LL12 57 E5
Acton Llan y Pwll Link Rd LL12 57 E3
Acton Park Way LL12 56 D6
Acton Rd LL11 60 C1
Adder Hill CH3 45 E1
Adderley Bank LL11 56 D3
Adelaide Rd CH1 38 D2
Adwy La LL11 54 C6
Adwy Wynt CH6 10 C4
Ael y Bryn, Brymbo LL11 54 D1
Ael y Bryn, Mold CH7 22 B5
Ael y Bryn, Wrexham LL11 56 C4
Ael y Ffynnon CH8 7 A5
Aerial Rd LL12 50 A3
Afon Vw CH5 13 C6
Afon Yr Rhos LL14 64 C2
Afondale CH6 10 B2
Afoneitha Rd LL14 64 C4
Agenora Cl CH5 13 C6
Ainsdale CH7 24 B3
Ainsdale Gro LL12 57 G5
Airfield Rd CH4 27 F4
Airfield Vw CH4 27 E1
Airoaks Cres LL12 50 B3
Alamein Rd CH2 35 H3
Albert Av CH6 10 D3
Albert Pl*, Fishermans Rd CH5 13 E6
Albert St, Chester CH1 4 D2
Albert St, Leeswood CH7 30 B2
Albert St, Wrexham LL13 5 D5
Albion Pl CH1 4 C5
Albion St CH1 4 B5
Alder Av CH5 20 A3
Alder Cl LL11 56 B1
Alder Gro CH2 41 E2
Alderberry Rd CH5 25 F1
Aldergrove LL11 54 A5
Alderley Pl CH1 35 F6
Aldersey Cl CH1 34 A2
Aldford Rd CH2 36 C5
Aldford Way LL12 57 F6
Aled LL14 65 C7
Aled Cres CH6 10 A4
Aled Ho*, Lakeside Bsns Village CH5 19 G5
Aled Way CH4 42 D3
Alexander Ct CH3 4 D3
Alexandra Ct CH7 24 C4
Alexandra Rd, Mold CH7 22 C5
Alexandra Rd, Wrexham LL13 5 A5
Alexandra St CH5 15 A7
Allans Cl CH5 20 B1
Allansford Av CH3 47 C5
Allerton Cl CH4 28 C2
Allington Cres LL12 51 E6
Allington Dr LL13 61 F2
Allington Pl CH4 40 C6
Allt Eisteddfod LL11 53 B3
Allt Goch CH6 10 C3
Allt y Golch CH8 8 A2
Allt y Pentref LL11 53 C3
Alltami Rd CH7 24 A1
Alma Rd LL20 66 A4
Alma St CH3 40 D4
Almond Gro LL13 61 F1
Alpraham Cres CH2 36 B5
Alun Cl CH7 18 B1
Alun Cres CH4 43 G2
Alundale Rd LL12 49 C5
Alvis Rd CH5 21 G2
Alwen LL14 65 C8
Alwen Av CH7 23 G3
Alwen Cl LL11 55 G6
Alwen Dr CH6 8 A5
Alwyn Cl CH7 22 B2
Alwyn Dr CH5 13 E7
Alwyn Gdns CH2 36 C3
Alyn Cl LL11 56 D3
Alyn Cres LL12 48 B3
Alyn Ct LL12 48 A1
Alyn Dale Av CH7 23 G4
Alyn Dr, Chester CH4 28 B5
Alyn Dr, Wrexham LL12 52 D4
Alyn Mdw CH7 22 C3
Alyn Pk CH5 19 H6
Alyn Rd, Buckley CH7 24 C4
Alyn Rd, Chester CH2 31 B2
Alyn St CH7 22 D3
Alyndale Rd, Chester CH4 42 D2
Alyndale Rd, Hope LL12 48 C1
Alyndale Rd, Wrexham LL12 56 D5
Amanda Gro LL14 59 G6
Ambleside CH2 36 D6
Ambleside Cl CH5 13 C6
Andrew Cres CH4 4 D6
Andrews Cl CH3 46 B2
Anfield Cl CH5 19 F1
Anglesey Cl LL12 57 F6
Annefield Pk LL12 51 E5
Annes Way CH4 4 D5
Ansell Rd LL13 57 G5
Anthony Eden Dr LL13 61 F3
Anvil Cl CH1 34 B2
Apple Tree Gro CH66 32 A1
Appleby Dr CH5 20 C4
Appledale Dr CH66 32 B1
Appleton Rd CH2 36 C6
Applewood LL13 60 D5
Appleyards La CH4 44 B1
Aragon Grn CH1 35 E6
Aran Cl CH7 23 G2
Aran Rd LL12 61 E1
Archers Way, Chester CH1 39 G3
Archers Way, Wrexham LL13 61 E2
Archway CH7 22 D6
Arden Cl CH3 46 C1
Arenig Cl LL11 55 H4
Arenig Rd LL13 61 G3
Arfryn LL11 55 F5
Argoed LL11 54 C2
Argoed Av CH7 23 E1
Argoed Hall La CH7 23 F3
Argoed Rd CH7 24 B3
Argoed Vw CH7 23 E1
Argyle St LL11 5 C3
Argyll Av CH4 39 G6
Arkle Ct CH3 41 F4
Arley Cl CH2 36 D6
Arley Rd LL11 56 D2
Army La CH7 25 E4
Arnhem Way CH3 45 E2
Arnold Gro CH5 13 E6
Arnolds Cres CH4 27 E5
Arosfa Cres LL20 67 D5
Arradon Ct CH2 36 C6
Arrowcroft Rd CH3 31 A6
Arthur St CH1 39 G3
Ascot Cl LL13 70 C5
Ash Cl, Ellesmere Port CH66 32 A1
Ash Cl, Wrexham LL11 55 G1
Ash Dr CH7 24 B1
Ash Gro, Acrefair LL14 65 B8
Ash Gro, Bagillt CH6 8 D6
Ash Gro, Buckley CH7 23 H3
Ash Gro, Chester CH4 43 H3
Ash Gro, Chirk LL14 68 E3
Ash Gro, Deeside CH5 15 B7
Ash Gro, Leeswood CH7 30 B1
Ash Gro, Llay LL12 50 C3
Ash Gro, Mold CH7 22 B3
Ash Gro, Wrexham LL13 61 F1
Ash Hay La CH2 37 F3
Ash La CH5 20 C5
Ash Lawn Ct*, Eversley Ct CH1 40 A1
Ash Rd LL13 62 C3
Ash Rd North LL13 62 C2
Ash Rd South LL13 62 C3
Ash Vw CH5 20 A1
Ashbourne Av LL11 55 H1
Ashburn Way LL13 61 F4
Ashby Pl CH2 4 D1
Ashfield Cres, Chester CH1 38 D1
Ashfield Cres, Deeside CH5 20 D3
Ashfield Rd, Deeside CH5 15 B7
Ashfield Rd, Wrexham LL11 56 B6
Ashleigh Cl, Chester CH4 43 E1
Ashleigh Cl, Deeside CH5 20 D4
Ashley Ct LL13 71 B5
Ashmount Enterprise Pk CH6 10 A1
Ashmuir Cl CH1 39 E3
Ashwood Ct CH2 41 E3
Ashwood La CH2 33 H5
Aspen Cl CH5 13 C6
Aspen Gro CH1 34 C5
Aspen Way CH2 41 F2
Assembly Rd LL11 58 B1
Aston Gro LL12 61 E1
Aston Hill CH5 19 H3
Aston Meads CH5 20 A3
Aston Park Rd CH5 20 A1
Aston Rd CH5 20 B2
Atis Cft CH6 10 E3
Atlea LL11 55 G6
Auckland Rd CH1 38 D1
Auden Cl CH5 25 F1
Audley Cres CH4 44 B1
Aughton Way CH4 27 G3
Augusta Dr LL13 57 G6
Austen Cl CH5 19 G6
Australia St LL14 64 D1
Avalon Ct LL13 60 D5
Avon Cl LL12 57 E6
Avon Ct CH7 22 C5
Avon Ct*, Welland Dr CH5 13 C7
Avon Dale Gro LL12 57 G5
Avondale Cres LL11 56 D2
Avondale Rd CH7 24 D4
Avonlea Cl CH4 43 E3
Awel y Mor CH8 7 D5
Awelfryn LL14 64 C4
Babbage Rd CH5 21 G2
Bache Av CH2 36 A6
Bache Dr CH2 36 B6
Bache Hall Ct CH2 36 A6
Bache Hall Est CH2 36 A6
Bache Mill Rd LL20 67 B5
Bachefield Av CH3 44 D2
Bachelors Ct*, Bachelors La CH3 41 E5
Bachelors La CH3 41 E5
Back Bridge St CH1 4 B4
Back Queen St CH1 4 C3
Back Watergate St CH1 4 B4
Backford Gdns CH1 32 A2
Bader Ct LL13 57 G5
Badgers Cl, Chester CH3 47 A2
Badgers Cl, Ellesmere Port CH66 32 A1
Badgers Rise CH5 13 C8
Badgers Walk CH2 36 C1
Bagillt Rd, Greenfield CH8 6 D2
Bagillt Rd, Holywell CH8 7 C6
Bailey Bridge Cl CH2 40 A2
Bakers Ct CH3 4 D3
Bakery Flds LL11 55 G5
Bala Av CH8 6 E4
Bala Ho*, Lakeside Bsns Village CH5 19 G5
Bala Rd LL13 61 G3
Ballater Cres CH3 41 E4
Ballerat Cl CH1 38 D1
Balmoral Cl, Flint CH6 10 A2
Balmoral Cl, Wrexham LL11 56 C6
Balmoral Pk CH1 39 H2
Balmoral Rd LL11 56 C6
Bangor Cl CH66 32 A2
Bangor Rd LL14 64 F2
Bank Cl CH2 36 C6
Bank Farm Mews CW6 46 B5
Bank La CH7 25 F2
Bank Pl CH8 7 B6
Bank Rd, Buckley CH7 24 B5
Bank Rd, Connahs Quay CH5 13 D5
Bank Row CH7 24 D4
Bank St, Ponciau LL14 64 D1
Bank St, Southsea LL11 55 E6
Bank St, Wrexham LL11 5 C3
Bank Villas CH7 22 C4
Banks Rd CH5 20 D4
Bannel La CH7 25 E4
Baptist St LL14 64 D1
Baristow Cl CH2 4 C1
Barkers La LL12 57 E4
Barkhill Rd CH3 41 E3
Barley Cft CH3 41 E6
Barmouth Cl CH5 13 C7
Barnes Cl CH1 35 F6
Barnfelde La LL12 52 B3
Barnfield LL13 5 C5
Barnston Ct CH3 71 C4
Barons Cl CH6 10 C2
Barons Rd LL13 61 E3
Barony Way CH4 43 E4
Barrel Well Hill CH3 40 D4
Barretts Hill LL11 56 B1
Barter Ct LL13 61 E5
Barter Rd LL13 61 E5
Bartholomew Way CH4 44 A2
Bartland Gro CH5 15 E7
Barton Cl LL13 60 D6
Barton Rd CH3 71 C4
Barwoods Dr CH4 43 F2
Basingwerk Av CH8 6 C2
Bath Rd LL13 5 B5
Bath St CH1 4 D4
Beacon Rd LL11 55 H4
Beaconsfield St CH3 4 D3
Beaumaris Cl CH7 24 D1
Beaumaris Rd CH5 13 C6
Beaumont Cl CH4 43 E2
Beaver Cl CH4 43 E2
Becketts La, Buckley CH7 24 B4
Becketts La, Chester CH3 41 E5
Bedevere Ct LL13 60 D5
Bedford Way CH7 22 B3
Bedward Row CH1 4 A4
Beech Av, Bradley LL11 56 B1
Beech Av, Gresford LL12 51 E5
Beech Dr CH7 22 B4
Beech Gdns LL13 5 D5
Beech Gro, Bagillt CH6 8 C6
Beech Gro, Chester CH2 40 D2
Beech Gro, Ellesmere Port CH66 32 B1
Beech Gro, Mold CH7 23 G3
Beech Rd, Buckley CH7 25 F3
Beech Rd, Deeside CH5 20 A2
Beech St, Rhosllanerchrugog LL14 64 D2
Beech St, Summerhill LL11 55 G1
Beech Tree Av LL12 50 B4
Beechcroft CH6 8 B4
Beechcroft Cl CH6 8 B4
Beechlands Av CH3 41 E4
Beechley Rd LL13 5 D6
Beechmuir CH1 39 E3
Beechtree Rd CH7 24 B3
Beechway CH2 36 A5
Beechwood Av CH5 13 D6
Beechwood Cl CH7 22 B2
Beechwood Rd CH4 43 E2
Bees Cotts CH1 38 C4
Beeston Pathway CH4 44 C1
Beeston Rd, Broughton CH4 27 F5
Beeston Rd, Higher Kinnerton CH4 29 H4
Beeston Vw CH4 40 C6
Belfry Cl LL13 57 H6
Belgrave Av CH4 43 E2
Belgrave Ct LL12 51 F5
Belgrave Pl CH4 4 C6
Belgrave Rd, Chester CH3 41 F6
Belgrave Rd, Wrexham LL13 5 C6
Belgrave St CH1 4 D2
Bell Ct LL13 61 E5
Bell Tower Walk CH1 4 B4
Bellard Dr CH2 41 E1
Belle Vue La CH3 31 A6
Bellevue Ct LL13 5 B4
Bellevue Rd LL13 5 A4
Bells Way LL13 71 B1

Belmont Av CH5 13 E7
Belmont Cres CH7 24 C2
Belmont Dr CH4 42 C1
Belmont Rd LL13 5 B6
Belvedere Cl CH5 20 C1
Belvedere Dr, Chester CH1 39 E1
Belvedere Dr, Wrexham LL11 60 A1
Benjamin Pl LL13 61 E3
Benjamin Rd LL13 61 E3
Benllech Cl CH5 13 C6
Bennetts La, Chester CH4 29 G4
Bennetts La, Deeside CH5 20 B4
Bennetts Rd LL11 55 F2
Bennetts Row CH6 10 F4
Bennions Rd LL13 5 C6
Bentley Av LL11 55 H1
Benton Dr CH2 40 A2
Berkley Dr CH4 44 B2
Bernard Rd LL13 61 E3
Bernfels Ct LL14 64 E1
Bernsdale Cl CH5 21 F3
Berse Gdns LL11 59 G1
Berse Rd, Bersham LL14 59 G5
Berse Rd, New Broughton LL11 59 G1
Bersham Rd, Bersham LL14 59 G5
Bersham Rd, New Broughton LL11 59 G1
Bersham Rd, Wrexham LL13, 14 5 A5
Bertie Rd LL13 61 E3
Berwyn LL14 64 F2
Berwyn Av, Chester CH4 28 B5
Berwyn Av, Wrexham LL14 69 D8
Berwyn Cl, Buckley CH7 24 C4
Berwyn Cl, Mold CH7 23 G2
Berwyn Cl, Wrexham LL13 71 B2
Berwyn Dr LL13 71 B1
Berwyn St LL20 67 A4
Berwyn Vw LL13 61 G3
Berwynfa LL20 70 C1
Bethania Rd LL14 65 A8
Beverley Cl LL13 61 G5
Bewley Ct CH3 41 E6
Bickerton Dr LL11 55 H3
Bickleywood Dr LL13 61 F1
Bidston Cl CH2 40 B1
Bieston Cl LL13 57 F4
Bilberry Cl CH4 28 C2
Birch Cft CH5 20 D4
Birch Cl CH7 24 C4
Birch Ct CH7 30 B1
Birch Ct*, Pen y Llan CH5 13 D5
Birch Dr LL12 51 F5
Birch Heath La CH3 41 H6
Birch Hill LL20 67 D5
Birch Rd CH4 43 F3
Birch Ridge CH6 10 A3
Birch Rise, Chester CH2 36 B6
Birch Rise, Deeside CH5 20 B5
Birch St LL13 5 D5
Birch Tree Cl LL11 55 G5
Birchfield Cres CH5 20 B2
Birchmuir CH1 39 E3
Birchwood Cl LL14 59 H5
Birkdale Av CH7 24 A2
Birkdale Cl LL13 57 G6
Birkdale Rd, Buckley CH7 24 A2
Birkdale Rd, Wrexham LL13 57 G6
Bishop St CH2 40 C2
Bishopgate CH2 41 E3
Bishops Ct CH4 27 G3
Bistre Av CH7 24 B3
Bistre Cl CH7 24 B3
Black Diamond St CH1 4 C1
Black Friars CH1 4 A5
Black Friars Ct CH1 4 A5
Blackbrook Av CH5 20 C3
Blackbrook Rd CH7 17 A5
Blacklane Rd LL11 55 F2
Blackthorn Cl, Chester CH3 45 E2
Blackthorn Cl, Wrexham LL12 51 F5
Blackthorne Av CH66 32 B1
Blackthorne Cl CH4 27 F5
Blacon Av CH1 35 E6
Blacon Hall Rd CH1 39 F1
Blacon Point Cl CH1 38 D2
Blacon Point Rd CH1 38 D2
Blaen Wern CH7 11 D5
Blake Cl CH1 35 F6
Blantern Rd CH4 29 H4
Blantern Way LL13 57 G6
Blast Rd LL11 54 C2
Blenheim Cl CH5 19 H5
Blue Bell La LL11 56 C3
Bluebell Cl CH3 45 E2
Bod Offa Dr CH7 23 H4
Bodafon Villas CH3 41 G5
Bodhyfryd, Holywell CH8 9 B4
Bodhyfryd, Wrexham LL12 5 D2
Bodlondeb CH6 10 D4
Bodlyn LL14 65 C7
Bodnant Gro CH5 13 C7
Bodwyn Cres LL12 51 E6
Bodwyn Pk LL12 51 E6
Bold Pl CH1 4 C3
Bold Sq CH1 4 D3
Bolesworth Rd CH2 36 C5
Boleyn Cl CH1 35 E5
Bolingbroke Heights*, Earl St CH6 10 C2
Bollam Cl CH5 13 C5
Bollands Ct CH1 4 B4
Bonc Wen LL14 64 C2
Border Retail Pk LL13 60 D2
Border Way CH3 41 F4
Borough Gro CH6 10 D2
Borras Park Rd LL12,13 57 F6
Borras Rd LL12 61 E1
Bottom Rd LL11 55 G1
Bottoms La CH4 40 C6
Boughton CH3 4 D3
Boughton Hall Av CH3 41 E4
Boughton Hall Dr CH3 41 F4
Boundary La CH4 43 E2
Bouverie St CH1 4 A1
Bowen Ct LL14 65 F7
Bowens La LL14 66 D2
Box La LL12 56 D5
Boxmoor Cl CH4 43 G3
Bracken Cl CH4 27 G5
Bracken Ct LL11 58 C1
Brackenwood Cl LL14 60 A5
Bradford Pl CH4 40 B6
Bradford St CH4 40 B6
Bradley Rd LL13 5 B3
Bradshaw Av CH4 42 C1
Braemar Cl CH3 41 F2
Braeside LL13 61 G5
Braeside Av CH5 20 C3
Brake Rd, Brymbo LL11 54 C2
Brake Rd, Moss LL11 55 F2
Bramble Cl, Buckley CH7 24 C4
Bramble Cl, Chester CH3 45 E1
Bramble Cl, Wrexham LL12 51 G5
Bramley Cl CH66 32 A1
Bramley Ct CW6 46 C5
Bramley La CH4 29 E4
Bramley Way CH5 19 G5
Bran LL14 65 C7
Brandon Gro LL12 52 D4
Brandy Brook LL14 64 E3
Brassey St CH3 40 D4
Bray Rd CH4 43 F1
Breck Cl LL13 71 B2
Brecon Cl LL12 57 F6
Breeze Hill CH5 13 F7
Brenig Ho*, Lakeside Bsns Village CH5 19 G5
Brennus Pl CH1 4 A3
Brentwood Rd CH1 35 E6
Breton Cl CH2 36 C6
Bretton Dr CH4 27 F4
Bretton Rd CH4 27 G3
Bretton Rd CH4 27 H4
Brewery Pl LL13 5 B3
Briar Dr CH7 24 D4
Briarswood LL11 56 B3
Brickbarn Cl CH7 24 B2
Brickfields CH7 25 E4
Bridge Ct, Chester CH2 40 D3
Bridge Ct, Holt LL13 71 B5
Bridge Ct, Southsea LL11 55 E6
Bridge Dr CH3 41 H6
Bridge Pl CH1 4 B5
Bridge Rd North LL13 62 D4
Bridge Rd South LL13 62 C5
Bridge St, Chester CH1 4 B4
Bridge St, Deeside CH5 15 A7
Bridge St, Holt LL13 71 B5
Bridge St, Llangollen LL20 67 B4
Bridge St, Mold CH7 22 C3
Bridge St, Pant LL14 64 C3
Bridge St, Penycae LL14 64 A4
Bridge St, Ruabon LL14 65 F7
Bridge St, Saltney CH4 42 D1
Bridge St, Southsea LL11 55 E6
Bridge St, Wrexham LL13 5 C4
Bridge Street Row CH1 4 B4
Bridge Ter CH3 41 E4
Bridge Vw CH5 15 E7
Bridgegate Chambers*, Duke St CH1 4 B5
Bridgeman Rd CH1 39 E2
Bridgend CH2 31 B2
Bridgewater Dr CH3 41 F3
Bridgewater Mws LL11 56 C2
Bridgeway East LL13 62 C5
Bridgeway West LL13 62 C6
Bright St LL13 5 A4
Brisbane Rd CH1 38 D2
Bristol Cl CH1 38 C1
Britannia Row CH7 30 B2
British Aerospace Aircraft Factory CH4 27 H2
Bro Alun CH7 22 C3
Bro Awelon LL14 64 A4
Bro Deg CH6 10 B3
Bro Dirion CH8 7 B5
Bro Gwilym LL14 66 D2
Broad Oak Av CH4 27 E4
Broad Oak Cl CH5 13 D7
Broad St LL14 64 D2
Broadacre Cl CH6 8 C6
Broadmead CH3 41 G4
Broadoaks LL12 52 E3
Broadway, Connahs Quay CH5 13 D8
Broadway, Ewloe CH5 19 G4
Broadway East CH2 40 B1
Broadway West CH2 40 B1
Brodie Cl CH2 36 A3
Brody Pl CH1 4 B5
Bromfield Av LL12 50 A4
Bromfield Cl CH7 22 D5
Bromfield Gro LL12 56 D6
Bromfield La CH7 22 D6
Bromfield Pk CH7 22 C5
Bromfield St LL14 64 E2
Bron Alyn LL12 50 C5
Bron Haul CH6 7 F5
Bron Llwyn CH6 10 C4
Bron y Coed LL13 60 C6
Bron y Dre LL13 5 A6
Bron y Gamlas LL20 66 B2
Bron y Nant, Mold CH7 22 D4
Bron y Nant, Wrexham LL13 60 B2
Bron y Wern CH6 8 B5
Bron yr Efail LL12 56 D3
Bron yr Eglwys CH7 23 F4
Bronallt LL14 64 C4
Bronalt CH7 30 B2
Broncoed Bsns Pk CH7 22 C6
Broncoed La CH7 22 C6
Broncoed Pk CH7 22 C5
Bronte Gro CH5 19 G5
Bronwylfa Rd LL14 59 F6
Broockhill Way CH7 24 B1
Brook Cl LL13 61 G5
Brook Dr CW6 46 C6
Brook La CH2 40 A2
Brook La CH4 21 H6
Brook Rd CH5 13 F7
Brook St, Buckley CH7 25 E4
Brook St, Llangollen LL20 67 C5
Brook St, Mold CH7 22 C5
Brook St, Northop CH7 17 B2
Brook St, Rhosllanerchrugog LL14 64 C2
Brook St, Rhosymedre LL14 66 E1
Brook St, Wrexham LL13 5 C4
Brook Street Bri CH1 4 D2
Brookdale Av, Connahs Quay CH5 13 D8
Brookdale Av, Flint CH6 10 B3
Brookdale Pl CH1 4 C3
Brookdale Way CH3 47 D4
Brooke Av CH2 36 C4
Brooke Cl CH5 19 G5
Brookes Av CH4 27 E5
Brookfield Dr CH2 40 C2
Brookleigh Av CH5 20 C3
Brookside, Buckley CH7 18 B2
Brookside, Chester CH3 41 E5
Brookside, Deeside CH5 15 E7
Brookside, Tarporley CW6 46 B6
Brookside Cres CH7 18 B2
Brookside Ter CH2 40 B2
Broom Cres CH3 46 C3
Broom Gro LL13 61 F2
Broomheath La CH3 46 C3
Brooms La CW6 46 C4
Broughton Hall Rd CH4 27 E4
Broughton Mills Rd CH4 42 A1
Broughton Rd LL11 55 E4
Broughton Retail Pk CH4 27 H3
Brown Heath Rd CH3 47 C2
Browning Cl CH1 35 F5
Browns La, Chester CH4 40 A6
Browns La, Wrexham LL14 66 D1
Browns Pl CH5 21 F3
Broxton Rd LL13 61 F2
Brunswick Pk CH7 24 D4
Brunswick Rd CH7 24 C3
Brunswood Grn CH5 19 H6
Brushwood Av CH6 10 A3
Bryd Clyd CH7 30 B2
Brymau Four Est CH4 42 D1
Brymau One Est CH4 43 E1
Brymau Three Est CH4 43 E1
Brymau Two Est CH4 43 E1
Brymbo Link Rd LL11 55 E5
Brymbo Rd LL11 53 D1
Bryn Aber, Bagillt CH6 8 B5
Bryn Aber, Holywell CH8 7 A5
Bryn Afon, Holywell CH8 6 B3
Bryn Afon, Wrexham LL14 64 C4
Bryn Av LL14 64 F2
Bryn Awel LL11 55 G6
Bryn Awelon, Buckley CH7 24 A4
Bryn Awelon, Mold CH7 22 D2
Bryn Barug CH7 30 C1
Bryn Cae Pl CH5 13 D5
Bryn Celyn, Brynteg LL11 55 F5
Bryn Celyn, Moss LL11 55 F1
Bryn Clwyd CH7 23 F2
Bryn Clywedog LL11 58 B1
Bryn Coch Cres CH7 22 B5
Bryn Coch La CH7 22 B5
Bryn Coed, Holywell CH8 7 B5
Bryn Coed, Wrexham LL11 55 G2
Bryn Coed Wepre CH5 19 E1
Bryn Derw, Flint CH6 10 D4
Bryn Derw, Wrexham LL12 49 C7
Bryn Derwen CH7 23 H4
Bryn Dr CH5 20 C3
Bryn Dyffryn CH8 8 D2
Bryn Dyrys CH6 8 B5
Bryn Eglwys Rd LL13 61 G3
Bryn Eitha LL14 64 B4
Bryn Eithin, Deeside CH5 19 E1
Bryn Eithin, Mold CH7 11 C6
Bryn Eryl LL20 66 B1
Bryn Estyn Ct LL13 61 H1
Bryn Ffynnon LL13 5 C3
Bryn Fynnon Rd LL14 64 B4
Bryn Garmon CH7 22 B4
Bryn Glas, Flint CH6 10 A4
Bryn Glas, Wrexham LL14 64 C3
Bryn Glas LL11 55 H2
Bryn Goleu LL11 55 F5
Bryn Gro LL13 61 G1
Bryn Gryffydd LL12 57 F5
Bryn Gwenfro LL11 54 D4
Bryn Gwyn CH6 10 D4
Bryn Gwyn La CH7 13 A8
Bryn Hafod LL13 61 F4
Bryn Hedd LL11 55 F5
Bryn Helyg CH6 10 D4
Bryn Heulog CH7 22 B4
Bryn Hilyn La CH7 22 D5
Bryn Hyfryd, Coedpoeth LL11 54 A6
Bryn Hyfryd, Connahs Quay CH5 13 B8
Bryn Hyfryd, Johnstown LL14 64 F2
Bryn Hyfryd, Soughton CH7 17 B5
Bryn La LL13 62 D1
Bryn Maelor LL11 55 F5
Bryn Mawr Rd, Buckley CH7 24 B4
Bryn Mawr Rd, Holywell CH8 7 B5
Bryn Nebo LL11 53 D2
Bryn Oddfa CH7 22 B3
Bryn Offa CH7 23 F4
Bryn Onnen CH6 10 D4
Bryn Pl LL12 50 C4
Bryn Rd, Brymbo LL11 54 D1
Bryn Rd, Buckley CH7 24 A1
Bryn Rd, Connahs Quay CH5 13 C6
Bryn Rd, Moss LL11 55 F1
Bryn Rd, Mynydd Isa CH7 23 G4
Bryn Rd, New Brighton CH7 23 F1
Bryn Rhedyn LL11 55 F6
Bryn Rhyd CH7 17 A2
Bryn Seion La CH7 17 B5
Bryn Seion Ter*, Bryn Seion La CH7 17 B5
Bryn Siriol, Flint CH6 10 D3
Bryn Siriol, Wrexham LL11 54 A6
Bryn St LL14 65 F6
Bryn Teg, Holywell CH8 7 D5
Bryn Teg, Soughton CH7 17 B5
Bryn Tirion CH8 9 B4
Bryn Way LL14 65 F5
Bryn Wood Dr CH7 24 B5
Bryn y Baal Rd CH7 23 F1
Bryn y Barcut LL14 64 B4

Bryn y Cabanau Rd LL13 5 D5
Bryn y Felin CH8 7 B5
Bryn y Ffynnon LL11 54 D1
Bryn y Gaer Rd LL11 55 F3
Bryn y Glyn LL11 56 B5
Bryn y Grog Hill LL13 71 A1
Bryn y Gwynt CH8 7 C5
Bryn y Wern LL11 54 A6
Bryn Ydd LL14 64 D1
Bryn Yorkin LL12 48 B3
Bryn Yorkin Rd LL12 49 A5
Bryn yr Onnen LL11 55 F5
Bryncoed Rd LL11 55 F1
Bryndraw Ter LL13 5 C4
Brynestyn Rd LL13 61 G1
Brynford Rd CH8 7 A8
Brynford St CH8 7 B6
Brynisa Rd LL11 55 G4
Brynmor Dr CH6 10 B3
Brynteg Cres LL11 55 F4
Bryntirion CH6 8 C5
Bryntirion Rd CH6 8 B6
Bryntirion Ter LL20 67 C5
Buckingham Av CH3 41 E3
Buckingham Rd LL11 56 C5
Bulkeley St CH3 40 D4
Bumpers La CH1 39 E6
Bunbury Cl CH2 33 H3
Bunce St CH1 4 B5
Burganey Ct CH4 52 E1
Burges St CH2 40 D2
Burgess Dr CH1 38 A1
Burnham Gdns LL13 61 F3
Burnham Rd CH4 43 F2
Burns Cl CH5 19 G6
Burns Way CH1 35 E6
Burntwood Ct CH7 25 F2
Burntwood Rd CH7 25 E1
Burton Ct CH5 13 D7
Burton Dr, Chester CH4 29 G4
Burton Dr, Wrexham LL12 56 D4
Burton Hall Rd LL12 52 A2
Burton Rd, Chester CH1 35 E6
Burton Rd, Wrexham LL12 52 B3
Burton Rise LL12 51 F5
Bury St LL13 5 D5
Bush Rd CH3 41 H6
Butcher St LL14 64 D1
Butler St CH5 15 A8
Butlers Hill LL20 67 B5
Butterbache Rd CH3 44 D1
Butterbur Cl CH3 45 E1
Buttermere Cl CH5 13 B6
Bwlch y Ddeufryn CH7 11 A2
Bye Pass Rd CH3 46 B1
Byron Cl, Chester CH1 35 F6
Byron Cl, Connahs Quay CH5 19 F1
Byron Cl, Ewloe CH5 19 G6
Bythom Cl CH3 45 H1

Cable St CH5 13 E6
Cadlas Cl CH5 19 E1
Cadnant Cl CH1 39 E2
Cadnant Ct CH4 27 G3
Cadnant Dr CH6 8 A4
Cae Adar La LL11 53 E2
Cae Berwyn CH7 17 B5
Cae Bracty CH7 22 C4
Cae Bychan CH6 10 D4
Cae Coch La LL14 66 D1
Cae Daniel LL14 64 D3
Cae Derw CH6 10 D3
Cae Derwen LL14 64 C4
Cae Gabriel LL14 64 B4
Cae Glas, Mold CH7 22 A5
Cae Glas, Soughton CH7 17 C5
Cae Glas, Wrexham LL11 54 B6
Cae Gwilym La LL14 66 D2
Cae Gwilym Rd LL14 66 D3
Cae Gywnedd CH8 6 B3
Cae Haf CH7 18 C1
Cae Hafod LL20 70 B2
Cae Hir, Flint CH6 10 D3
Cae Hir, Mold CH7 22 A4
Cae Isa CH7 23 F1
Cae Llys Cl CH5 13 B8
Cae Merfyn LL11 54 D4
Cae Mynach CH7 30 C5
Cae Pentre LL11 55 F4
Cae Penty Rd LL12 49 A8
Cae Petit CH6 10 D3
Cae Plas Teg LL20 70 B2
Cae Rhug La CH7 11 A1
Cae Thomas LL20 67 B5
Cae Vaunog CH4 28 B4
Cae y Dderwen CH8 6 B3
Caegwyn LL20 70 C2
Caer Efail LL11 53 D1
Caer Eglwys LL14 64 D1
Caer Ffynnon CH6 7 F5
Caer Fron CH6 7 B7
Caer Haf LL11 55 G1
Caer Llan LL14 65 F6
Caer Mul CH7 11 B2
Caer Ysgol LL20 70 C2
Caerllew LL13 71 B5
Caernarvon Cl CH5 15 A8
Caernavon Rd LL12 57 F6
Caesar Av CH6 10 E3
Caia Gdns LL13 61 E3
Caia Rd LL13 5 D4
Cairndale Av CH5 13 C7
Cairns Cres CH1 38 D1
Cairnton Cres CH8 6 D3
Caldbeck Cres CH5 13 B6
Caldy Av*, Welland Dr CH5 13 C7
Caldy Cl CH2 36 B6
Caldy Valley Rd CH3 45 E2
Callin Ct CH1 4 A5
Camberley Dr LL12 61 E1
Camberley Rise LL12 61 E1
Cambrian Av CH3 41 F3
Cambrian Cl, Connahs Quay CH5 13 D7
Cambrian Cl, Mold CH7 22 D6
Cambrian Ct, Chester CH1 39 H3
Cambrian Ct, Wrexham LL11 54 D1
Cambrian Rd CH1 4 A2
Cambrian Way CH5 19 H3
Cambridge Rd CH2 40 D1
Cambridge Sq LL11 56 D4
Camor Afon LL20 70 C2
Campbell Cl LL12 52 D4
Campbell St LL14 64 C1
Campion Cl CH3 45 E2
Camrose Cl CH5 19 E1
Canadian Av CH2 40 D2
Canal Side CH3 4 D3
Canal St CH1 4 A3
Canal Wood Ind Est LL14 69 C5
Canberra Way CH1 38 D2
Canning St CH1 4 B3
Cannon Way CH4 29 G4
Canol y Bryn CH7 23 G2
Canon Dr CH6 8 B6
Canterbury Cl CH66 32 A1
Canterbury Rd CH1 39 F1
Capeland Cl CH4 43 E3
Capesthorne Rd CH3 47 C3
Cappers Hill LL11 55 G4
Car St CH1 4 D2
Carden Park Way LL13 57 G6
Cardigan Rd LL12 57 F6
Carlines Av CH5 19 H4
Carlisle Rd CH1 39 E1
Carlson Dr LL11 56 D4
Carlton Av CH4 42 D2
Carlton Cl CH2 31 A3
Carlton Dr LL11 55 H2
Carlton Pl CH2 41 E1
Carmel Cl CH1 38 D2
Carmel Rd CH8 8 A2
Carnoustie Cl LL13 61 H1
Carrick Rd CH4 39 G6
Carter Av CW6 46 C6
Carter St CH1 4 D2
Cartmel Cl LL13 61 F5
Carton Rd CH7 23 G4
Castle Cl, Chester CH4 27 F1
Castle Cl, Pulford CH4 52 F1
Castle Cl, Tarporley CW6 46 C6
Castle Cl, Wrexham LL11 56 C4
Castle Cres LL14 69 D6
Castle Croft Rd CH4 43 G2
Castle Dr CH1 4 B6
Castle Dyke St CH6 10 C1
Castle Gdns LL13 71 B5
Castle Grange LL12 48 B4
Castle Heights*, Chapel St CH6 10 C2
Castle Hill CH4 52 E1
Castle Hill St CH5 20 B1
Castle Ind Pk CH6 10 C1
Castle Mews CH5 13 F7
Castle Park Av CH5 19 E1
Castle Rd, Flint CH6 10 D2
Castle Rd, Wrexham LL14 69 D7
Castle Rise CH5 20 D6
Castle St, Caergwrle LL12 48 B3
Castle St, Chester CH1 4 B5
Castle St, Flint CH6 10 C1
Castle St, Holt LL13 71 B6
Castle St, Llangollen LL20 67 B5
Castle St, Ponciau LL14 64 D1
Castle Ter LL11 58 C1
Castle Walks LL14 69 D6
Castlemere Cl CH4 27 E5
Castletown Rd LL11 55 F2
Catherine Dr CH5 19 H4
Catherine St CH1 39 H4
Caughall Rd CH2 36 C1
Cavalier Dr CH1 35 E5
Cavendish Ct LL12 51 F5
Cavendish Rd CH4 43 H1
Cavendish Sq LL12 57 E4
Cawdor Dr CH3 41 E3
Caxton Pl LL13 5 B2
Cecil St CH3 40 D4
Cedar Av, Connahs Quay CH5 13 C5
Cedar Av, Garden City CH5 16 B4
Cedar Cl, Bradley LL11 56 B1
Cedar Cl, Buckley CH7 24 B2
Cedar Cl, Gresford LL12 51 F6
Cedar Cl, Wrexham LL12 57 F4
Cedar Ct*, Pen y Llan CH5 13 D5
Cedar Dr, Chester CH2 41 F2
Cedar Dr, Wrexham LL11 55 G1
Cedar Gdns CH5 20 A2
Cedar Gro, Chester CH2 41 E1
Cedar Gro, Mold CH7 22 B3
Cedar Mews CH1 39 E1
Cedar Pk CH3 41 G4
Cedardale Dr CH66 32 B1
Cefn La LL11 53 E1
Cefn Parc*, Stryt Issa LL14 64 B3
Cefn Rd, Brynteg LL11 55 E3
Cefn Rd, Bwlchgwyn LL11 53 E1
Cefn Rd, Connahs Quay CH5 13 D5
Cefn Rd, Wrexham LL13 61 G1
Cefn y Bedd LL12 49 C5
Cefndre LL13 61 G4
Ceiriog Cl LL14 69 D6
Ceiriog Rd LL13 61 G3
Celandine Cl CH3 45 E1
Celmar Gro LL14 59 G5
Celtic St CH5 13 F6
Celyn Av CH5 13 D7
Celyn Cl, Holywell CH8 8 A2
Celyn Cl, Wrexham LL11 55 H4
Celyn Cres CH4 42 D2
Celyn Dr LL12 48 B2
Celyn Nurseries CH5 19 G4
Celyn Pk CH8 8 A2
Celyn Pl LL11 58 C1
Cement Pl CH1 4 C3
Cemetery Rd, Coedpoeth LL11 58 A1
Cemetery Rd, Rhosllanerchrugog LL14 64 D3
Cemlyn Cl CH1 39 E2
Centenary Rd LL13 60 A4
Central Av LL12 57 E6
Central Dr CH5 20 A1
Central Rd LL13 5 A2
Central Trading Pk CH4 43 E1
Cerney Rd LL11 55 F1
Cestrian St CH5 13 E6
Chainmakers Row CH4 43 E1
Challinor St CH3 40 D4
Chambers La CH7 23 G4
Chancel Dr CH6 8 C6
Chandos Cl CH4 44 C2
Chanticleer Cl LL13 61 F1
Chantry Ct CH1 39 E4
Chapel Cl, Rowton CH3 47 B4
Chapel Cl, Saughall CH1 34 A3
Chapel Ct, Connahs Quay CH5 13 E6
Chapel Ct, Wrexham LL11 55 E6
Chapel Grn CW6 46 B5
Chapel La, Chester CH3 41 E4
Chapel La, Chirk LL14 69 D5
Chapel La, Holt LL13 71 B6
Chapel La, Llay LL12 50 B2
Chapel La, Rossett LL12 52 D3
Chapel Pl LL13 5 B5
Chapel Rd LL11 59 G1
Chapel St, Acrefair LL14 65 A8
Chapel St, Chester CH3 4 D3
Chapel St, Connahs Quay CH5 13 E6
Chapel St, Flint CH6 10 C2
Chapel St, Holt LL13 71 B6
Chapel St, Johnstown LL14 64 E2
Chapel St, Llangollen LL20 67 B5
Chapel St, Mold CH7 22 C4
Chapel St, Penycae LL14 64 A4
Chapel St, Rhostyllen LL14 59 G6
Chapel St, Rhosymedre LL14 66 E1
Chapel St, Wrexham LL13 5 C4
Chapel Ter CH6 8 A4
Charles Av LL20 66 B1
Charles Cres CH4 4 D6
Charles Dr CH6 10 C3
Charles Rd CH2 35 H3
Charles St, Chester CH1 4 C2
Charles St, Chirk LL14 68 D4
Charles St, Hoole CH2 40 C2
Charles St, Johnstown LL14 64 E2
Charles St, Mold CH7 22 C6
Charles St, Wrexham LL13 5 D4
Charlotte Ct CH1 4 C3
Charlotte St CH1 39 H4
Charlton Ct CH2 40 D1
Charmleys La CH5 20 A1
Charterhall Dr CH2 40 C4
Chaser Ct CH1 39 F3
Chatheralls Ind Est CH7 24 B1
Chatsworth Dr, Chester CH2 37 E6
Chatsworth Dr, Wrexham LL11 55 H4
Chatsworth Gdns LL11 56 D2
Chaucer Cl CH5 19 G6
Chelford Cl CH1 39 F4
Chelford Mews*, Pearl La CH3 41 F4
Chelston Av LL13 57 F4
Chemistry La CH5 21 E1
Chepstow La LL13 61 G5
Cheriton CH5 19 E1
Cherry Dale Rd CH4 26 D5
Cherry Dr CH7 23 G2
Cherry Fld LL11 55 G5
Cherry Gdns CH3 41 E4
Cherry Grove Rd CH3 41 E4
Cherry Hill Dr LL12 57 F5
Cherry Orch LL13 71 B6
Cherry Orchard Rd CH5 26 B2
Cherry Rd CH3 41 E4
Cherrytree Rd LL11 56 B1
Chesham St CH1 4 D2
Cheshire La CH7 24 C2
Cheshire Vw, Brymbo LL11 54 C1
Cheshire Vw, Wrexham LL13 61 E2
Chesnut Cres CH5 19 H6
Chester St CH7 22 C4
Chester Aerospace Pk CH4 27 F2
Chester App CH4 44 A1
Chester Bank Ind Est CH4 38 C6
Chester Bsns Pk CH4 43 H5
Chester Cl CH5 15 A8
Chester Enterprise Centre CH2 4 D1
Chester Rd, Broughton CH4 27 E2
Chester Rd, Buckley CH5,7 25 E4
Chester Rd, Ewloe CH5 19 H4
Chester Rd, Flint CH6 10 E3
Chester Rd, Great Sutton CH66 32 A1
Chester Rd, Huntington CH3 44 D1
Chester Rd, Mold CH7 22 D4
Chester Rd, Penyffordd CH4 28 B3
Chester Rd, Rossett LL12 51 G2
Chester Rd, Saltney CH4 42 A2
Chester Rd, Sandycroft CH5 20 D
Chester Rd, Tarporley CW6 46 C5
Chester Rd, Whitby CH65 32 B
Chester Rd, Wrexham LL11,12 5 D
Chester Rd East CH5 20 D
Chester Rd West CH5 15 A
Chester Retail Pk CH1 39 G3
Chester Ring Rd CH3 41 F
Chester Southerly By-Pass CH3,4 43 G
Chester St, Chester CH4 43 F
Chester St, Flint CH6 10 D
Chester St, Wrexham LL13 5 D
Chester Way LL13 70 C
Chester West Employment Pk CH1 39 E4
Chesterton Av CH5 19 G
Chesterton Ct CH2 40 B
Chestnut Av, Summerhill LL11 55 G
Chestnut Av, Wrexham LL11,12 56 D
Chestnut Cl, Chester CH2 41 E
Chestnut Cl, Flint CH6 10 A
Chestnut Cl, Soughton CH7 17 A
Chestnut Cl, Wrexham LL12 51 E
Chestnut Cres CH5 19 H
Chestnut Ct LL11 55 G
Chestnut Ct*, Pen y Llan CH5 13 D
Chestnut Grange CH4 39 H
Chestnut Gro CH5 20 C
Chestnut Rd, Mold CH7 22 A

Chestnut Rd, Wrexham LL11 56 B1
Chetwyn Ct LL12 51 F5
Cheviot Cl LL11 55 H4
Chevron Cl CH1 39 E2
Chevron Hey CH1 39 E2
Chevrons Rd CH5 20 B1
Cheyney Rd CH1 4 A1
Chichester St CH1 4 A2
Chiltern Cl, Chester CH4 43 H3
Chiltern Cl, Connahs Quay CH5 13 C8
Chiltern Cl, Wrexham LL11 55 H4
Chirk Cl CH2 36 D5
Chirk Rd LL14 69 E7
Christleton Rd CH3 40 D4
Church Bank CW6 46 C5
Church Cl, Buckley CH7 18 C1
Church Cl, Holywell CH8 6 C2
Church College Cl CH1 39 H2
Church Ct CH3 71 B4
Church Grn LL12 50 D5
Church Hall Cl CH1 39 F1
Church La, Backford CH2 32 C5
Church La, Chester CH3 71 B4
Church La, Ewloe CH5 19 H3
Church La, Guilden Sutton CH3 31 B6
Church La, Gwernaffield CH7 11 B2
Church La, Hawarden CH5 20 C5
Church La, Mold CH7 22 C3
Church La, Stoak CH2 33 H2
Church La, Upton CH2 36 B4
Church Rd, Brynteg LL11 55 G4
Church Rd, Buckley CH7 24 C1
Church Rd, Chester CH4 27 G3
Church Rd, Connahs Quay CH5 13 D5
Church Rd, Eccleston CH4 44 C6
Church Rd, Farndon CH3 71 C4
Church Rd, Minera LL11 53 D4
Church Rd, Northop CH7 17 B2
Church Rd, Saughall CH1 34 A3
Church Rd, Southsea LL11 55 E6
Church St, Chester CH1 4 C2
Church St, Connahs Quay CH5 13 C5
Church St, Farndon CH3 71 C4
Church St, Flint CH6 10 C2
Church St, Gwersyllt LL11 55 H2
Church St, Holt LL13 71 B5
Church St, Llangollen LL20 67 B4
Church St, Penycae LL14 64 A4
Church St, Rhosllanerchrugog LL14 64 D3
Church St, Rhostyllen LL14 59 G6
Church St, Rhosymedre LL14 66 E1
Church St, Ruabon LL14 65 F7
Church St, Tarporley CW6 46 C5
Church St, Tarvin CH3 46 C1
Church St, Wrexham LL13 5 C4
Church St North CW6 46 C5
Church View Ct LL13 71 C2
Church Vw, Chirk LL14 69 E6
Church Vw, Deeside CH5 21 E2
Church Vw, Ruabon LL14 65 E7
Church Walk CH6 8 B5
Church Walks CH3 41 H5
Church Way CH1 35 E6
Churchill Cl CH5 20 A5
Churchill Dr LL13 61 F2
Churchward Cl CH2 40 A1
Churton Dr LL13 61 E2
Churton Rd CH3 41 E4
Churton St CH3 41 E4
Cil Coed LL14 68 E3
Cilcen Gro LL12 56 D6
Cileen LL11 55 G1
Cilnant CH7 22 A4
Cinder Cl CH3 31 B6
Cinder La CH3 31 B6
Circular Dr, Chester CH4 43 E3
Circular Dr, Deeside CH5 19 G3
City Quays*, Leadworks La CH1 4 D3
City Rd CH1 4 D3
City Walls CH1 4 A3
City Walls Rd CH1 4 A3
City Way CH1 4 D3
Clair Av CH5 21 F3
Clappers La LL12 50 D5
Clare Av CH2 40 D2
Claremont Av CH5 15 E8
Claremont Walk CH1 4 C3
Clarence Av CH3 41 E3
Clarence Rd LL11 56 C6
Clarence St CH5 15 A8
Clarendon Av LL11 56 B5
Clarendon Cl CH4 44 C1
Clarke Rd LL12 57 F5
Clarke St LL14 64 D2
Claverton Ct CH4 4 D5
Clawdd Offa LL14 64 E2
Clay La CH5 20 C1
Claypit La LL12 51 F5
Claypit Rd CH4 43 H2
Claypits La CH3 47 A5
Clayton Ct CH7 22 A4
Clayton Rd, Mold CH7 22 A4
Clayton Rd, Wrexham LL11 55 E1
Cleaver Rd CH1 39 E2
Cledwen Dr CH7 23 G3
Cledwen Rd CH4 27 G3
Cleggs Cl CH3 45 F1
Clemley Cl CW6 46 C4
Cleveland Gro CH5 15 E7
Cleveland St LL14 65 F6
Cleves Cl CH1 35 E5
Clifford Dr CH4 43 F3
Clifton Cl LL13 61 E4
Clifton Dr CH1 39 E2
Clifton Park Av CH5 13 C5
Cliveden Rd CH4 43 F3
Clivedon Rd CH5 13 C7
Clos Ascot LL13 61 G5
Clos Coed CH5 20 D2
Clos Lindum CH7 23 F1
Clos Llewelyn LL11 54 B6
Clos y Capel CH7 24 C2
Clos y Meillion CH5 19 G5
Clos Ystrad LL13 60 C5
Clover La CH4 43 F3
Clover Pl CH4 43 F3
Clwedog East Rd LL13 62 B4
Clwedog Rd North LL13 62 C5
Clwedog Rd South LL13 62 B5
Clwyd Av, Holywell CH8 6 D4
Clwyd Av, Mold CH7 23 G4
Clwyd Cl CH4 27 F1
Clwyd Gro CH7 24 B4
Clwyd Ho*, Lakeside Bsns Village CH5 19 G5
Clwyd St CH5 20 B2
Clwyd Wen LL13 61 E4
Clydesdale Rd CH7 25 F2
Clywd Cres CH7 23 F1
Clywedog Cl LL11 55 H4
Cobden Pl LL11 58 B1
Cobden Rd LL13 5 A3
Cobham Cl LL13 60 D6
Coed Aben LL13 61 G3
Coed Aben Rd LL13 62 C4
Coed Afon LL20 67 C5
Coed Bach CH6 10 A3
Coed Efa La LL11 55 G5
Coed Onn Rd CH6 10 C3
Coed Richard LL14 65 B8
Coed Terfyn CH4 28 C1
Coed y Bryn LL13 61 G4
Coed y Felin Cl LL11 54 D1
Coed y Felin Rd LL11 54 D1
Coed y Ffynnon LL13 60 C5
Coed y Fron CH8 7 A6
Coed y Graig, Chester CH4 28 B2
Coed y Graig, Wrexham LL14 64 D4
Coed y Nant, Penycae LL14 64 B4
Coed y Nant, Wrexham LL13 60 C5
Colchester Sq CH4 43 F3
Colemere St LL13 5 B5
Coleridge Cl CH1 35 G6
Coleshill Lea*, Coleshill St CH6 10 C2
Coleshill Pl CH5 13 C5
Coleshill St, Flint CH6 10 C2
Coleshill St, Holywell CH8 7 B6
College Grn CH4 44 B1
College Hill LL11 55 E5
College St LL13 5 C4
College Vw CH5 13 C5
Colliers La CH7 23 H4
Colliery La CH5 20 C2
Colliery Rd, Chirk LL14 69 D6
Colliery Rd, Southsea LL11 55 E5
Colliery Rd, Wrexham LL11 56 B6
Collins Ct LL13 61 E5
Coltsfoot Cl CH3 45 E2
Columbine Cl CH3 45 E2
Colwyn Rd LL13 61 E3
Common La, Chester CH3 47 C5
Common La, Tarporley CW6 46 C6
Commonhall St CH1 4 B4
Compton Pl CH4 43 G1
Concorde Row LL13 57 G5
Congleton Rd CH4 27 G4
Conifer Cl CH66 32 B1
Coningsby Ct LL13 57 G5
Coniston Cl*, Machynlleth Way CH5 13 C7
Coniston Dr CH7 24 D2
Coniston Rd CH2 36 D6
Connahs Quay Rd CH7 17 B2
Connaught Av CH5 15 A8
Connor Cres LL13 61 E4
Constitution Hill CH7 30 C1
Conway Av CH7 24 D4
Conway Cl, Caergwrle LL12 48 B3
Conway Cl, Chester CH4 42 D2
Conway Cl, Flint CH6 10 B4
Conway Cl, Gwersyllt LL11 56 A2
Conway Ct CH5 13 C7
Conway Dr LL13 61 G2
Conway Ho*, Lakeside Bsns Village CH5 19 G5
Conway St CH7 22 C5
Coopers Cft CH3 45 E1
Coopers Cl LL13 61 F1
Coopers La CH5 13 C5
Copeswood Cl CH4 27 F5
Coppa Vw CH7 24 D4
Coppack Cl CH5 19 E1
Coppafield Cl CH7 24 D3
Copper Beech Cl CH4 27 F4
Copperas Hill LL14 64 B4
Coppi Ind Est LL14 64 B1
Coppins Cl CH3 41 E3
Cornfield Cl CH66 32 A1
Cornish Cl LL13 60 D5
Cornist Dr CH6 10 B2
Cornist La CH6 10 A3
Cornist Rd CH6 10 B2
Cornwa Rd CH5 20 B1
Cornwall Rd, Chester CH2 36 C5
Cornwall Rd, Deeside CH5 20 B1
Cornwall St CH1 4 C1
Coronation Dr LL14 69 E5
Coronation St, Cefn-mawr LL14 66 D3
Coronation St, Chester CH4 43 F1
Coronation St, New Broughton LL11 55 G6
Corporation St CH6 10 C1
Corun y Bryn CH5 19 E1
Corwen Cl CH5 13 C7
Corwen Way CH4 28 B4
Cosford Cl LL13 57 G5
Cotebrook Dr CH2 36 C5
Cotes Pl CH1 39 E2
Cotgreaves Cl CH4 43 H2
Cotswold Cl, Boughton CH3 40 D4
Cotswold Cl, Upton CH2 36 D5
Cottage Cl LL12 52 F2
Cottage Gdns CH7 24 D3
Cottage La CH5 20 C3
Cottage Rd CH4 43 H3
Cotterill Cl CH5 13 C8
Cotton La CH3 47 D1
Coulson Ct*, Mason St CH1 4 B2
Council St LL12 50 B4
Countess Ct CH1 39 H1
Countess Way CH1 39 H1
County Rd CH7 30 C3
Courbet Dr CH5 13 B6
Court Rd LL13 5 A6
Courtland Dr CH5 20 A2
Courtney Rd CH4 43 E3
Cousens Way CH1 39 H1
Coventry Av CH66 32 A1
Cowhey Cl CH4 43 H2
Cowthorne Dr CH3 47 B5
Cox La LL12 51 G4
Crabwall Pl CH1 35 F6
Craig Cl LL14 69 E5
Craig Way LL12 57 E6
Craigle LL14 64 D1
Craigmillar Cl LL12 5 D1
Cranbrook Cl CH5 13 D7
Crane Bank CH1 39 H4
Crane St LL14 66 D2
Cranford Ct CH4 43 G3
Cranford Rd LL13 61 F2
Cranleigh Cres CH1 39 H2
Crathie Pl LL11 56 C6
Crathie Rd CH3 41 E3
Crawford Walk CH2 40 D3
Crecas La CH8 8 B2
Crescent Cl LL13 61 E2
Crescent Rd LL13 5 D3
Crewe La CH3 71 C5
Crewe La South CH3 71 C6
Crewe St CH1 4 D2
Cricceth Cl CH7 24 D1
Cripps Av LL11 55 F6
Crispin La LL11 5 A1
Cristionydd LL14 64 B4
Croes Atti La CH6 10 E4
Croesfoel Ind Pk LL14 59 G6
Croeshowell Hill LL12 51 E1
Croeshowell La LL12 51 E1
Croesnewydd Rd LL13 5 A3
Croft Av CH5 13 D8
Croft Cl CH3 47 B4
Croft La CH5 20 B2
Croft Mews CH1 34 A3
Crofters Way, Chester CH1 34 A3
Crofters Way, Deeside CH5 20 D4
Cromar Cres LL12 52 E3
Crompton Cl CH4 29 G4
Cromwell Av CH7 24 B2
Cromwell Cl, Chester CH4 28 B3
Cromwell Cl, Deeside CH5 19 H5
Crook St CH1 4 B4
Crookenden Cl CH2 36 A3
Crookenden Rd CH2 36 A3
Crosfield Rd CH8 6 B3
Cross Grn CH2 36 C5
Cross Hey CH4 4 D6
Cross La, Llangollen LL20 67 B5
Cross La, Wrexham LL11 55 F3
Cross Lanes CH3 46 D3
Cross Rds CH8 7 B6
Cross St, Chester CH2 40 D4
Cross St, Holywell CH8 7 A6
Cross St, Southsea LL11 55 F6
Cross St, Wrexham LL11 5 C1
Cross Tree Ct CH7 19 F5
Cross Tree La CH5 20 C5
Crossfields CH3 46 B2
Crossley Cres CH2 41 E1
Crossways, Caergwrle LL12 48 C4
Crossways, Chester CH4 28 B2
Crossways, Ewloe CH5 19 H4
Crossways, Mancot CH5 20 D2
Crossways, Shotton CH5 15 A8
Crossways, Wrexham LL13 61 E2
Croughton Rd, Croughton CH2 33 G4
Croughton Rd, Stoak CH2 33 H3
Crown Pl LL12 50 B4
Crud y Gwynt CH7 23 H4
Culfan LL14 64 C3
Cumbrae Dr CH65 32 D1
Cunliffe St, Mold CH7 22 C5
Cunliffe St, Wrexham LL11 5 C1
Cunliffe Walk LL11 56 D5
Cunningham Av LL13 61 E2
Cuppin St CH1 4 B5
Curzon Cl CH4 39 G6
Curzon Pk North CH4 39 H5
Curzon Pk South CH4 43 G1
Curzon St CH4 43 F1
Cwm Cl CH7 23 F4
Cwm Eithin LL12 57 E3
Cwm Eithion CH6 10 D4
Cwrt Brenig CH7 24 D4
Cwrt Cwellyn CH5 27 E1
Cwrt Dinas CH5 27 E1
Cwrt Erwain CH4 43 E1
Cwrt Leighton CH5 13 D5
Cwrt Ogwen CH5 27 F1
Cwrt Onnen CH5 20 D4
Cwrt Telford CH5 13 D8
Cyman Cl CH1 38 D2
Cymau Rd LL12 49 A5
Cynlas LL11 55 F5
Cynlas St LL14 64 D2

Dafydd Cl CH7 23 G3
Daisy Bank Cl LL14 60 A4
Daisy Hill Rd CH7 24 D3
Daisy Rd LL11 55 G4
Dale Ct LL11 55 G6
Dale Dr CH2 36 B4
Dale Rd, Deeside CH5 20 A1
Dale Rd, Wrexham LL11 55 G6
Dale St, Chester CH3 41 E4
Dale St, Wrexham LL13 61 E3
Daleside, Buckley CH7 24 A4
Daleside, Chester CH2 36 B4
Daleside Av LL12 57 G5
Dalton Cl CH1 39 E2
Dane Cl, Chester CH4 43 F3
Dane Cl, Wrexham LL11 55 H3
Dane Gro CH2 31 A2
Daneswood LL13 71 C2
Daniel Ct*, Bridge St CH5 15 A7

Daniel Owen Centre*, Earl Rd CH5 22 C4
Daniell Way CH3 45 E1
Daniels Dr LL14 65 F5
Darby Rd LL11 55 F5
Darland Cl LL12 52 E3
Darland La LL12 52 E2
Darland Vw LL12 52 E3
Darlington Cres CH1 34 A3
Darwen Dr CH4 28 C2
Darwin Rd CH1 38 D2
Daulwyn Rd CH7 25 E2
Dauncey Cl CH2 36 A3
Davey Cl LL11 56 B5
Davies Av LL11 54 C1
Davies Ct LL13 61 E5
Davy Way LL12 49 F5
Dawn Cl CH7 24 B4
Dawpool Cl CH2 40 B1
Dawson Dr CH1 40 A2
Daytona Dr CH7 18 C2
Ddol LL14 59 G5
Ddol Awel CH7 22 A4
Dean Cl LL13 57 F6
Dean Rd LL13 57 F6
Deanery Cl CH1 40 A2
Deans Av CH5 13 E6
Deans Cl, Bagillt CH6 8 B6
Deans Cl, Chester CH2 36 B5
Deans Cl, Tarvin CH3 46 B3
Deans Pl CH5 13 E6
Deans Way CH3 46 B2
Deansbury Cl CH6 10 A2
Deansway CH4 29 H3
Dee Av LL12 57 E6
Dee Banks CH3 40 D6
Dee Cotts CH6 10 D2
Dee Cres CH3 71 B4
Dee Ct, Chester CH3 71 B4
Dee Ct, Wrexham LL13 70 C5
Dee Fords Av CH2 40 D5
Dee Hills Pk CH3 4 D3
Dee Ho*, Lakeside Bsns Village CH5 19 G5
Dee La, Chester CH3 4 D3
Dee La, Llangollen LL20 67 B4
Dee La, Wrexham LL13 71 B6
Dee Mdws LL13 71 B6
Dee Pk LL13 71 B6
Dee Rd, Chester CH2 31 A2
Dee Rd, Connahs Quay CH5 13 E7
Dee Rd, Garden City CH5 15 F7
Dee View Cres CH5 20 C1
Dee View Rd, Connahs Quay CH5 13 D5
Dee View Rd, Holywell CH8 6 C3
Dee Vw CH3 71 B4
Deeside LL13 71 B5
Deeside Ct CH3 40 C4
Deeside Enterprise Centre CH5 15 B7
Deeside Ind Est CH5 16 A2
Deeside Ind Pk CH5 14 C3
Deganwy Cl CH7 24 D1
Degas Cl CH5 13 B6
Deiniol Av LL13 71 C2
Deiniols Rd CH5 20 D3
Delamere Av, Buckley CH7 24 D4
Delamere Av, Wrexham LL11 55 H1
Delamere St CH1 4 B2
Delfryn LL14 64 C4
Delph La LL14 64 D1
Delph Rd LL14 65 A5
Delta Ct CH4 42 C1
Delves Way CH3 45 E1
Delvine Dr CH2 36 B6
Delyn LL14 64 F2
Delyn Rd CH8 6 C3
Demage La, Backford CH1 32 A6
Demage La, Upton CH2 36 B4
Demage La South CH2 36 B4
Denbigh Cl, Buckley CH7 24 D1
Denbigh Cl, Wrexham LL12 57 F6
Denbigh Rd CH7 22 A1
Denbigh St CH1 39 H3
Denford Cl CH4 27 G4
Denhall Cl CH2 36 B6
Denning Rd LL12 57 F5
Dennis Ct LL14 65 F7
Dennis Dr CH4 43 H2
Denson Dr CH5 19 H4
Denstone Dr CH4 43 G3
Dentith Dr CH1 35 E6
Derby Pl CH2 40 C2
Derby Rd, Caergwrle LL12 48 B2
Derby Rd, Wrexham LL13 60 D3
Derwen LL14 68 E3
Derwen Cl CH5 13 D6
Derwen Deg CH7 30 B2
Derwent Cl LL12 56 D6
Derwent Cres LL12 56 D6
Derwent Rd CH2 36 D6
Deva Av, Chester CH4 43 E1
Deva Av, Connahs Quay CH5 13 C6
Deva Av, Holywell CH8 7 B5
Deva Bsns Pk CH5 16 B4
Deva Cl CH6 10 E3
Deva Ct CH2 40 C3
Deva Heights CH3 40 D6
Deva La CH2 36 A5
Deva Link CH1 39 G3
Deva Ter CH3 4 D4
Deva Way LL13 61 F2
Devon Cl, Connahs Quay CH5 13 C8
Devon Cl, Wrexham LL11 56 D4
Devon Rd CH2 36 D6
Devonshire Pl CH4 4 C6
Devonshire Rd CH4 27 G4
Dewi Av CH8 7 A6
Dicksons Dr CH2 40 B1
Dig La CH5 20 D6
Dinas LL14 65 C8
Dinas Cl CH1 38 D3
Dinas Dr LL20 67 D5
Dinbren Rd LL20 67 B1
Dinghouse Wood CH7 25 F1
Dingle Bank CH4 40 A6
Dingle La CW6 46 D4
Dingle Pl LL12 50 B4
Dingle Rd CH7 30 B1
Dirty Mile CH7 25 F4
Disraeli CH5 19 H6
Dock Rd CH5 13 E5
Dodds Dr CH5 13 E6
Dodds La LL11 56 A3
Dodleston La CH4 52 E1
Dog La CW6 46 A5
Dol Acton LL11 56 B5
Dol Awel CH5 19 G5
Dolphin Ct CH4 43 G1
Dolydd La LL14 66 C2
Dolydd Rd, Cefn-mawr LL14 66 D2
Dolydd Rd, Wrexham LL13 5 A3
Donne Pl CH1 35 F6
Donnington Way CH4 43 F1
Doran LL14 64 F2
Dorchester Rd CH4 43 F3
Dorfold Way CH2 36 C5
Dorin Ct CH2 36 B5
Dormer Cl CH3 47 B4
Dorset Dr LL11 56 D4
Dorset Pl CH2 41 E1
Dorset Rd CH2 36 C5
Douglas Pl CH4 43 E2
Dover Rd CH4 43 G2
Dovey Cl, Connahs Quay CH5 13 C7
Dovey Cl, Flint CH6 10 B4
Downham Pl CH1 39 E2
Downsfield Rd CH4 43 G2
Downswood Ct CH1 40 A1
Downswood Dr CH1 40 A1
Dreflan CH7 22 B3
Drive A CH5 16 A1
Drive B CH5 16 B1
Drive C CH5 16 B2
Drive D CH5 16 B2
Drome Rd CH5 16 B2
Drury La, Buckley CH7 24 D2
Drury La, Leeswood CH7 30 B2
Drury La Ind Est CH7 25 E2
Drury New Rd CH7 25 F2
Drws y Coed LL13 60 C6
Dryden Cl CH5 19 G5
Dryersfield CH3 41 E5
Duchess Pl CH2 4 B1
Duckers La CH5 21 E4
Duckworth Row CH5 21 F3
Duffryn Cl CH7 24 D4
Duke Rd LL14 64 D2
Duke St, Chester CH1 4 B5
Duke St, Chirk LL14 69 D5
Duke St, Flint CH6 10 C2
Duke St, Rhosllanerchrugog LL14 64 D2
Duke St, Ruabon LL14 65 F7
Duke St, Soughton CH7 17 B5
Duke St, Wrexham LL11 5 B3
Dukes Ct CH1 4 C5
Dukesfield Cl CH7 24 D3
Dukesfield Dr CH7 24 C3
Dukesway CH2 36 C4
Dulas Ct CH2 36 C4
Dulverton Av CH3 41 G3
Dunbar Cl CH5 13 C5
Dundas St CH5 15 D8
Dunham Way CH2 36 C5
Dunlin Av CH5 13 D6
Dunster Rd LL13 63 E4
Durban Av CH3 41 G6
Durham Rd CH1 39 E1
Dutton Rd LL13 63 E3
Duttons La, Chester CH2 36 D3
Duttons La, Tarporley CW6 46 C5
Dwyfor Av CH7 23 G3
Dyfed Dr CH5 20 C1
Dyke St LL11 54 C1
Dylan Cl CH5 19 G6
Dyserth Rd CH1 39 E2

Eagle Mdw LL13 5 D4
Eagles Pl LL11 55 F2
Eardswick Cl CH2 4 C1
Earl Rd CH7 22 C4
Earl St CH6 10 C2
Earle St LL13 5 C5
Earles Cres CH5 21 E2
Earles La CW6 46 C5
Earls Lea*, Earl St CH6 10 C2
Earls Oak CH2 36 B4
Earlston Ct CH3 4 D4
Earlsway CH4 39 G6
East Av, Ruabon LL14 65 F6
East Av, Wrexham LL11 56 C6
East Cl CH7 23 F4
East Grn CH5 16 B6
East St LL20 67 B4
East Vw, Mold CH7 23 F1
East Vw, Wrexham LL11 56 C3
Eastern Pathway CH4 4 C6
Eastfield Ct LL13 61 G5
Eastfields Gro CH1 34 B3
Eastgate Row CH1 4 B4
Eastgate St CH1 4 B4
Eastleigh Cl LL11 56 C5
Eastwood Ct CH4 27 F1
Eaton Av, Chester CH4 44 B1
Eaton Av, Connahs Quay CH5 13 E8
Eaton Cl LL12 52 E4
Eaton Cl CH4 27 G3
Eaton Dr LL13 61 F2
Eaton Gro CH4 43 E2
Eaton Mews CH4 44 B1
Eaton Rd CH4 40 B6
Ebury Pl CH4 40 B6
Eccleston Av CH4 44 B1
Eccleston Rd CH4 29 G4
Echo Cl CH4 43 E2
Edale Dr CW6 46 C5
Edgar Cotts CH4 4 C6
Edgar Pl CH4 4 C6
Edge Gro CH2 40 D3
Edinburgh Rd LL11 56 C5
Edinburgh Way CH4 4 D5
Edingburgh Av LL12 48 A2
Edmund St CH7 22 C,D6
Edna St CH2 40 C3
Edward St LL13 5 A5
Edwards Av LL11 54 C2
Edwards Ct CH1 4 B4
Edwards Rd CH4 43 G2
Edwin Dr CH6 10 C3
Egerton Ct CW6 46 B5
Egerton Dr CH2 36 B6
Egerton Rd CH1 35 E6
Egerton St, Chester CH1 4 C2
Egerton St, Wrexham LL11 5 C3
Egerton Walk LL11 56 D5
Eggbridge La CH3 47 B5
Eglwys Cl CH7 24 A3
Eglwysfan LL14 66 E1
Eighth Av LL12 50 B3
Eirlys Gdns CH7 23 G4
Elder Cl LL12 51 F6
Elder Dr CH4 43 E3
Eldon Gro LL14 59 H5
Eleventh Av LL12 50 B4
Elfed Dr CH7 24 B2
Elgin Cl CH3 41 E3
Elidie Cl CH5 13 C6
Eliot Cl CH5 19 G6
Elizabeth Cl CW6 46 D6
Elizabeth Cres CH4 40 C5
Elizabeth Ct*, Pen y Llan CH5 13 D5
Ellesmere Av, Broughton CH4 27 G3
Ellesmere Av, Chester CH2 40 B1
Ellesmere Rd CH7 23 G4
Ellice Way LL11 60 A2
Elliot Ho CH1 35 G6
Ellis St LL14 64 E1
Elm Av, Connahs Quay CH5 13 D7
Elm Av, Flint CH6 10 A2
Elm Cft CH5 20 D4
Elm Ct LL12 52 C4
Elm Dr, Buckley CH7 18 B1
Elm Dr, Mold CH7 22 B3
Elm Gro, Buckley CH7 24 B4
Elm Gro, Chester CH4 43 E2
Elm Gro, Ellesmere Port CH66 32 B1
Elm Gro, Wrexham LL12 57 E6
Elm Grove Way LL12 57 E6
Elm Rd, Deeside CH5 20 A2
Elm Rd, Wrexham LL13 63 E2
Elm Sq CH4 43 F2
Elm Walk, Mold CH7 23 H3
Elm Walk, Wrexham LL12 50 B3
Elm Way CH5 19 G4
Elmanoak Gro LL12 50 B3
Elmuir CH1 39 E3
Elmwood Av CH2 40 C2
Elmwood Cl CH5 20 A1
Elstree Av CH3 41 F3
Elwy Cl CH7 23 G3
Elwy Cres CH6 10 A4
Elwy Ho*, Lakeside Bsns Village CH5 19 G5
Elwyn Dr LL13 71 B2
Embassy Cl CH1 38 C1
Emlyn Ter LL14 64 D1
Emlyn Williams Ct*, Fishermans Rd CH5 13 E6
Emmanuel Gro LL14 66 D2
Empress Rd LL13 5 A5
Enderby Rd CH1 4 A2
Endsleigh Cl CH2 36 C4
Endsleigh Gdns CH2 36 C3
Eneurys Rd LL11 56 D6
Englefield Av, Chester CH4 42 D1
Englefield Av, Connahs Quay CH5 13 C6
Englefield Cres CH7 23 G3
Englefield Dr CH6 10 E3
Englefield Rd CH8 6 C2
Ennerdale Rd CH2 36 D6
Enth Av LL12 50 B4
Epsom Cl CH1 39 H3
Epsom Way LL13 61 F5
Epworth Cl LL11 55 F2
Erddig Cl LL14 59 H6
Erddig Rd LL13 5 B6
Erith St CH7 30 B2
Erlas Gro LL13 61 G2
Erlas La LL13 62 B1
Erlas Park Rd LL13 57 G6
Ermine Rd CH2 4 D1
Ernest Parry Rd LL13 61 G2
Ersto Cres CH5 19 H5
Erw Deg, Llangollen LL20 67 C6
Erw Deg, Wrexham LL14 65 A7
Erw Fach CH7 23 F2
Erw Ffynnon CH7 30 B5
Erw Gaer LL11 55 F2
Erw Gerrig LL14 64 C2
Erw Goed CH7 23 F2
Erw Las LL14 64 D3
Erw Lwyd LL14 64 C3
Erw Wladys LL20 70 C1
Erw'r Llan CH7 30 C5
Esless La LL14 60 A5
Essex Cl LL11 56 D4
Essex Rd CH2 40 D1
Estuary Vw CH5 20 A3
Estyn Cl LL12 48 C1
Ethelda Dr CH2 37 E6
Etna Rd CH7 24 D2
Ettrick Pk CH3 41 E3
Eurgain Av CH5 13 B8
Evans St CH6 10 C1
Evansleigh Dr CH5 21 F3
Eversley Ct CH2 40 A1
Eversley Pk CH2 40 A1
Ewart St, Chester CH4 38 B6
Ewart St, Wrexham LL14 68 D4
Ewloe Barns Ind Est CH7 18 D5
Ewloe Pl CH7 24 C1
Exeter Pl CH1 39 F1
Expressway Bsns Pk CH5 15 D8
Exton Pk CH1 4 A1
Eyton Grange LL12 51 F

Factory Pool La CH7 22 A
Factory Rd CH5 21 E1
Fagl La LL12 48 A1
Fair Haven CH8 7 D
Faircroft Ct LL13 61 G
Fairfield LL11 54 D
Fairfield Av CH5 13 D
Fairfield Rd, Buckley CH7 25 F
Fairfield Rd, Chester CH2 40 D
Fairfield Rd, Deeside CH5 15 C
Fairfield St LL13 5 C
Fairford Rd CH4 43 F
Fairholme Cl CH1 34 B
Fairmeadow CH4 52 F
Fairmount Rd LL13 57 G
Fairoaks Cres LL12 50 B
Fairoaks Dr CH5 13 B
Fairview, Chester CH4 28 B
Fairview, Holt LL13 71 B
Fairview, Rhostyllen LL14 59 H
Fairway CH5 21 F
Fairway Cl CH5 13 C
Fairway Gdns LL11 55 H
Fairy Rd LL13 5 B
Falcon Rd LL13 61 G
Fammau View Dr CH4 28 B
Farbailey Cl CH4 43 G
Farm Cl CH7 24 B
Farm Dr CH5 13 B
Farm Rd, Buckley CH7 24 B
Farm Rd, Deeside CH5 15 E
Farm Side LL12 57 F
Farmfield Cl CH5 20 A
Farndon Cl CH4 27 G
Farndon St LL12 5 D
Farne Cl CH65 32 D

Farriers Walk LL12 51 F5
Faulkner St CH2 40 C2
Faulkners Cl CH4 29 G4
Faulkners La CH3 41 H6
Feather St CH6 10 C2
Feathers Lea*, Feathers St CH6 10 C2
Fedwen Arian CH4 28 C1
Feilden Ct CH1 35 F2
Felin Puleston LL13 60 A5
Fellows La LL12 48 B3
Fennant Rd LL14 64 E1
Fenwick Dr LL13 61 F2
Fern Cl CH6 10 A3
Fern Ct*, Pen y Llan CH5 13 D5
Fern Gro CH5 20 A3
Ferndale LL13 61 F2
Ferndale Av LL14 59 G6
Ferndale Cl CH4 28 C2
Ferndale Rise LL11 56 A4
Fernham Dr LL13 57 E4
Fernhill Rd CH1 35 E6
Fernlea Ct CH1 34 A3
Fernside Rd CH5 20 A1
Ferry Cl CH5 16 B5
Ferry La CH1 38 C5
Fferm Llidiart Werdd LL11 54 A6
Ffordd Aber CH8 9 C4
Ffordd Aelwyd CH8 8 B2
Ffordd Aeron LL11 54 B6
Ffordd Alafon LL12 57 F4
Ffordd Aled LL12 57 E4
Ffordd Almer LL12 56 D3
Ffordd Alun LL12 57 E4
Ffordd Argoed CH7 22 D3
Ffordd Beuno CH8 8 C2
Ffordd Brenig CH7 23 G3
Ffordd Brigog CH7 23 H4
Ffordd Bryn Estyn CH7 22 A4
Ffordd Bryn Madoc LL11 53 C3
Ffordd Cae Llwyn CH5 19 E1
Ffordd Caerfyrddin LL11 56 B5
Ffordd Carreg y Llech CH7 30 A4
Ffordd Celyn, Leeswood CH7 30 B3
Ffordd Celyn, Soughton CH7 17 B4
Ffordd Corwen CH7 30 A6
Ffordd Cwm LL13 60 C5
Ffordd Cynan LL12 57 F4
Ffordd Dawel CH7 17 A5
Ffordd Ddreiniog CH8 8 A2
Ffordd Ddyfrdwy CH8 9 B5
Ffordd Derwyn CH4 28 A4
Ffordd Dewi LL14 64 E3
Ffordd Dolgoed CH7 22 B5
Ffordd Dwyfor CH8 6 B3
Ffordd Dyfed, Rhosllanerchrugog LL14 64 D2
Ffordd Dyfed, Wrexham LL12 61 F1
Ffordd Dylan LL12 61 E1
Ffordd Edgeworth LL12 61 E1
Ffordd Edwin CH7 17 B2
Ffordd Eisteddfod LL11 53 B3
Ffordd Elan LL12 57 E5
Ffordd Eldon CH7 17 B4
Ffordd Elfed LL12 61 E1
Ffordd Elwy LL12 57 E5
Ffordd Estyn LL11 56 C4
Ffordd Fer, Holywell CH8 7 B5
Ffordd Fer, Mold CH7 23 F3
Ffordd Ffynnon CH5 19 H6
Ffordd Frondeg LL13 60 D6
Ffordd Fynnon CH8 8 B2
Ffordd Ganol CH7 17 B5
Ffordd Garmonydd LL12 56 D3
Ffordd Gerwyn LL13 60 D6
Ffordd Glyn, Mold CH7 22 A5
Ffordd Glyn, Wrexham LL13 60 C5
Ffordd Glyndwr, Flint CH6 10 D3
Ffordd Glyndwr, Northop CH7 17 B2
Ffordd Gryffydd LL12 50 A4
Ffordd Gwenllian LL12 50 C3
Ffordd Gwilym LL12 57 E6
Ffordd Gwynedd, Northop CH7 17 B2
Ffordd Gwynedd, Rhosllanerchrugog LL14 64 D3
Ffordd Gwynedd, Wrexham LL11 56 C5
Ffordd Haearn CH4 28 B3
Ffordd Hendre LL13 60 D6
Ffordd Hengoed CH7 22 B6
Ffordd Hiraethog CH8 9 C5
Ffordd Hooson LL12 61 E1
Ffordd Ifor LL14 64 C4
Ffordd Iorwerth LL12 50 C3
Ffordd Isaf LL11 53 C3
Ffordd Jarvis LL12 57 E6
Ffordd Kayton LL14 66 E3
Ffordd Kinderley CH5 13 D8
Ffordd Las, Chester CH4 28 B2
Ffordd Las, Soughton CH7 17 B5
Ffordd Lerry LL12 57 E3
Ffordd Llanarth CH5 13 B5
Ffordd Llanerch LL14 64 C4
Ffordd Llanfynydd CH7 30 D5
Ffordd Llewelyn CH6 10 D3
Ffordd Llywelyn LL12 57 E3
Ffordd Mabon LL12 50 A4
Ffordd Maddoc LL12 50 A4
Ffordd Madoc LL12 57 E4
Ffordd Maelor LL12 61 E1
Ffordd Mailyn LL13 60 D5
Ffordd Meillion CH5 19 E1
Ffordd Meirionydd LL11 56 C5
Ffordd Mon LL11 56 C5
Ffordd Morgan, Llay LL12 50 A4
Ffordd Morgan, Wrexham LL12 56 D3
Ffordd Morgannwg LL11 56 C5
Ffordd Mynydd Isa LL14 64 C3
Ffordd Nercwys CH7 30 A4
Ffordd Neuadd CH8 8 B2
Ffordd Newydd, Deeside CH5 19 E1
Ffordd Newydd, Mold CH7 22 A5
Ffordd Newydd, Wrexham LL11 53 C2
Ffordd Offa, Cefn-mawr LL14 66 E3
Ffordd Offa, Mold CH7 23 G4
Ffordd Offa, Rhosllanerchrugog LL14 64 E3
Ffordd Ogwen CH7 23 G3
Ffordd Owain, Brymbo LL11 54 D2
Ffordd Owain, Wrexham LL12 57 E3
Ffordd Owen CH7 17 B2
Ffordd Pandarus CH8 9 C4
Ffordd Pant Gwyn CH5 13 B8
Ffordd Parc y Fron CH8 7 B6
Ffordd Pedrog LL12 57 F4
Ffordd Pelydryn CH5 19 H6
Ffordd Pennant, Holywell CH8 9 B5
Ffordd Pennant, Mold CH7 22 B2
Ffordd Pentre, Deeside CH5 20 D1
Ffordd Pentre, Holywell CH8 8 B2
Ffordd Pentre, Mold CH7 22 D4
Ffordd Pentre, Wrexham LL14 64 F2
Ffordd Powell LL11 59 G1
Ffordd Powys LL14 64 D3
Ffordd Siarl CH7 30 B2
Ffordd Tegid, Deeside CH5 19 G5
Ffordd Tegid, Wrexham LL12 57 F4
Ffordd Tegla LL12 57 E4
Ffordd Tirion CH7 17 B5
Ffordd Top y Rhos CH7 30 B4
Ffordd Trefaldwyn LL11 56 C5
Ffordd Trefin LL12 57 F4
Ffordd Trem y Foel CH7 22 B5
Ffordd Tudno LL12 57 E4
Ffordd Ty Mawr LL14 66 E3
Ffordd Tyn y Cestyll Rd LL20 70 B3
Ffordd Uchaf LL11 53 C3
Ffordd Welfor CH8 8 B2
Ffordd y Bont, Leeswood CH7 30 B3
Ffordd y Bont, Treuddyn CH7 30 C5
Ffordd y Ffynnon CH8 9 B4
Ffordd y Fran CH6 10 D4
Ffordd y Gaer LL11 56 B1
Ffordd y Gilrhos CH7 30 A5
Ffordd y Glyn CH8 6 B3
Ffordd y Llan CH7 30 B4
Ffordd y Rhos CH7 30 A6
Ffordd yr Odyn CH7 30 A6
Ffordd yr Ysgol, Flint CH6 10 A2
Ffordd Yr Ysgol, Wrexham LL11 53 C3
Ffordd Ysgubor CH8 9 B5
Ffordd Ystrad LL13 60 C5
Ffrwd Rd LL12 49 B6
Fiddlers La CH1 34 B2
Field Cl, Chester CH3 46 B2
Field Cl, Flint CH6 10 B3
Field Farm Rd CH7 24 B2
Field La CH3 46 B2
Field Pl CH5 19 F1
Field Vw, Deeside CH5 21 E2
Field Vw, Wrexham LL13 61 E2
Fielding Cl CH5 19 G5
Fieldside CH5 20 C4
Fieldway CH1 34 B2
Fifth Av, Flint CH6 10 C4
Fifth Av, Wrexham LL12 50 B3
Filkins La CH3 41 E4
Finchett Dr CH1 39 H3
Finney Cl LL11 56 B5
Fir Gro CH7 22 B3
Fir Tree Av CH4 43 H3
Fir Tree La CH3 41 H4
Fir Tree Rd LL11 56 B1
Firbeck Cl CH4 27 F5
Firbrook Av, Connahs Quay CH5 13 E7
Firbrook Av, Hawarden CH5 20 C3
Firemans Sq CH1 4 B3
Firgrove Cnr LL12 57 F5
First Av, Deeside CH5 16 A1
First Av, Flint CH6 10 C3
First Av, Llay LL12 50 A3
First Av, Summerhill LL11 55 G2
First Av, Wrexham Ind Est LL13 63 E3
Firtree Gro CH66 32 B1
Fisher Rd CH1 39 E2
Fishermans Rd CH5 13 E6
Fishermans Wharf*, Fishermans Rd CH5 13 E6
Five Ashes Rd CH4 43 G3
Five Crosses Ind Est LL11 54 A5
Flag La North CH2 36 C3
Flag La South CH2 36 C4
Flat La CW6 46 B5
Flaxmere Dr CH3 41 E6
Fleming Dr LL11 56 B6
Flintshire Retail Pk CH6 10 B1
Flookers Brook CH2 4 D1
Florita Cl CH5 13 C5
Foel Gron CH6 8 B5
Fontwell Cl LL13 61 G5
Foregate St CH1 4 C4
Forest Dr CH4 27 F4
Forest Pines LL13 57 H6
Forest Rd LL12 50 B3
Forest St CH1 4 C4
Forest Walk CH7 25 E4
Forge Cl LL11 55 F6
Forge Rd LL11 55 F5
Forge Way CH4 43 F4
Foster Rd LL11 5 C1
Foundry Rd LL13 5 C4
Fourth Av, Deeside CH5 14 D4
Fourth Av, Flint CH6 10 C3
Fourth Av, Gwersyllt LL11 55 H3
Fourth Av, Llay LL12 50 A3
Fourth Rd LL13 63 E2
Fowler Rd CH1 38 D2
Fox Cover CH3 31 B6
Fox Covert La CH2 37 E1
Fox Hill CW6 46 C6
Fox La CH3 47 C4
Fox Lea CH1 34 A3
Foxcote Cl CH1 39 E1
Foxes Cl CH5 21 E2
Foxes La CH5 15 E7
Foxes Walk, Chester CH3 41 E6
Foxes Walk, Higher Kinnerton CH4 29 G4
Foxglove Cl CH3 45 E1
Foxwist Cl CH2 4 B1
Foxwood Dr LL14 60 A4
Frances Av LL12 56 D4
Francis Ct CH1 4 D3
Francis La, Holt LL13 71 A6
Francis La, Wrexham LL13 62 D1
Francis Rd LL11 55 F2
Francis St CH1 4 C2
Fraser Ct CH4 40 B6
Frazer Dr CH7 24 B4
Fredrick St LL14 64 E2
Friars Cl LL12 57 E4
Friars Ct, Deeside CH5 20 B5
Friars Ct, Wrexham LL13 70 C4
Friars Mws LL13 70 C4
Frodsham Ct CH1 4 B3
Frodsham Row*, Frodsham St CH1 4 C3
Frodsham Shopping Mall CH1 4 C3
Frodsham Sq*, Frodsham St CH1 4 C3
Frodsham St CH1 4 C3
Frog La, Holt LL13 71 A5
Frog La, Wrexham LL13 61 G5
Fron Bache LL20 67 B5
Fron Castell LL20 67 B5
Fron Deg CH6 8 A4
Fron Heolog CH5 19 G5
Fron Las, Holywell CH8 7 D5
Fron Las, Wrexham LL11 58 B1
Fron Park Rd CH8 7 A5
Fron Rd CH5 13 F7
Fronheulog Hill LL11 53 C2
Fulbrooke CH8 6 C3
Furnace Cl LL11 54 D1
Furnace Rd LL12 49 B7
Furne Rd CH1 39 E1
Gabriel Cl LL13 57 G6
Gadlys La CH6 8 A5
Gainford Av CH5 13 C7
Gainsborough Rd LL12 57 F5
Gala Cl CH4 27 G5
Galaxy Gro LL11 55 G5
Gamford La LL12 52 F3
Gamul Pl CH1 4 B5
Gamul Ter CH1 4 B5
Gardd Eithin CH7 18 C1
Gardd Estyn LL11 56 D5
Gardd Francis LL14 64 A4
Gardd yr Gwanwyn CH7 18 D1
Gardden Ind Est LL14 65 E5
Gardden Rd LL14 64 E2
Gardden Vw LL14 65 F5
Garden City Ind Est CH5 15 E6
Garden Ct, Chester CH1 4 A3
Garden Ct, Rhosllanerchrugog LL14 64 D2
Garden Ct, Wrexham LL11 56 D5
Garden La CH1 4 A2
Garden Pl CH7 24 C5
Garden Rd LL11 5 B1
Garden Row CH8 9 C5
Garden Ter CH1 4 A2
Garden Way CH5 13 F7
Gardenside CH7 24 D3
Gardners Row CH6 10 E4
Garner Rd LL13 61 E2
Garratt Cl CH5 13 E6
Garth Dr CH2 40 A1
Garth Ganol CH6 10 D4
Garthorpe Av CH5 13 D6
Garthorpe Cl CH5 13 D6
Gas La CH7 22 C5
Gate Rd LL20 66 B2
Gatefield LL13 60 D4
Gatesheath Dr CH2 36 B5
Gateway LL12 56 D6
Gatewen Rd LL11 55 G5
Gawer Pk CH1 40 A1
Gaymoore Cl CH1 4 A1
Gayton Cl, Chester CH2 36 C6
Gayton Cl, Connahs Quay CH5 13 D7
Gedington Cl LL13 57 H5
Gegin Rd LL11 53 F3
Gele Av LL11 56 A2
Gelfft Rd CH5 13 B8
George Av LL20 66 B1
George Kenyon Mews CH4 43 E2
George St, Chester CH1 4 B3
George St, Chirk LL14 68 D4
George St, Llangollen LL20 67 B4
George St, Wrexham LL11 5 B1
Ger y Ddol LL20 67 A4
Ger y Llan CH7 11 D5
Ger Y Nant LL20 67 A5
Gerald St LL11 5 B1
Gerddi LL14 64 C1
Gerrards Av CH3 41 E5
Gibson St LL13 5 A4
Gilwern Cl CH1 40 A1
Gladstone Av CH1 39 H4
Gladstone Rd, Broughton CH4 27 F4
Gladstone Rd, Chester CH1 39 H3
Gladstone St, Mold CH7 22 C4
Gladstone St, Queensferry CH5 15 C8
Gladstone St, Shotton CH5 15 A8
Gladstone Ter CH5 21 E2
Gladstone Way CH5 20 C4
Gladwyn Rd LL12 56 D4
Glamis Cl CH3 41 E3
Glan Aber LL12 61 E1
Glan Aber Cl LL11 56 A3
Glan Aber Ct CH4 43 G1
Glan Aber Dr CH4 43 F1
Glan Aber Pk CH4 43 G1
Glan Alun CH7 22 C5
Glan Garth LL12 61 E2
Glan Gors, Flint CH6 10 D4
Glan Gors, Wrexham LL13 61 G3
Glan Llyn Rd LL11 56 A2
Glan y Don CH8 6 E4
Glan y Fferi CH5 15 E8
Glan y Morfa Ct CH5 13 E6
Glanrafon LL14 64 C2
Glanrafon Rd CH7 22 C5
Glas Coed Way LL11 55 H4
Glasdir CH7 30 B5
Glasfryn LL14 64 F2
Glasllwyn CH5 20 B1
Glaslyn LL14 65 C8
Glastonbury Av CH2 36 D4
Glebe Mdws CH2 31 B2
Glen Avon LL12 61 E1
Glendale Av CH5 21 F3
Gleneagles LL13 61 G1
Gleneagles Cl CH3 41 F3

Glenesk Ct CH5 15 E7
Glenside Cl CH1 34 D6
Globe Way CH7 19 E6
Gloomscroft CH5 20 B5
Gloucester Av CH5 15 A8
Gloucester Cl CH66 32 A1
Gloucester Dr LL11 60 A1
Gloucester St CH1 4 B2
Glovers Loom CH3 41 E6
Gloverstone Ct CH1 4 B5
Glyn Abbott Av CH8 7 D5
Glyn Av LL12 57 E5
Glyndwr Ct CH7 22 C6
Glyndwr Rd, Mold CH7 11 C6
Glyndwr Rd, Wrexham LL12 56 D5
Glynne St, Connahs Quay CH5 13 E6
Glynne St, Queensferry CH5 20 D1
Glynne Way CH5 20 C6
Glynnedale Pk CH5 19 H5
Glyon La LL12 49 A8
Glyteg CH7 22 B5
Godre'r Coed CH7 11 D5
Godre'r Mynydd CH7 11 D5
Godstall La CH1 4 B4
Golftyn Dr CH5 13 B5
Golftyn La CH5 13 A7
Gonsley Cl CH2 4 B1
Goodwood Cl CH1 39 H3
Goodwood Gro, Buckley CH7 18 C2
Goodwood Gro, Leeswood CH7 30 A1
Goodwood Gro, Wrexham LL13 61 F5
Gordon La CH2 32 C4
Gornal Av CH5 13 D6
Gorse Cl CH4 28 C2
Gorse Cres LL12 51 F5
Gorse Stacks CH1 4 C3
Gorse Way CH3 45 E2
Gosforth Pl CH2 40 D2
Gosmore Rd CH7 23 F1
Goss St CH1 4 B4
Goulbourne Av LL13 57 G6
Gourton Sq LL13 57 G5
Gowy Cres CH3 46 C2
Gowy Rd CH2 31 A2
Goya Cl CH5 13 C6
Grafton Mews CH2 4 B1
Graham Rd CH1 39 F2
Graigwen Rd LL11 55 F3
Granby Ct CH5 13 D7
Grange Av LL11 56 C6
Grange Cl LL12 57 E5
Grange La CH8 8 C3
Grange Rd, Chester CH2 40 A1
Grange Rd, Deeside CH5 20 B1
Grange Rd, Llangollen LL20 67 B5
Grange Rd, Vicars Cross CH3 41 F4
Grange Rd West CH3 41 F4
Grangeside CH2 36 B4
Grango La LL14 64 D1
Granston Ct CH5 19 E1
Grant Dr CH5 20 A4
Granville Rd CH1 39 H3
Grasmere Cl CH5 13 B6
Grasmere Cres CH7 24 D2
Grasmere Rd CH2 40 D1
Grays Rd CH7 23 G4
Greek Rd LL14 64 D1
Green Bank CH4 44 B2
Green Cl LL14 66 E1
Green Ct LL11 55 E1
Green La, Chester CH4 29 H5
Green La, Ewloe CH5 19 E4
Green La, Lache CH4 43 E3
Green La, Llangollen LL20 67 B4
Green La, Saughall CH1 34 C5
Green La, Shotton CH5 15 A8
Green La, Tarporley CW6 46 C6
Green La, Vicars Cross CH3 41 F4
Green La, Wrexham LL14 68 F3
Green La East CH5 16 C2
Green La Estate CH5 16 C3
Green La West CH5 16 B1
Green Lawns Dr CH66 32 A1
Green Mdws, Deeside CH5 20 A5
Green Mdws, Wrexham LL11 59 G1
Green Pk, Chester CH4 28 B2
Green Pk, Connahs Quay CH5 13 E7
Green Pk, Wrexham LL13 60 B5
Green Rd LL11 55 E1
Green St LL13 71 B5
Greenacre Dr CH6 8 C5
Greenacre Rd CH4 43 F4
Greenacres Ct CH2 36 D3
Greenbank Dr CH6 10 A3
Greenbank Rd, Chester CH2 41 E1
Greenbank Rd, Deeside CH5 20 A1
Greenbank St LL13 5 D5
Greenfield LL11 60 C1
Greenfield Av CH4 29 H4
Greenfield Bsns Centre CH8 6 D2
Greenfield Bsns Pk CH8 6 E3
Greenfield Cres CH3 47 C4
Greenfield La CH2 37 E6
Greenfield Rd, Broughton CH4 27 F4
Greenfield Rd, Holywell CH8 6 B4
Greenfield Rd, Waverton CH3 47 C4
Greenfield Rd, Wrexham LL11 54 B6
Greenfield St CH8 7 B5
Greenfields CH2 36 C2
Greenfields La CH3 47 A4
Greenhill Av CH5 20 A5
Greenside CH7 22 B4
Greensway CH4 39 G6
Greenway, Farndon CH3 71 C4
Greenway, Saughall CH1 34 B2
Greenway St CH4 4 B6
Greenway Vw LL12 51 E5
Greenways LL13 61 G5
Greenways Ct CH4 27 F5
Greenwood Av CH4 44 B1
Grenadin Cl LL11 55 G5
Grenville Av CH5 19 G4
Gresford Av CH2 4 D1
Gresford Ind Pk LL12 56 D2
Gresford Pk LL12 51 E5
Gresford Rd, Hope LL12 48 C1
Gresford Rd, Llay LL12 50 B2
Gresford Way LL12 56 D4
Grey Cl CH5 19 G6
Grey Friars CH1 4 A5
Grey Friars Ct CH1 4 A4
Greyhound Park Rd CH1 39 F3
Greyhound Retail Pk CH1 39 F3
Greystones Rd CH3 41 F5
Greythorn Cl LL12 51 E5
Griffin Cl CH1 35 F6
Griffiths Ct CH5 13 F8
Griffiths Rd LL11 55 H4
Grindley Bank CH2 31 A3
Groesfan LL14 64 A4
Groesffordd CH8 6 C2
Grogen LL14 68 E3
Groomsdale La CH5 20 A5
Grosvenor Cres LL12 52 D4
Grosvenor Ct CH1 4 D3
Grosvenor Dr CH7 24 C3
Grosvenor Park Rd CH1 4 D3
Grosvenor Park Ter CH1 4 D4
Grosvenor Pl CH1 4 B5
Grosvenor Precinct CH1 40 B5
Grosvenor Rd, Chester CH4 4 A6
Grosvenor Rd, Deeside CH5 20 B1
Grosvenor Rd, Tarvin CH3 46 A2
Grosvenor Rd, Wrexham LL11 5 B2
Grosvenor St, Chester CH1 4 B5
Grosvenor St, Mold CH7 22 C4
Grove Av CH3 41 F3
Grove Gdns CH3 41 H4
Grove Lodge Cl LL11 60 D1
Grove Park Rd LL13 5 C2
Grove Rd, Chester CH1 32 A5
Grove Rd, Wrexham LL11 5 C1
Grub La CW6 46 C5
Grw Las LL12 61 E1
Guilden Grn CH3 31 A6
Guilden Sutton La CH3 41 F2
Guildford Cl CH4 43 F2
Gun St LL12 52 D4
Gutter Hill LL14 64 E2
Guy La CH3 47 C4
Gwalia, Caergwrle LL12 48 B3
Gwalia, Johnstown LL14 64 F2
Gwalia Rd, Brymbo LL11 54 D2
Gwalia Rd, Moss LL11 55 F2
Gwel Afon CH8 8 D3
Gwel y Mynydd CH7 24 B2
Gwenffrwd Rd CH8 7 A6
Gwenfro LL13 61 F3
Gwern La LL12 48 E2
Gwernaffield Rd CH7 11 B2
Gwernygaseg Rd LL11 54 A4
Gwydyr Way LL13 60 D5
Gwylanan Av CH5 13 D6
Gwynant LL14 65 C8
Gwynedd Dr CH6 10 C2
Gypsy La CH1 35 F1

Hackett Ct LL13 61 E5
Hadfield Cl CH5 19 F1
Hadley Cl LL14 69 E6
Hadrian Dr CH1 35 E5
Hafan Deg, Holywell CH8 8 D2
Hafan Deg, Mold CH7 22 B6
Hafan Deg, Treuddyn CH7 30 B5
Hafan Glyd CH5 15 B8
Hafod CH6 10 B3
Hafod Cl, Chester CH1 38 D2
Hafod Cl, Connahs Quay CH5 13 C5
Hafod Pk, Connahs Quay CH5 13 C5
Hafod Pk, Mold CH7 22 A4
Hafod Rd, Mold CH7 11 C4
Hafod Rd, Wrexham LL14 60 A6
Hafod Wen LL14 64 F3
Hafod y Ddol Rd CH8 9 D6
Hafod y Glyn*, Maelor Rd LL14 64 E2
Hafod y Wern CH7 11 D6
Haig Rd LL13 5 D6
Halkett Cl CH4 43 E2
Halkyn Rd, Chester CH2 4 D1
Halkyn Rd, Flint CH6 10 B4
Halkyn Rd, Holywell CH8 7 B6
Halkyn St, Flint CH6 10 B2
Halkyn St, Holywell CH8 7 B6
Halkyn Vw CH5 19 F1
Hall La, Connahs Quay CH5 13 D7
Hall La, Tarporley CW6 46 C4
Hall La, Wrexham LL14 64 A1
Hall St, Llangollen LL20 67 A5
Hall St, Penycae LL14 64 A4
Hall St, Rhosllanerchrugog LL14 64 C1
Hall Vw LL11 59 H1
Hallfield Cl CH6 10 A2
Hallfields Rd CH3 46 B2
Hallows Cl CW6 46 B6
Hallows Dr CW6 46 C6
Hallowsgate Ct CW6 46 C6
Hals Cl CH5 13 B5
Halstonwood Cl LL13 61 F1
Halton La LL14 68 D3
Halton Rd CH2 36 C5
Hamilton Av CH5 21 F3
Hamilton Cl LL13 57 G6
Hamilton Pl CH1 4 B4
Hamilton Rd CH5 13 C5
Hamilton St CH2 40 D2
Hamlington Av LL11 55 H3
Hampden Way LL14 65 B8
Hampdon Rd LL13 5 A5
Hampshire Dr LL11 56 D4
Hampson Av LL13 61 E4
Hampton Av CH5 20 D2
Hampton Rd CH4 43 F1
Hancocks La CH7 24 B4
Hand La LL14 64 D1
Handbridge CH4 4 C6
Handford Rd CH2 36 C6
Hankelow Cl CH2 4 C1
Hanover Way LL13 60 D4
Harding Rd CH2 35 H3
Hare La CH3 41 F2
Harebell Cl CH3 45 E2
Harlech Av CH5 13 C7
Harlech Cl CH7 24 D1
Harrington Cl CH2 36 A3
Harrington Rd CH2 36 A3
Harrison Gro CH5 21 G3
Harrowby Rd CH7 22 C4
Hartford Mews*, Pearl La CH3 41 F4
Hartford Way CH1 39 F4
Harthill Rd CH1 35 E6
Hartington St CH4 40 B6
Hartley Cl CH4 29 G4
Harwd Rd LL11 54 D1
Harwoods La LL12 52 D4
Haslin Cres CH3 41 G6
Hatchmere Dr CH3 41 E6
Hatherton Way CH2 4 B1
Hatton Bldgs CH2 4 D1
Hatton Rd CH1 35 E6
Haulfre LL11 58 C1
Haulfryn CH7 17 B5
Havard Way LL13 61 F3
Hawarden Dr CH7 25 F2
Hawarden Ind Pk CH4 27 F1
Hawarden Rd, Chester CH4 28 B3
Hawarden Rd, Wrexham LL12 48 C1
Hawarden Way CH5 20 D3
Hawker Cl CH4 27 G4
Hawkesbury Rd CH7 24 C2
Hawklane Cl CH5 13 C8
Hawkstone Way LL13 61 G1
Hawthorn Av CH7 22 A3
Hawthorn Cl CH5 20 A2
Hawthorn Rd, Chester CH4 43 F2
Hawthorn Rd, Christleton CH3 41 H6
Hawthorn Rd, Wrexham LL12 51 G6
Hawthorne Av, Buckley CH7 24 D4
Hawthorne Av, Connahs Quay CH5 13 D7
Hawthorne Av, Wrexham LL14 65 A8
Hawthorne Vw CH5 16 A4
Hawthorne Way LL12 50 A4
Haydan Ct CH2 40 B2
Haydock Cl, Chester CH1 39 H3
Haydock Cl, Leeswood CH7 30 A1
Haydock Rd LL13 70 C4
Haydon Way CH5 15 E7
Hayes Pk CH1 4 A1
Hayfield Rd LL12 51 F5
Haygarth Heights CH1 4 D3
Haymakers Cl CH4 43 F4
Haymakers Way CH1 34 B3
Haytor Rd LL11 56 C5
Hazel Av LL11 55 H3
Hazel Cl CH66 32 A1
Hazel Ct CH6 10 A3
Hazel Dr CH4 28 C2
Hazel Gro, Mold CH7 22 B3
Hazel Gro, Wrexham LL12 56 D6
Hazel Rd CH4 43 F2
Hazelwood Cl CH5 13 C8
Hazelwood Cres CH5 25 F1
Health St CH5 15 B7
Heath Bank CH3 41 G1
Heath Cl, Chester CH3 41 E5
Heath Cl, Tarvin CH3 46 B3
Heath Dr CH3 46 B2
Heath La, Chester CH3 41 E5
Heath La, Stoak CH2 33 E,G2
Heath Rd CH2 36 B5
Heath Ter CH2 36 C4
Heathcote Cl CH2 40 A2
Heather Ct CH3 41 E5
Heatherdale Cl LL11 55 H4
Heathfields Cl CH2 40 A2
Heathwood Cl LL11 55 H4
Heber Mt LL13 61 F2
Hedgeway Cl LL14 59 H5
Helens Pl CH5 13 E6
Helfa Bach LL14 68 E3
Hen Blas CH7 22 B5
Henblas Rd LL14 59 G6
Henblas Sq Shopping Centre LL13 5 C3
Henblas St LL13 5 C3
Henblas Ter LL14 59 H6
Hendy Rd CH7 22 A4
Henffordd CH7 22 C3
Henley Av CH5 13 E8
Henley Rd CH4 43 F2
Henodyn CH7 17 B2
Henrietta St CH5 15 A8
Henry Pl CH1 4 C2
Henry St, Rhostyllen LL14 59 H5
Henry St, Ruabon LL14 65 F6
Henry Taylor St CH6 10 D2
Henry Wood Ct CH4 43 E2
Henshall St CH1 4 A2
Heol Abon LL14 66 D3
Heol Bathafarn LL11 58 C1
Heol Bennion LL14 66 D3
Heol Berwyn LL14 66 D3
Heol Briniog LL11 54 C6
Heol Bronwydd*, Heol Maelor LL14 64 F3
Heol Cadfan LL11 58 C
Heol Camlas LL11 55 H
Heol Caradoc, Coedpoeth LL11 54 B6
Heol Caradoc, Rhosllanerchrugog LL14 64 C
Heol Cefn LL11 55 G
Heol Cefnydd LL14 66 C
Heol Celyn LL11 54 C
Heol Craigfab LL14 66 D
Heol Dafydd LL12 57 E
Heol Ddyfrdwy LL14 64 F
Heol Dinas LL12 57 E
Heol Dirion LL11 58 C
Heol Eifion LL14 64 E
Heol Esgob LL20 67 C
Heol Fammau CH7 23 F
Heol Glyndwr LL11 58 C
Heol Gryffudd LL11 54 B
Heol Gwenallt LL11 58 B
Heol Hafod, Coedpoeth LL11 54 C
Heol Hafod, Johnstown LL14 64 F
Heol Horeb LL11 58 B
Heol Hyfryd LL11 55 G
Heol Hyfrydle LL11 58 B
Heol Islwyn LL11 58 C
Heol Kenyon LL14 64 F
Heol Llani LL12 48 B
Heol Llawhaden LL12 57 E
Heol Llewelyn LL11 54 B
Heol Mabon LL14 64 C
Heol Maelor, Coedpoeth LL11 58 C
Heol Maelor, Johnstown LL14 64 F
Heol Mona LL11 54 B
Heol Offa, Coedpoeth LL11 58 D

Heol Offa,
Johnstown LL14 64 F3
Heol Offa,
Tanyfron LL11 54 D5
Heol Orsaf LL14 64 F3
Heol Pedr LL11 55 H2
Heol Penally LL12 57 E3
Heol Penderyst LL20 66 B2
Heol Penyfelin LL11 58 B2
Heol Wen LL11 58 C1
Heol y Brenin CH8 7 B5
Heol y Bryn,
Flint CH6 10 D4
Heol y Bryn,
Wrexham LL14 64 C4
Heol y Castell LL11 58 B1
Heol y Coed LL11 55 G2
Heol y Cyngor LL14 64 F3
Heol y Derwen CH7 30 B2
Heol y Fferm LL11 55 H2
Heol y Ffordd LL11 56 B1
Heol y Ffynnon LL11 56 B1
Heol y Gelli LL11 58 C1
Heol y Goron CH7 30 B2
Heol y Nant LL11 58 B1
Heol y Pac LL11 58 B1
Heol y Parc LL11 56 A1
Heol y Pelin LL14 64 C2
Heol y Plas LL14 66 E3
Heol y Vro LL11 54 C6
Heol y Waen LL11 56 A1
Heol y Wal LL11 56 A1
Heol y Wern CH7 11 D5
Heol yr Efail LL11 58 B1
Heol yr Eglwys LL11 55 H2
Herbert Jennings Av
LL12 56 D5
Hereford Av CH66 32 A1
Hereford Pl CH1 39 G1
Hereward Rd CH3 41 E5
Heritage Cl LL14 59 G5
Heritage Sq CH7 30 B6
Hermitage LL20 67 B5
Hermitage Ct CH1 34 A3
Hermitage Dr LL13 60 D5
Hermitage Rd CH1 34 A3
Heron Cl CH3 71 C4
Heron Pl CH2 4 B1
Herons Cl CH4 27 F4
Herons Way CH4 43 H4
Herriot Gro CH5 19 G5
Heulwen Cl LL12 48 C3
Hewitt St CH2 40 D3
Hewitts La CH7 24 B3
Hickmore Heys CH3 31 A6
High Meadow Ct
CH6 10 A2
High Pk,
Deeside CH5 20 B5
High Pk, Mold CH7 11 B2
High St, Bagillt CH6 8 A4
High St,
Bangor-on-Dee
LL13 70 C5
High St,
Brymbo LL11 54 D1
High St,
Caergwrle LL12 48 B3
High St,
Cefn-mawr LL14 66 D1
High St,
Coedpoeth LL11 54 A6
High St,
Connahs Quay CH5 13 E6
High St,
Farndon CH3 71 B4
High St,
Gresford LL12 50 D5
High St, Holywell CH8 7 B6
High St,
Johnstown LL14 64 E3
High St,
Llangollen LL20 70 B2
High St, Mold CH7 22 C3
High St, Moss LL11 55 F2
High St,
Northop CH7 17 B2
High St,
Rhosllanerchrugog
LL14 64 D2
High St,
Rhostyllen LL14 59 G6
High St,
Rhosymedre LL14 66 E1
High St,
Ruabon LL14 65 F7
High St, Saltney CH4 42 D1
High St,
Southsea LL11 55 E6
High St,
Summerhill LL11 55 H1
High St, Tarvin CH3 46 B1
High St,
Wrexham LL13 5 C4
Highcliffe Av CH1 39 H2
Highcroft CH5 20 A1
Higher Berse Rd
LL11 58 D1
Higher Cl CH5 13 B7
Higher Common Cl
CH7 24 C2
Higher Common Rd
CH7 24 C2
Higher Common Way
CH7 24 C2
Higher La LL12 50 C1
Highfield CH5 20 C5
Highfield Av,
Deeside CH5 20 A3
Highfield Av,
Mold CH7 23 H3
Highfield Dr CH7 24 D5
Highfield Rd,
Bagillt CH6 8 B4
Highfield Rd,
Chester CH1 38 D1
Highfields Rd LL11 55 H4
Highfields Villas CH7 22 C5
Highgrove Cl LL14 59 G6
Highland Av CH5 20 A2
Highmere Dr CH5 13 B6
Highmore Ct LL13 61 G5
Highridge Dr LL14 60 A4
Hightown Rd LL13 60 D3
Highvale CH5 13 B7
Hilary Cl CH3 41 F5
Hilary Gro CH7 24 B4
Hilbre Rd CH5 13 D5
Hill Cl LL14 64 A4
Hill Cres LL12 61 E2
Hill Ct LL13 61 E5
Hill Rd CH4 44 B6
Hill St,
Cefn-mawr LL14 66 D2
Hill St,
Llangollen LL20 67 B5
Hill St,
Newbridge LL14 66 E3
Hill St,
Pentre Broughton
LL11 55 F3
Hill St, Penycae LL14 64 A4
Hill St,
Rhosllanerchrugog
LL14 64 D2
Hill St,
Rhostyllen LL14 59 G6
Hill St,
Summerhill LL11 55 G2
Hill St, Wrexham LL11 5 C3
Hill Top Cl CH5 19 G3
Hill Vw CH7 23 G2
Hillbury Rd LL13 60 C5
Hillcourt Av CH6 8 C6
Hillcrest Rd CW6 46 D4
Hillock La LL12 51 F5
Hills Lea*,
Coleshill St CH6 10 C2
Hillsdown Dr CH5 13 C8
Hillside CH5 20 C4
Hillside Av CH5 13 C6
Hillside Cres,
Buckley CH7 24 C4
Hillside Cres,
Mold CH7 22 B2
Hillside Ct CH8 7 B5
Hillside Rd,
Blacon CH1 39 E2
Hillside Rd,
Penyffordd CH4 28 B2
Hillside Rd,
Tarporley CW6 46 C6
Hillside Way CH6 10 B3
Hillsview Rd CH7 24 B4
Hilltop Dr LL12 51 F4
Hilltop Rd CH3 31 A6
Hilltop View Rd LL12 57 F5
Hilton Cl LL11 55 H1
Hinsley Dr LL13 57 G6
Hobart Way CH1 38 D1
Hockenhull Av CH3 46 B2
Hockenhull Cres CH3 46 B2
Hockenhull La CH3 46 B3
Holbein Cl CH4 44 B1
Holborn Cres LL11 55 F5
Holland Rd LL11 55 E1
Hollands La CW6 46 B4
Hollins La CH5 25 F1
Hollowbrook Dr CH5 13 C8
Holly Cl,
Buckley CH7 24 B3
Holly Cl, Chester CH2 31 B2
Holly Cl,
Connahs Quay CH5 13 C5
Holly Ct,
Leeswood CH7 30 B1
Holly Ct,
Wrexham LL12 51 E5
Holly Ct*,
Pen y Llan CH5 13 D5
Holly Dr,
Chester CH4 28 C2
Holly Dr, Mold CH7 22 B3
Holly Grange CH5 13 C6
Holly Gro,
Deeside CH5 20 B2
Holly Gro,
Wrexham LL13 61 F1
Holly Leigh Ct LL11 60 C1
Holly Rd CH4 43 F2
Holly Tree Cl CH5 19 G4
Holly Walks LL12 5 D1
Hollybush Cl LL11 56 B2
Hollyfields LL12 51 F5
Holm Oak Way CH66 32 A1
Holme St CH3 46 A2
Holmwood Av LL14 59 G6
Holt Rd, Rossett LL12 52 D4
Holt Rd,
Wrexham LL13 5 D3
Holt St LL13 5 D3
Holway Ct CH8 8 C2
Holway Rd CH8 8 D2
Holyhead Rd LL14 68 D2
Holyrood Cres LL11 56 C6
Holyrood Way CH3 41 E3
Holywell Rd,
Deeside CH5 19 G3
Holywell Rd,
Flint CH6 10 B1
Holywell St CH6 10 C1
Home Cl CH3 45 H1
Home Pk CH1 35 F3
Homestead La LL14 60 A3
Honeysuckle Cl,
Chester CH4 27 F5
Honeysuckle Cl,
Ellesmere Port
CH66 32 A1
Hoole Gdns CH2 41 E2
Hoole La CH3 40 C4
Hoole Pk CH2 40 D3
Hoole Rd CH2 4 D1
Hoole Way CH1 4 C2
Hope Hall Dr LL12 48 C1
Hope Rd CH4 27 F4
Hope St,
Caergwrle LL12 48 B3
Hope St,
Chester CH4 43 F1
Hope St,
Gwersyllt LL11 56 A3
Hope St,
Rhosllanerchrugog
LL14 64 C2
Hope St,
Wrexham LL11 5 C3
Hope View Ct CH7 24 C3
Hornbean Av CH7 25 E3
Hornesby Cl CH5 13 B6
Horrocks Rd CH2 36 C6
Horseshoe Pass Vw
LL20 67 C5
Horsley Dr LL12 56 D4
Hoseley La LL12 51 G4
Hough Grn CH4 43 G1
Hougton Cl CH2 40 D3
Hourd Way CH66 32 A1
Housesteads Dr CH2 40 D3
Housman Cl CH1 35 G6
Howard Rd CH4 42 D2
Howard St CH5 13 E6
Howards Cl CH4 28 B3
Howe Rd CH4 43 H1
Hudsons Hill LL12 51 G6
Huges Row LL14 65 B7
Hugh St CH4 40 A6
Hugmore La LL13 62 D1
Hullah La LL13 61 F1
Hulleys Cl CH4 28 C2
Hunter St CH1 4 A3
Hunters Cft CH4 29 G4
Hunters Cres CH3 46 C3
Hunters Dr CH3 46 C3
Hunters Walk CH1 4 B3
Hunters Way LL12 50 A4
Huntroyde Av LL13 5 C6
Hunts Cl CH3 41 F5
Huntsman Cnr LL12 57 F4
Hurlestone Cl CH2 31 A2
Hurstwood CH3 47 B5

Idwal LL14 65 C7
Idwal Cl LL11 55 G6
Imperial Av CH1 38 C1
Ince Dr CH3 71 C5
Ingham Cl CH3 40 D4
Institute La CH7 18 C2
Irvings Cres CH4 43 E2
Is y Coed CH7 22 C6
Isabella Ct CH4 43 E2
Isglan Rd CH8 6 A1
Island Grn Shopping
Centre LL13 5 B3
Islay Cl CH65 32 D1
Issa Fm CH7 23 G2
Ithens Way LL13 60 D6
Iver Cl CH2 36 C4
Iver Rd CH2 36 C4
Ivy Cl LL11 56 C5
Ivy Cres CH7 22 B3
Ivy Ct*,
Pen y Llan CH5 13 D5
Ivy Mews CH2 41 E1

Jackson Ct CH4 27 F1
James Pl CH2 40 D3
James St,
Chester CH1 4 C2
James St,
Wrexham LL14 59 G6
Jamieson Cl CH3 40 D4
Jarman Av LL13 5 C6
Jarvis Way LL12 57 E6
Jasmine Cres CH7 22 B3
Jasmine Ct LL11 55 G6
Jefferson Rd CH5 19 H4
Jeffreys Cl LL12 57 E5
Jeffreys Rd LL12 57 E4
Jesmond Rd CH1 39 H3
John Henry Ct*,
Bryn y Gwynt CH8 7 C5
John St, Chirk LL14 68 D4
John St,
Llangollen LL20 67 B4
John St,
Ruabon LL14 65 F6
Johns Ct LL12 52 B3
Johnson St LL14 64 D1
Johnsons Cl CH4 43 H2
Jonathans Way CH1 39 E1
Jones St LL14 64 C2
Jubilee Ct CH7 24 C4
Jubilee Rd,
Buckley CH7 24 C4
Jubilee Rd,
Wrexham LL13 5 B4
Jubilee St CH5 15 B7
Julius Cl CH6 10 E3
Juniper Cl,
Connahs Quay CH5 13 C6
Juniper Cl,
Gresford LL12 51 G6
Juniper Cl,
Wrexham LL12 57 F4
Juniper Ct CH2 41 F2
Juniper Dr CH66 32 A1
Juniper Gro CH66 32 A1
Jupiter Dr CH1 39 E4
Jutland Av LL11 55 H3

K.U.S.
Ind Pk CH4 27 E1
Kaleyards CH1 4 C3
Kathen Ct LL12 51 F6
Katkins Cft CH3 41 F5
Kearsley Av CH5 20 A5
Keats Cl,
Deeside CH5 19 G6
Keats Cl,
Ellesmere Port CH66 32 A1
Keats Ter CH1 39 G1
Kelsall Hill CW6 46 D4
Kelsborrow Way
CW6 46 C6
Kelsterton Ct CH5 13 B5
Kelsterton La CH5 12 A4
Kelsterton Rd CH5 12 B4
Kelvin Gro CH2 40 C1
Kempton Cl CH1 39 H3
Kendal Cl CH2 36 D6
Kendal Way LL12 57 E4
Kenfig Pl LL14 66 D2
Kennedy Cl CH2 37 E6
Kennedy Dr CH5 20 C3
Kensington Av CH5 15 A8
Kensington Cl,
Chester CH4 43 G1
Kensington Cl,
Wrexham LL14 59 G5
Kensington Grn CH4 43 F1
Kensington Gro LL12 57 E4
Kensington Rd CH4 43 F1
Kenstone Cl CH7 22 D5
Kent Av CH5 15 A8
Kent Cl CH4 28 C2
Kent Dr LL11 56 D4
Kent Gdns CH2 36 D6
Kent Rd,
Chester CH2 36 D6
Kent Rd,
Connahs Quay CH5 13 C6
Kent Rd,
Wrexham LL11 55 E3
Kenyon Av LL11 56 C5
Keristal Av CH3 44 D1
Kerry Pl LL12 61 E1
Kestrel Cl CH5 13 C8
Keswick Cl CH2 36 D6
Ketlan Ct CH4 43 E1
Ketland Cl CH5 15 B8
Ketland Pl CH5 15 B8
Killins La CH5 13 F8
Kilmorey Park Av
CH2 40 C2
Kilmorey Park Rd
CH2 40 C2
Kilmorey Pk CH2 40 C2
Kiln Cl, Buckley CH7 24 B2
Kiln Cl, Flint CH6 10 B2
Kiln La LL12 48 C1
Kimberley Ter*,
Watertower Vw
CH3 40 D4
King Edward Dr CH6 10 C4
King Edward St CH5 15 A7
King George Ct LL11 53 D1
King George St CH5 15 A8
King St,
Acrefair LL14 65 A8
King St,
Cefn-mawr LL14 66 D1
King St, Chester CH1 4 A3
King St,
Leeswood CH7 30 B2
King St, Mold CH7 22 C4
King St,
Rhosllanerchrugog
LL14 64 D2
King St,
Wrexham LL11 5 B3
Kingfisher Cl CH3 71 D4
Kingfisher Ct CH2 4 B1
Kings Av, Flint CH6 10 D3
Kings Av,
Holywell CH8 6 C3
Kings Cft*,
Kings Rd CH5 13 D5
Kings Cl,
Chester CH4 43 F3
Kings Cl, Mold CH7 22 D5
Kings Cl,
Wrexham LL13 61 E4
Kings Cres East CH3 41 E5
Kings Cres West CH3 41 E5
Kings Ct CH1 4 A3
Kings La LL14 66 D1
Kings Mews CH1 4 A3
Kings Oak Ct LL13 61 E5
Kings Rd CH5 13 D5
Kingsbury Cl CH6 10 A2
Kingsfield Ct CH4 43 H4
Kingsley Gdns CH3 41 E5
Kingsley Rd,
Chester CH3 41 E5
Kingsley Rd,
Deeside CH5 15 E7
Kingsmead CH2 36 A4
Kingsmills Rd LL13 5 D5
Kingston Ct CH1 34 B2
Kingston Dr CH5 13 C7
Kingstown LL12 61 E1
Kingsway,
Chester CH2 40 C1
Kingsway,
Deeside CH5 15 A7
Kingsway,
Wrexham LL12 48 C2
Kingsway West CH2 40 C1

Kingswood Av CH1 34 D2
Kingswood La CH1 34 C3
Kingswood Walk CW6 46 C5
Kinnaird Ho CH1 4 D3
Kinnerton Cl CH4 43 E3
Kinnerton Heights CH4 29 H4
Kinnerton La CH4 26 B6
Kinnerton Old Rd CH4 26 A4
Kinnerton Rd CH4 29 E6
Kinnington Way CH1 32 A2
Kipling Cl CH5 19 G6
Kipling Rd CH1 35 F6
Kirby Cl CH2 40 B1
Kirkett Av CH4 29 G4
Kirkwood Cl CH3 41 E3
Kitchen St CH1 39 H5
Knights Grn CH6 10 C2
Knightsbridge Ct CH1 4 C4
Knowle La CH7 24 D3
Knowsley Rd CH2 40 D1
Knutsford Way CH1 39 F4
Kohima Cres CH3 45 F2
Kynaston Dr CH4 42 C1
Kynaston Pl LL14 66 D2

Laburnum Ct LL12 50 B4
Laburnum Gro, Chester CH4 43 E2
Laburnum Gro, Ellesmere Port CH66 32 B1
Laburnum Way LL13 71 B5
Lache Gdns CH4 43 G3
Lache Hall Cres CH4 43 F4
Lache La CH4 43 E6
Lache Park Av CH4 43 G1
Lake Vw, Gresford LL12 50 D5
Lake Vw, Wrexham LL12 57 F5
Lakeside CH4 43 H6
Lakeside Bsns Village CH5 19 G5
Lakeside Cl, Buckley CH7 24 C1
Lakeside Cl, Wrexham LL12 50 D5
Lakewood CH4 43 G5
Lambourne Cl CH66 32 A1
Lambpit St LL11 5 C3
Lambs La CH7 24 D4
Lampit St LL14 64 A4
Lancaster Dr CH3 41 E3
Lancaster Pk CH4 27 E5
Lancaster Ter LL14 65 B8
Lance Vw LL12 52 E3
Langdale Av, Buckley CH7 24 D2
Langdale Av, Wrexham LL14 59 H6
Langford Cl LL13 57 G6
Langford Cres CH7 24 A4
Langford Ct CH3 46 C2
Langollen Ter*, Rock Rd LL14 66 E1
Langport Dr CH3 41 G3
Lansbury Gro LL11 55 F5
Lansdown Rd CH4 27 F4
Lansdowne Gro CH4 43 G1
Lansdowne Rd CH5 13 C5
Larch Av CH5 20 B1
Larch Gro LL13 61 F2
Larch Way CH4 43 E2
Larchdale Cl CH66 32 B1
Larchfields CH1 34 B3
Larchwood Rd LL12 57 F5
Larkspur Cl CH4 43 F3
Larne Dr CH4 27 G3
Laurel Cl LL12 51 F6
Laurel Dr CH7 24 D4
Laurel Gro, Chester CH2 40 D2
Laurel Gro, Wrexham LL14 64 F3
Laurels Av LL13 70 C5
Lavender Ct CH5 15 B8
Lavister Gdns LL12 56 D4
Lavister Walks LL12 52 E2
Law St CH2 40 C3
Lawn Dr CH2 36 B4
Lawrence St CH5 21 F3
Laws Gdns CH3 41 E6
Lawson Cl LL12 61 E1
Lawson Rd LL12 60 D1
Laxton Cl CH66 32 A1
Lea Dr CH7 24 C4
Lea Rd LL13 5 B4
Leaches Cl CH5 21 E3
Leaches La CH5 20 D4
Leadbrook Dr CH6 10 F4
Leadworks La CH1 4 D3
Leahurst Cl CH2 40 D1
Leahurst Way LL11 56 A2
Leaside Rd CH1 35 E6
Ledsham La CH5 25 H2
Lee St CH1 4 D3
Leen La CH1 4 B4
Leeswood Rd CH7 24 B4
Leighstone Ct CH2 4 B1
Leonard St CH1 39 H2
Lesters La CH4 26 D5
Level Rd CH5 19 H6
Lexham Green Cl CH7 24 C3
Leyfield Ct CH4 43 F3
Leyland Dr CH4 42 C1
Lichfield Cl LL13 57 G5
Lichfield Rd CH1 39 F1
Lightfoot St CH2 4 D1
Lilac Dr CH4 28 B3
Lilac Gro CH66 32 B1
Lilac Way LL11 60 B2
Lime Av LL12 51 E5
Lime Cl CH5 13 C7
Lime Gro, Hoole CH2 40 D2
Lime Gro, Saltney CH4 43 E2
Lime Tree Cl CH66 32 B2
Lime Tree Dr CH3 71 C4
Lincoln Cl LL13 57 G6
Lincoln Dr CH2 37 E6
Lincoln Rd, Chester CH1 39 F1
Lincoln Rd, Deeside CH5 20 A4
Lindale Cl CH5 13 B6
Linden Av, Chirk LL14 68 D3
Linden Av, Connahs Quay CH5 13 C6
Linden Av, Wrexham LL13 61 E4
Linden Cl CH66 32 A1
Linden Dr, Chester CH2 31 B2
Linden Dr, Mold CH7 22 A5
Linden Gro, Chester CH2 41 E2
Linden Gro, Saltney CH4 42 D2
Linden Gro, Wrexham LL12 50 B3
Linderick Av CH7 24 A3
Lindfields CH4 43 F2
Linen Hall Pl CH1 4 A4
Linkside Way CH66 32 A2
Linksway CH2 36 A4
Linley Av LL14 64 F3
Linley Pl LL11 56 C4
Linthorpe Cl CH7 24 C3
Linthorpe Gdns CH7 24 D3
Linthorpe Rd CH7 24 C3
Linwood Cl CH4 28 C2
Lisburne Gro LL13 57 F3
Little Abbey Gateway CH1 4 B3
Little Acton Dr LL12 56 D5
Little Heath CH3 41 H5
Little Heath Rd CH3 41 H4
Little Mdws LL11 56 A2
Little Mere CH3 41 H5
Little Mountain Rd CH7 25 F5
Little Roodee CH5 27 E1
Little St John St CH1 4 C4
Little Stanney La CH2 33 F1
Littleton La CH3 41 H3
Liverpool Rd, Buckley CH7 24 C2
Liverpool Rd, Chester CH2 4 B2
Liverpool Rd, Dunkirk CH1 32 A2
Liverpool Rd, Moston CH2 36 A1
Liverpool Rd, Upton CH2 36 A4
Llafar y Nant LL20 70 B2
Llandore Cl CH5 19 E1
Llanfair Cres CH5 19 E1
Llangoed Ter LL11 58 C1
Llangollen Rd, Llangollen LL20 66 A2
Llangollen Rd, Wrexham LL14 65 A8
Llangollen Wharf LL20 67 B4
Llay Ct LL12 50 B4
Llay Hall Av LL12 50 A4
Llay Hall Ind Est LL12 49 D7
Llay Ind Est LL12 48 F4
Llay New Rd LL11,12 50 A3
Llay Place Av LL12 50 A3
Llay Rd, Cefn-y-bedd LL12 49 D5
Llay Rd, Rossett LL12 52 B4
Llewellyn St CH5 13 F8
Llewelyn Dr CH7 23 G2
Llewelyn Rd LL11 54 C4
Lloyd Cl CH3 71 C4
Lloyd Dr CH65 33 E1
Lloyd Pl CH1 39 E1
Lloyd St, Flint CH6 10 C1
Lloyd St, Wrexham LL14 64 C1
Lloyds La LL14 69 E5
Llwyn Alun LL12 48 B1
Llwyn Bach CH7 22 A5
Llwyn Bedw CH7 11 B2
Llwyn Clwyd CH5 20 B1
Llwyn Derw CH7 23 F2
Llwyn Eglwys LL12 48 C2
Llwyn Eithin CH7 22 B5
Llwyneinion Rd LL14 64 C1
Llwyni Dr CH5 19 E1
Llwynon Cl CH7 23 G3
Llyndir La LL12 52 D2
Llys Adarn CH5 19 G5
Llys Allun LL11 55 H2
Llys Alyn CH5 19 E1
Llys Ambrose CH7 22 A6
Llys Ann CH7 30 B2
Llys Argoed CH7 23 F4
Llys Ben CH7 18 C1
Llys Berllan CH7 24 A3
Llys Brenig CH5 19 G5
Llys Bryn Eglwys CH7 22 C3
Llys Caer CH4 27 E5
Llys Caer Glo CH7 17 B5
Llys Ceibren CH5 20 B1
Llys Daniel Owen CH7 22 B2
Llys David Lord LL13 5 A4
Llys Dedwydd CH7 23 F4
Llys Degwm CH7 30 B5
Llys Derw LL14 64 D1
Llys Derwen, Chester CH4 29 G3
Llys Derwen, Mold CH7 22 D4
Llys Eithin CH7 18 C1
Llys Enfys CH7 11 C6
Llys Fammau CH7 23 F3
Llys Gwynant CH7 23 G2
Llys Iorwg CH7 22 C3
Llys John Dafis CH7 22 B2
Llys Maes Teg CH8 6 E4
Llys Mai CH7 24 B2
Llys Menden CH7 22 A4
Llys Mervyn CH7 22 B2
Llys Nercwys CH7 22 D6
Llys Owain LL12 50 A4
Llys Pant Derw CH5 13 B8
Llys Penuel LL14 64 D1
Llys Pont y Felin CH7 22 C3
Llys Pont y Garreg CH7 22 C5
Llys Preswylfa CH7 22 B4
Llys Tudela CH7 22 A4
Llys Wylfa CH7 23 F3
Llys y Berllan CH8 6 B3
Llys y Brenin CH8 7 B6
Llys Y Coed LL11 60 C1
Llys y Coed*, The Firs CH5 22 D6
Llys y Felin CH6 10 B4
Llys y Fron, Holywell CH8 7 B6
Llys y Fron, Mold CH7 22 A4
Llys y Graig, Mold CH7 23 G2
Llys y Graig, Wrexham LL14 66 E1
Llys y Mor CH8 8 B2
Llys y Wennol CH7 18 D1
Llys y Wern, Soughton CH7 17 B5
Llys y Wern, Treuddyn CH7 30 B5
Llys yr Awel CH7 22 D6
Llys yr Coed CH7 22 D6
Llys yr Efail CH7 22 C4
Llys yr Foel CH7 22 D5
Llys yr Nant CH7 22 D6
Lodge La CH1 34 A1
Lodge Rd LL11 56 B6
Lon Bryn Coch CH7 22 B5
Lon Cae Del, Deeside CH5 19 H5
Lon Cae Del, Mold CH7 22 A5
Lon Castanwydden CH7 30 B2
Lon Celyn CH5 13 C6
Lon Dderwen CH5 13 C6
Lon Goed CH8 8 C2
Lon Groes CH6 10 B3
Lon Gwynant CH5 19 G5
Lon Isaf CH7 22 D4
Lon Llwyni CH5 13 B8
Lon Nwy CH7 22 D5
Lon y Becws CH6 10 C2
Lon y Berth CH7 22 A5
Lon y Parc CH7 22 B5
Lon yr Orsaf CH7 22 D4
London Rd CH7 17 B5
Long La, Saughall CH1 34 B1
Long La, Upton CH2 36 C4
Long La, Waverton CH3 47 D6
Long La, Wrexham LL11 55 E2
Longacre Dr CH6 8 C5
Longburgh Cl CH2 40 D3
Longdale Dr CH1 38 D1
Longfellow Av CH5 19 G6
Longfield LL14 69 E6
Longfield Av CH2 36 C4
Longley Av CW6 46 C4
Longueville LL13 60 C5
Longview Rd LL11 55 F3
Lonsdale Ct CH4 43 F3
Lord St, Chester CH3 40 D4
Lord St, Wrexham LL11 5 B3
Lorne St, Chester CH1 4 A2
Lorne St, Wrexham LL11 5 C1
Louise St CH1 4 A2
Love La CH7 22 C3
Love St CH1 4 C4
Lower Aston Hall La CH5 20 B3
Lower Bridge St CH1 4 B5
Lower Brook St CH5 13 C5
Lower Farm Cl LL11 56 A2
Lower Mill Dr LL11 59 G1
Lower Minster LL12 57 E4
Lower Mountian Rd CH4 28 C4
Lower Park Rd CH4 4 D5
Lower Rd LL11 58 B1
Lowerfield Rd CH4 43 G3
Lucerne Cl CH3 45 E1
Ludlow Cl LL13 70 D4
Ludlow Rd, Chester CH1 39 G1
Ludlow Rd, Wrexham LL13 70 D4
Ludwell Cl CH4 43 H2
Lumley Pl CH1 4 C4
Lumley Rd CH2 40 A1
Lundy Dr CH65 32 D1
Lupin Dr CH3 45 E1
Lyme Gro CH7 24 D4
Lyndale Gro LL12 56 D4
Lynfield Cl CH5 13 D7
Lynton Cl CH4 43 F2
Lynton Pl CH4 27 F4
Lynwood Rd CH1 35 F6
Lyon St CH1 4 C2
Lytham Ct LL13 57 H6

Machynlleth Way CH5 13 C7
Madeira Hill LL13 5 C5
Madeley Cl CH4 27 G4
Maelor Av LL14 64 C4
Maelor Cl CH7 24 D4
Maelor Pl LL14 65 F7
Maelor Rd LL14 64 E2
Maelor Vw LL13 71 C2
Maengwyn Av CH5 13 C7
Maes Afon CH6 10 B3
Maes Alarch CH8 9 A4
Maes Alaw CH6 10 D3
Maes Alun LL12 48 B2
Maes Bache LL20 67 B6
Maes Bodlonfa CH7 22 B4
Maes Brenin LL13 62 C5
Maes Celyn, Northop CH7 17 A2
Maes Celyn, Wrexham LL13 60 C5
Maes Cibyn LL12 48 C4
Maes Collen LL20 67 B5
Maes Crimond LL11 55 E6
Maes Eithen LL11 55 G5
Maes Enion LL14 64 C1
Maes Glan LL14 64 C2
Maes Glanrafaon*, Brook St CH7 22 C5
Maes Glas, Deeside CH5 19 G5
Maes Glas, Flint CH6 10 B
Maes Glas, Treuddyn CH7 30 B5
Maes Gruffydd CH7 17 A5
Maes Grug LL14 64 D1
Maes Gwalia CH7 17 B5
Maes Gwern CH7 22 B
Maes Gwyn CH6 10 D
Maes Hyfryd, Coedpoeth LL11 54 C
Maes Hyfryd, Flint CH6 10 C
Maes Hyfryd, Gwersyllt LL11 56 B
Maes Isaf LL14 64 F
Maes Llan CH7 11 B
Maes Madoc LL14 65 B
Maes Meillion LL11 53 F
Maes Pengwern LL20 67 C
Maes Teg, Flint CH6 10 C
Maes Teg, Wrexham LL14 64 B
Maes Telford LL20 66 B
Maes Tyddyn LL11 54 C
Maes Uchaf CH5 19 E
Maes Wepre CH5 19 E
Maes y Coed, Flint CH6 10 B
Maes y Coed, Wrexham LL11 56 A
Maes y Dre Av CH6 10 D
Maes y Dyffryn CH8 6 C
Maes y Ffynnon Rd LL11 53 C
Maes y Ficerdy LL14 64 E
Maes y Gornel LL14 64 C
Maes y Llan Rd LL14 65 F
Maes y Meillion CH7 30 B
Maes y Nant LL14 64 A
Maes y Plwm CH8 8 C
Maes y Waun LL14 69 D
Maes y Wennol LL14 69 E
Maes y Ysgol LL14 69 D
Maes yr Afon CH8 7 D
Maes yr Haf, Mold CH7 22 E
Maes yr Haf, Wrexham LL12 56 D
Maes yr Haul CH7 22 E
Maes yr Odyn CH8 7 C
Maes yr Ysgol CH6 10 E
Maesgwyn Rd LL11 5 A
Maesmawr Rd LL20 67 D
Maesteg, Brynteg LL11 55 F
Maesteg, Gwynfryn LL11 53 E
Maes-y-Coed CH4 43 E
Maesydre Rd LL12 5 D
Magazine La CH7 18 D
Main Rd, Broughton CH4 27 F
Main Rd, Higher Kinnerton CH4 29 G
Main Rd, Soughton CH7 17 A
Main Rd, Wrexham LL11 56 E
Mainwaring Dr CH4 42 C
Maitland Way CH1 38 D
Makepeace Cl CH3 41 C

Maldwyn Cl CH6 10 C3
Mallard Ct CH2 36 C4
Mallow Cl CH3 45 E2
Malta Rd CH2 35 H2
Malvern Dr LL11 55 H4
Malvern Rd CH1 39 G1
Manbry Cl CH5 13 C6
Mancot La CH5 20 D3
Mancot Royal Cl CH5 20 D3
Mancot Way CH5 20 D3
Manley Ct CH5 15 A7
Manley Rd, Coedpoeth LL11 58 B1
Manley Rd, Wrexham LL13 60 D3
Mannings La CH2 37 E6
Mannings La South CH2 41 E1
Manor Cl, Chester CH4 21 H6
Manor Cl, Wrexham LL12 50 A4
Manor Cres CH4 21 H6
Manor Dr, Bagillt CH6 8 D6
Manor Dr, Buckley CH7 24 D3
Manor Dr, Chester CH3 41 F5
Manor Farm Cl CH2 31 A3
Manor Farm Cotts CH3 41 G6
Manor Ind Est CH6 8 D6
Manor La, Deeside CH5 27 E2
Manor La, Wrexham LL12 51 H1
Manor Pk CH7 17 B5
Manor Rd, Chester CH4 43 H3
Manor Rd, Deeside CH5 16 B6
Mansfeild Av CH5 19 H5
Maple Av LL12 57 E6
Maple Cl LL12 51 F5
Maple Cres CH5 19 H6
Maple Dr LL14 65 B8
Maple Gro, Buckley CH7 25 F3
Maple Gro, Ellesmere Port CH66 32 B1
Maple Gro, Hoole CH2 41 E2
Maple Gro, Saltney CH4 43 E2
Maple Wood Av CH5 15 E7
Maplehurst Cl LL14 59 H5
Maplewood Gro CH1 34 B3
Marbury Av CH7 24 D4
Marbury Rd CH3 41 F4
Marcella Cres LL13 71 C2
Mare Hey La CH5 19 G4
Marford Hights LL12 51 G3
Marford Hill LL12 51 G4
Marford Row LL11 54 A6
Marian CH6 10 C4
Marian Dr CH3 41 E5
Marina Dr, Chester CH2 36 C4
Marina Dr, Deeside CH5 15 A8
Mark Cl CH2 40 D3
Market Sq CH6 10 C1
Market St, Llangollen LL20 67 A4
Market St, Rhosllanerchrugog LL14 64 C2
Market St, Wrexham LL13 5 D3
Marl Cft CH3 41 E6
Marl Heys CH2 36 C4
Marlborough Av CH5 19 H5
Marlborough Ct*, Derby Pl CH2 40 C2
Marlborough Rd LL13 63 E4
Marley Way CH4 43 E1
Marlow Av CH2 36 D5
Marlowe Av CH5 13 E8
Marlowe Cl CH1 35 G6
Marlston Av CH4 43 G2
Marlwood Pl CH4 27 E5
Marnel Dr CH5 20 D2
Marsh Cres LL12 57 E6
Marsh La CH6 10 D2
Marsh Vw CH5 13 F6
Martin Cl CH2 36 A3
Martin Rd, Broughton CH4 27 G4
Martin Rd, Moston CH2 36 A3
Masefield Dr CH1 35 E6
Mason Av LL13 5 C6
Mason St CH1 4 B2
Masonic Pl CH1 4 C4
Matthew Cl CH2 40 D3
Matthias Rd LL11 55 F3
Maude St CH5 13 F6
Mawddwy Av LL11 56 C6
Maxwell Av CH5 20 D3
Maxwell Cl, Buckley CH7 24 D3
Maxwell Cl, Wrexham LL12 51 E6
Maxwell Dr CH7 30 B1
Maybury Av LL20 70 B2
Maydor Av CH4 42 D1
Mayfield Ct LL12 50 B4
Mayfield Dr CH7 24 A3
Mayfield Mews CH7 24 A3
Mayfield Rd CH1 34 D6
Mayflower Dr LL12 51 F5
Maytree Av CH3 41 F3
Mayville Av, Llay LL12 50 B5
Mayville Av, Wrexham LL11 60 C1
McKeown Cl CH5 13 C8
Meadow Av CH7 25 F2
Meadow Bank, Holywell CH8 8 D2
Meadow Bank, Tarporley CW6 46 C6
Meadow Cl, Farndon CH3 71 C5
Meadow Cl, Tarvin CH3 46 B2
Meadow Cres LL12 48 B2
Meadow Ct CH1 35 F2
Meadow La CH3 44 D2
Meadow Lea LL13 61 E2
Meadow Pl CH7 22 C4
Meadow Rd CH4 27 F4
Meadow Rise, Chester CH4 28 B4
Meadow Rise, Wrexham LL12 50 B3
Meadow View Ct CH5 25 H4
Meadow Villas CH8 6 C4
Meadow Vw, Buckley CH7 25 F4
Meadow Vw, Deeside CH5 16 B5
Meadow Vw, Wrexham LL11 54 D4
Meadowcroft, Higher Kinnerton CH4 29 G4
Meadowcroft, Saughall CH1 34 B2
Meadowfield Rd CH4 43 G3
Meadows La, Chester CH4 4 C6
Meadows La, Saughall CH1 34 A3
Meadows Pl CH4 4 D6
Meadows Vw LL12 51 F5
Meadowside CH7 22 A2
Meadowside Mews CH1 39 H2
Meadowsway CH2 36 B4
Meadway Cl LL11 56 A2
Mechanics La CH5 20 D2
Medlar Cl CH4 43 F3
Megs La CH7 24 C5
Meifod Pl LL13 5 B5
Melbourne Rd, Buckley CH7 24 B4
Melbourne Rd, Chester CH1 38 D1
Melbreck Av CH5 20 A5
Melford Pl CH5 19 F1
Melin y Dre CH8 6 B4
Melkridge Cl CH2 40 D3
Melrose Av, Chester CH3 41 E3
Melrose Av, Deeside CH5 20 B1
Melrose Dr CH66 32 A1
Melverley Dr CH1 38 C1
Melwood Cl CH4 28 C2
Melyd Av LL14 64 F2
Menai Ho*, Lakeside Bsns Village CH5 19 G5
Menai Rd LL13 61 G3
Menai Way LL11 55 H2
Mendip Cl LL11 55 H4
Menuhin Ho CH2 36 B6
Mercer Way CH4 43 F2
Mercia Dr CH7 23 G3
Mercury Ct CH1 39 E3
Mere Cres LL13 57 G5
Merecroft CH2 40 D5
Meredith St LL13 5 A6
Mereilian Av LL12 51 G5
Merlin Rd LL12 57 E4
Merlin St LL14 64 E2
Merllyn Av CH5 13 D7
Merllyn Ct CH6 8 B5
Merllyn La CH6 8 B5
Merton Dr CH4 43 G4
Mertyn La CH8 8 B2
Methodist Hill LL20 66 B4
Meynell Pl CH1 35 G6
Middle Rd LL11 58 B1
Middle St LL14 66 E3
Middlecroft CH3 31 A6
Middleton Ter LL14 69 E5
Milborne Cl CH2 36 C6
Mile Barn Rd LL13 57 G5
Milford St CH7 22 C3
Mill Cft CH6 10 E3
Mill Cl CH2 36 B5
Mill Cross CH3 47 C4
Mill Flds LL11 55 G6
Mill La, Buckley CH7 24 C3
Mill La, Cefn-mawr LL14 66 D2
Mill La, Chester CH2 36 A6
Mill La, Connahs Quay CH5 13 F7
Mill La, Penycae LL14 64 A4
Mill St, Chester CH4 4 C6
Mill St, Llangollen LL20 67 B4
Mill View Rd CH5 13 F8
Mill Wharf CH3 47 C4
Millais Cl CH5 13 B6
Millards Ct*, High St LL14 64 E2
Millbank Rise LL13 61 E4
Millbrook La LL13 70 D6
Millbrook Rd LL13 61 G5
Millers Cl CH3 47 B5
Millers Ct CH7 24 C3
Millfield Cl CH3 71 C4
Millstone Pk CH4 28 B3
Millway CH3 47 C4
Milton Rd CH1 35 F6
Milton St CH1 4 C3
Min Awel CH6 10 C4
Min y Coed LL20 67 C5
Min y Graig Av LL11 54 D1
Min y Grug LL11 53 F4
Min yr Aber LL11 56 B1
Minafon LL13 61 F3
Minera Hall Rd LL11 53 F4
Minera Rd, Cefn-y-bedd LL12 49 A7
Minera Rd, Minera LL11 54 A4
Miners Rd LL12 49 F5
Minerva Av CH1 39 E4
Minerva Ct CH1 39 E3
Minffordd LL20 67 B4
Minffordd Flds CH7 11 D6
Mission Mews*, Hoole La CH3 40 D4
Moel Fammau Rd CH7 23 F1
Moel Ganol CH7 22 A4
Moel Gron CH7 23 F3
Moel Parc CH6 10 D4
Moel View Dr CH7 18 C2
Moel View Rd CH7 24 C5
Moelwyn Cl CH7 23 G3
Mold By-Pass CH7 22 C3
Mold Rd, Broughton CH4 27 E4
Mold Rd, Buckley CH7 24 A3
Mold Rd, Caergwrle LL12 48 A1
Mold Rd, Cefn-y-bedd LL12 49 D7
Mold Rd, Connahs Quay CH7 13 A8
Mold Rd, Deeside CH5 19 E4
Mold Rd, Deeside CH5 19 G4
Mold Rd, Mold CH7 23 E4
Mold Rd, Penyffordd CH4 28 C1
Mold Rd, Wrexham LL11 5 A1
Mold Rd Est LL11 55 H3
Mold Way CH5 19 G4
Moldsdale Rd CH7 22 D5
Mollington Ct CH1 35 E2
Monet Cl CH5 13 B5
Monger Rd LL13 61 E5
Monmouth Rd LL12 57 G6
Montgomery Rd LL13 61 E2
Montrose Ct CH4 43 F1
Montrose Gdns LL13 61 F2
Monza Cl, Buckley CH7 18 D2
Monza Cl, Mold CH7 23 H4
Moor Av CH8 8 C2
Moor Cft CH7 23 F1
Moor La, Chester CH3 47 B4
Moor La, Deeside CH5 21 E5
Moor La, Holywell CH8 8 D2
Moorcroft Av CH3 41 F5
Moorcroft Cres CH3 41 G1
Moorcroft Ct CH3 41 F5
Moorcroft Mews CH4 42 D1
Moorcroft Ter CH4 42 D1
Moorfield Ct CH5 20 A3
Moorfield Rd CH5 20 A3
Moorfields, Buckley CH7 24 D3
Moorfields, Holywell CH8 8 D2
Moorhead Cl LL12 61 E1
Moorhouse Cl CH2 36 B6
Moorland Av LL13 61 E2
Moreton Av LL14 64 F3
Moreton St LL14 64 E2
Morgan Av LL11 56 C6
Morgan Cl CH1 35 F6
Morley Av CH5 13 D7
Morley Cl CH2 31 B2
Mornington Cres CH7 25 E2
Mortlake Cres CH3 40 D4
Morton Rd CH1 39 E2
Moss Bank CH1 40 A2
Moss Grn LL12 52 E4
Moss Gro CH4 43 E2
Moss Hill LL11 55 F2
Moss Rd LL11 55 F2
Moss Valley Rd LL11 55 G5
Mossley Ct CH5 20 C6
Moston Rd CH2 36 A2
Mostyn Pl CH1 35 E6
Mostyn Rd, Holywell CH8 6 A1
Mostyn Rd, Wrexham LL11 58 B2
Mostyn St CH5 15 A7
Mount Cl CH7 23 F4
Mount Flds LL13 69 D5
Mount Hill LL11 54 D2
Mount Isa Dr LL11 54 D1
Mount Pl CH3 40 D4
Mount Pleasant, Chester CH4 43 F1
Mount Pleasant, Wrexham LL14 66 D2
Mount Pleasant Av CH6 10 B3
Mount Pleasant Rd CH7 25 E2
Mount St, Rhostyllen LL14 59 G6
Mount St, Wrexham LL13 5 D4
Mount Tabor Cl CH4 28 C1
Mount Zion LL11 54 B1
Mountain Cl LL12 48 C1
Mountain St LL14 64 C1
Mountain View Cl CH5 19 F1
Mountain Vw, Brymbo LL11 54 C1
Mountain Vw, Chester CH4 43 E2
Mountain Vw, Hope LL12 48 C1
Mountain Vw, Mold CH7 23 H3
Mountfield Rd CH5 20 A3
Mountway CH3 47 B5
Muir Rd CH1 39 E2
Muirfield Cl LL13 61 H1
Muirfield Rd CH7 24 A3
Music Hall Pass CH1 4 B4
Mwyn Ffordd LL11 53 F4
Myrica Gro CH2 41 F2
Myrtle Av CH4 29 H4
Myrtle Gro CH2 41 E2
Myrtle La CH8 7 C6
Myrtle Rd, Buckley CH7 24 A3
Myrtle Rd, Wrexham LL12 51 F6

Nant Ct LL11 58 B1
Nant Derw CH7 22 A4
Nant Eos CH8 8 D2
Nant Garmon CH7 22 B4
Nant Glyn CH7 24 B5
Nant Mawr Cres CH7 24 B4
Nant Mawr Ct CH7 24 B4
Nant Mawr Rd CH7 24 A3
Nant Peris CH1 38 D2
Nant Rd, Connahs Quay CH5 13 D6
Nant Rd, Wrexham LL11 53 B1
Nant Sq*, Tudor St LL11 58 B1
Nant View Ct CH7 24 B4
Nant y Coed, Holywell CH8 7 C5
Nant y Coed, Mold CH7 22 B5
Nant y Gaer Rd LL12 50 B4
Nant y Glyn CH6 8 A5
Nantyr Rd LL20 70 A3
Naomi Cl CH1 35 E6
Napier Rd CH2 36 A3
Napier Sq LL13 61 E4
Narrow La LL12 51 E5
Nayland Av LL12 51 F6
Nebo Hill LL11 53 D1
Nefyn Cl CH5 13 C7
Nelson St, Chester CH1 4 D2
Nelson St, Deeside CH5 15 B7
Nelson St, Wrexham LL13 61 E4
Neston Dr CH2 36 B6
Netherfield Ct CH4 44 B1
Neville Cres LL12 56 D6
Neville Dr CH3 41 E5
Neville Rd CH3 41 E5
Nevin Rd CH1 38 D2
New Brighton Rd, Bagillt CH6 7 F5
New Brighton Rd, Soughton CH7 17 B5
New Crane Bank CH1 39 H4
New Crane St CH1 4 A4
New Hall Rd LL14 65 F6
New High St LL14 65 F6
New House Av LL12 50 B4
New Park Rd CH5 20 A2
New Rd, Brymbo LL11 55 E2
New Rd, Brynteg LL11 55 F4
New Rd, Cefn-mawr LL14 66 C2
New Rd, Coedpoeth LL11 58 C1
New Rd, Deeside CH5 25 H4
New Rd, Holywell CH8 7 A5
New Rd, Llangollen LL20 70 B2
New Rd, New Broughton LL11 55 G6
New Rd, Southsea LL11 55 F6
New Rd, Wrexham LL11 56 C5
New Roskell Sq CH6 10 C1
New St, Connahs Quay CH5 13 F6

New St, Mold CH7 22 B4
New St, Rhosllanerchrugog LL14 64 D2
New St, Summerhill LL11 55 G1
New Union St CH5 13 D5
Newbridge Rd LL14 66 E2
Newbrigg Rd LL12 56 D4
Newbury Cl LL13 61 G5
Newbury Rd CH4 43 F2
Newby Walk CH5 13 B6
Newcroft CH1 34 B2
Newell Dr LL14 65 F5
Newgate Row CH1 4 B4
Newgate St CH1 4 C4
Newhall Ct CH2 36 C5
Newhall Rd CH2 36 C5
Newmarket Rise LL13 61 G5
Newport Cl LL13 61 F5
Newquay Dr LL13 61 F5
Newry Ct CH2 40 B2
Newry Pk CH2 40 B1
Newry Pk East CH2 40 A1
Newthorn Pl CH7 24 C4
Newton Cl CH7 18 B1
Newton Dr CH7 25 F2
Newton Hall Ct CH2 36 D6
Newton Hall Dr CH2 36 C6
Newton Ho CH2 36 C6
Newton La CH2 40 C1
Newton Mews CH2 36 D6
Newton Park Vw CH2 40 B1
Newton St LL13 61 E4
Newtown LL12 51 E5
Newtown Cl CH1 4 C2
Nicholas Ct CH1 4 A4
Nicholas St CH1 4 A4
Nicholas Street Mews CH1 4 A4
Nickolson Cl CH2 31 B2
Nield Ct CH2 36 B4
Nightingdale Cl CH3 71 C4
Ninth Av LL12 50 B4
Noddfa Ct LL14 64 F3
Norfolk Rd, Chester CH2 40 D1
Norfolk Rd, Wrexham LL12 57 F4
Norley Dr CH3 41 F4
Norman Cl CH66 32 A1
Norman Ct LL11 55 G1
Norman Rd LL13 5 C6
Norman St CH5 20 B1
Norman Way CH1 35 E6
Normanby Dr CH5 13 C7
Normandy Rd CH2 36 A2
Norris Rd CH1 35 E6
Norse Cl LL11 55 H3
North Av LL14 65 F5
North Grn CH5 16 B6
North Rd, Holywell CH8 7 A6
North Rd, Wrexham LL14 64 D1
North St, Chester CH3 40 D4
North St, Saltney CH4 38 B6
North St, Sandycroft CH5 21 G3
North St, Shotton CH5 15 B8
North Wood LL12 57 F5
Northern Pathway CH4 4 D6
Northgate Av CH2 4 B2
Northgate St CH1 4 B3
Northleigh Gro LL11 56 C5
Northop Cl CH5 13 C8
Northop Rd CH6 10 C4
Northop Rd CH7 17 B4
Northway CH4 39 G6
Norton Av CH4 42 D2
Norton Rd CH3 41 F3
Norwood Dr CH4 43 H2
Nuns Rd CH1 4 A4
Ny Ct CH4 52 F1

Oak Alyn Ct LL12 49 D7
Oak Bank La CH2 37 F5
Oak Cl, Bradley LL11 56 B1
Oak Cl, Connahs Quay CH5 13 C6
Oak Cl, Summerhill LL11 55 G1
Oak Dr, Buckley CH7 24 B1
Oak Dr, Chester CH4 29 H4
Oak Dr, Gresford LL12 51 F5
Oak Dr, Leeswood CH7 30 B1
Oak Dr, Wrexham LL12 56 D6
Oak Gro CH6 8 D6
Oak Mdws LL11 54 D4
Oak Pk CH7 30 B1
Oak Rd, Acrefair LL14 65 B8
Oak Rd, Chester CH4 43 F2
Oak Rd, Ponciau LL14 64 E1
Oak Rd, Wrexham Ind Est LL13 63 E5
Oak St LL20 67 B4
Oak Tree Av LL12 50 A4
Oak Tree Cl, Buckley CH7 24 D3
Oak Tree Cl, Deeside CH5 20 A1
Oakcroft LL14 69 D6
Oakdale Cl CH4 27 F5
Oakfield Av CH2 36 C3
Oakfield Dr CH2 36 C3
Oakfield Rd, Buckley CH7 24 C4
Oakfield Rd, Chester CH1 38 C1
Oakfield Rd, Deeside CH5 20 A4
Oakhurst LL13 61 G1
Oaklands CH3 31 A6
Oaklands Av LL13 57 F6
Oaklands Rd LL14 69 E7
Oaklea Av CH2 40 D2
Oakley La LL13 71 C2
Oakley Rd CH5 20 D3
Oakmere Dr, Chester CH3 41 E6
Oakmere Dr, Ellesmere Port CH66 32 A1
Oaktree Ct CH2 41 E3
Oakwood Cl CH7 22 B3
Oakwood Ct LL14 59 H5
Oakwood Villas CH5 13 E7
Ochr y Waen CH7 24 B2
Offa LL14 68 D3
Offa St, Brymbo LL11 54 C1
Offa St, Johnstown LL14 64 E2
Ogwen LL14 65 C8
Ogwen Cl LL11 55 F6
Old Aston Hill CH5 19 H3
Old Bank La CH7 24 B5
Old Chester Cl CH5 19 H4
Old Chester Rd CH6 7 B7
Old Coach Rd CW6 46 B5
Old Dee Bri CH1 4 C5
Old Farm Rd LL14 59 H5
Old Hall Cl LL14 59 H5
Old Hall Gdns CH2 4 D1
Old Hall Pk CH3 31 B6
Old Hall Pl CH1 4 B4
Old Hall Rd CH5 20 A5
Old Hope Rd CH4 28 D1
Old La CH4 52 F1
Old Liverpool Rd CH5 19 F4
Old London Rd, Bagillt CH6 8 B5
Old London Rd, Bedol CH6 8 C6
Old London Rd, Flint CH6 10 A2
Old Meadow Ct LL12 50 B3
Old Mill Ct CH2 36 B5
Old Minera Rd LL11 53 E3
Old Mold Rd, Deeside CH5 19 G4
Old Mold Rd, Wrexham LL11 55 H2,3
Old Rd LL20 70 C1
Old Ruthin Rd LL11 53 B2
Old School Ct, Ruabon LL14 65 E6
Old School Ct, Wrexham LL12 48 C4
Old Seals Way CH1 39 G3
Old Smelt Rd LL11 54 A6
Old Womans La CH3 45 G1
Old Wrexham Rd, Chester CH4 44 A1
Old Wrexham Rd, Wrexham LL12 57 F1
Oldfield Cres CH4 43 F3
Oldfield Dr CH3 41 F3
Oldfield Mews CH3 41 F4
Oldwood LL11 55 G5
Onslow Rd CH1 38 D1
Orchard Cft CH3 31 A6
Orchard Cl, Buckley CH7 24 C3
Orchard Cl, Chester CH2 36 B6
Orchard Cl, Deeside CH5 20 D3
Orchard Ct LL12 51 E5
Orchard Ct*, Chapel La CH3 41 E4
Orchard Gdns LL11 56 C5
Orchard Gro CH3 71 C5
Orchard La LL12 48 E3
Orchard Lea CH5 19 E4
Orchard Pl CH4 28 B4
Orchard St CH1 4 A2
Orchard Vw LL12 51 E5
Orchard Way, Deeside CH5 15 F7
Orchard Way, Mold CH7 22 B3
Orchard Way, Tarporley CW6 46 C5
Orchid Cl CH3 45 E1
Ormonde Rd CH2 40 A1
Ormonde St CH1 4 D2
Osborne Cl LL11 56 C6
Osborne St LL14 64 C3
Osbourne Ct CH5 13 D5
Osprey Ct CH2 4 B1
Oswold Way LL12 57 E6
Oulton Av CH2 36 C5
Oulton Pl CH1 4 B2
Overdale Av CH7 23 G4
Overlea Cres CH5 20 B4
Overlea Dr CH5 20 B4
Overleigh Ct CH4 40 B6
Overleigh Dr, Mold CH7 23 H4
Overleigh Dr, Wrexham LL13 57 G5
Overleigh Rd CH4 44 A1
Overleigh Ter*, Browns La CH4 40 A6
Overton Cl CH7 24 C4
Overton Rd LL13 70 C5
Overton Way LL12 57 E6
Overwood Av CH1 35 E3
Overwood La, Chester CH1 38 C1
Overwood La, Mollington CH1 35 E3
Owen Cl CH1 35 E5
Owens St LL14 64 C1
Oxford Rd CH4 43 F2
Oxford St LL13 61 E3

Padarn Cl CH4 42 D2
Paddock Cl LL14 59 H5
Paddock Rd CH4 44 C6
Paddock Row, Chester CH1 4 B4
Paddock Row, Wrexham LL14 65 F7
Paddock Way, Chester CH4 29 G4
Paddock Way, Gwernymynydd CH7 11 D6
Padeswood Ct CH7 24 C4
Padeswood Dr CH7 25 E6
Padeswood Rd CH7 24 C3
Palace Cl CH6 10 A2
Palatine Cl CH1 35 E6
Palgrave Cl CH1 35 G6
Palm Gro CH66 32 B1
Palmer St LL13 61 E3
Palmerston Cres CH5 19 H6
Palmerstone Cl CH1 39 G2
Pandy Ind Est LL11 56 C3
Pandy La LL11 56 D3
Pant Glas CH7 17 B5
Pant Hill LL14 64 C3
Pant Isa CH7 17 B5
Pant La LL12 51 E5
Pant Olwen LL12 51 E5
Pant Ucha CH7 17 B5
Pant y Fownog Dr CH7 23 H4
Panton Pl, Chester CH2 40 D2
Panton Pl, Holywell CH8 7 B6
Panton Rd CH2 40 D2
Parade St LL20 67 B4
Paradise CH4 4 C6
Paradise La CH5 19 G5
Parc Alun CH7 22 C3
Parc Bryn Castell CH5 19 E1
Parc Bychan LL11 56 C5
Parc Derwen CH7 30 B1
Parc Hendy CH7 22 A4
Parc Plas Aney CH7 22 A5
Park Av, Chester CH4 29 G4
Park Av, Flint CH6 10 C2
Park Av, Hawarden CH5 20 C4
Park Av, Holywell CH8 8 C2
Park Av, Llangollen LL20 67 A4
Park Av, Mold CH7 22 B3
Park Av, Mynydd Isa CH7 23 G3
Park Av, Saltney CH4 43 E1
Park Av, Saughall CH1 34 B1
Park Av, Shotton CH5 15 B8
Park Av, Wrexham LL12 5 D2
Park Cl CH3 46 B1
Park Cres, Chester CH4 28 B4
Park Cres, Holywell CH8 8 C2
Park Ct, Chester CH1 4 D4
Park Ct, Wrexham LL12 52 D4
Park Dr, Chester CH2 41 E1
Park Dr, Holywell CH8 8 B2
Park Dr South CH2 41 E2
Park Gro CH5 13 E8
Park Hall Rd CH8 6 C3
Park Hill Av LL11 56 A2
Park Issa CH7 23 H2
Park La, Chester CH4 28 B4
Park La, Holywell CH8 7 B6
Park La, Wrexham LL12 51 H6
Park Mws LL14 64 E2
Park Rd, Bagillt CH6 8 C6
Park Rd, Buckley CH7 24 C3
Park Rd, Holywell CH8 8 B2
Park Rd, Ponciau LL14 64 D1
Park Rd, Rhosymedre LL14 66 E2
Park Rd, Tanyfron LL11 54 D5
Park Rd West CH4 43 G1
Park St, Chester CH1 4 C5
Park St, Johnstown LL14 64 E3
Park St, Ruabon LL14 65 F7
Park St, Wrexham LL11 60 C1
Park Vw, Buckley CH7 25 F3
Park Vw, Northop CH7 17 C2
Park Vw, Wrexham LL14 64 E2
Park Walk CH2 40 B1
Park Wall Rd LL11 56 A1
Park Way, Buckley CH7 24 D3
Park Way, Chester CH1 34 B2
Park West CH1 39 E3
Parkend Walk LL14 59 G5
Parker Dr CH3 71 C5
Parker Dr South CH3 71 C5
Parkers Bldgs CH1 4 C3
Parkers Cl LL11 56 C6
Parkfield Rd CH4 27 G4
Parkgate Ct CH1 39 H1
Parkgate Rd CH1 4 A1
Parkland Walk LL14 65 F7
Parkleigh Ct LL12 61 E2
Parkside LL13 5 B5
Parkside CH7 24 C3
Parkway, Deeside CH5 14 E4
Parkway, Mold CH7 22 B5
Parkway Bsns Centre CH5 14 E4
Parliament Way CH66 32 A1
Parsonage Cl LL12 51 E5
Parsons La CH2 35 H5
Pasture Cl CW6 46 B6
Patten Cl CH5 19 G6
Peach Fld CH3 45 F1
Pear Tree Cl CH5 20 A1
Pear Tree Way, Chester CH2 36 D6
Pear Tree Way, Ellesmere Port CH66 32 A1
Pearl La CH3 41 F,G4
Pearson St LL14 64 D1
Peckforton Way CH2 36 C5
Peel St LL13 5 A4
Peel Ter CH1 4 D2
Pemba Dr CH7 24 C3
Pemberton Rd CH1 4 A3
Pembroke Cl, Chester CH4 44 C1
Pembroke Cl, Deeside CH5 20 D1
Pembroke Rd LL12 57 G6
Pembry Rise CH5 13 B6
Pen Lon CH8 6 F4
Pen y Ball Hill CH8 7 A6
Pen y Ball St CH8 7 A6
Pen y Bryn, Hope LL12 48 C1
Pen y Bryn, Mold CH7 22 B4
Pen y Bryn, Soughton CH7 17 B5
Pen y Bryn, Wrexham LL13 5 B5
Pen y Coed Rd CH7 25 E2
Pen y Garreg Cl CH7 23 H3
Pen y Glyn CH6 8 A4
Pen y Graig Rd LL11 54 C2
Pen y Llan Ct*, Pen y Llan CH5 13 D5
Pen y Llan St CH5 13 D5
Pen y Llyn LL11 56 A3
Pen y Lon CH7 23 F4
Pen y Maes, Buckley CH7 24 A4
Pen y Maes, Mold CH7 23 F4
Pen y Maes Gdns CH8 7 C6
Pen y Maes Rd CH8 7 B6
Pen y Nant CH6 8 B4
Pen y Pentre CH7 17 B5
Pen y Waun LL14 69 E5
Pen y Wern LL14 64 D3
Pencoed LL20 66 B1
Penderyn Way LL12 50 A4
Pendine Way LL11 55 H4
Pendragon Ct LL13 60 D5
Pendwll Rd LL11 55 F1
Penfold Hey CH2 36 B4
Pengwern LL20 67 C5
Pengwladys Av CH5 13 D8
Penlan LL14 64 F2
Penlan Dr CH5 20 B4
Penley Rd CH7 24 C4
Penllwyn LL14 64 F2
Penmon Cl CH1 38 D2
Pennant St CH5 13 E6
Penny Bank Cl CH4 26 D5
Penrallt LL11 55 E2
Penrho Est CH8 9 D6
Penrhos LL11 55 G1
Penrhos Ct CH5 19 E1
Penrhyn, Holywell CH8 7 D5
Penrhyn, Wrexham LL13 71 B2
Penrhyn Dr LL11 56 A2
Pensby Av CH2 36 B6
Pentland Cl CH3 40 D3
Pentre Felin LL13 5 B4
Pentre Gwyn LL13 61 G4
Pentre Ind Est CH5 21 E2
Pentre La, Buckley CH7 24 B1
Pentre La, Wrexham LL12 50 B5
Pentre St LL12 50 B5
Pentredwr LL14 64 C1
Penybryn LL12 50 B4
Penyffordd By-Pass CH4 28 A4
Penygelli Av LL11 58 B1

Penygelli Rd LL11 58 B2
Penygraig LL14 64 D2
Penymaes Av LL12 5 D1
Penymynydd Rd CH4 28 C1
Penypalmant Rd LL11 53 F4
Pepper St CH1 4 B5
Percival Cl CH2 36 A4
Percival Rd CH2 36 A3
Percy Rd, Chester CH4 4 C6
Percy Rd, Wrexham LL13 5 C5
Peris LL14 65 C8
Peris Cl LL11 55 G6
Peter St LL14 64 D2
Petit Cl LL12 49 C5
Philips Cl LL12 57 F5
Philips Rd LL11 55 H3
Phillip St, Chester CH2 4 D1
Phillip St, Deeside CH5 21 F3
Phillips Rd CH1 39 E2
Phoenix St CH5 21 F3
Pickering Mews*, Pickering St CH2 40 C2
Pickering St CH2 40 C2
Pickmere Dr CH3 41 E6
Picton Gorse La CH2 37 F4
Picton La CH2 37 G1
Pierce St CH5 15 C8
Pierces Sq LL13 5 B4
Piercy Av LL13 71 B2
Pierpoint La CH1 4 B4
Pigeon House La LL12 48 A1
Pikey La LL12 57 F1
Pilgrim Way LL13 62 B5
Pilgrims Cl CH7 17 B2
Pillbox Prom CH1 4 A4
Pine Cl LL11 55 G1
Pine Crest CH6 10 A3
Pine Gdns CH2 36 A6
Pine Gro, Chester CH3 41 E2
Pine Gro, Ellesmere Port CH66 32 B1
Pine Gro, Mold CH7 23 G4
Pine Gro, Wrexham LL12 50 B3
Pinedale Cl CH66 32 B1
Pinetree Cl CH4 27 F4
Pinewood Av CH5 13 D7
Pinewood Cl LL14 59 H5
Pinewood Rd CH7 25 F2
Pinfold Ct CH4 44 B1
Pinfold La, Buckley CH7 18 D3
Pinfold La, Chester CH4 44 B,C1
Pinfold La, Wrexham LL12 50 A3
Pingot Cft CH3 41 E6
Pipers Ct CH2 41 E1
Pipers Grn CH3 41 E3
Pipers La CH2 41 E1
Pippins Cl CH5 15 A8
Pisgah Hill LL11 55 F3
Pistyll CH8 7 C8
Pistyll Hill LL12 51 G5
Pitmans La CH5 20 B5
Pitts Cl CH3 46 C2
Plas Acton Cl LL12 56 D3
Plas Acton Rd LL11 56 B3
Plas Alyn LL11 55 G2
Plas Angharad LL14 59 H5
Plas Bennion Rd LL14 65 C6
Plas Coch Rd LL11 60 B1
Plas Coch Retail Pk LL11 56 B6
Plas Darland LL11 5 C1
Plas Dur LL11 55 E2
Plas Gwenfrewi CH8 7 A5
Plas Gwyn LL12 61 E1
Plas Hafan LL14 64 F2
Plas Howell LL11 58 C1
Plas Isaf LL14 66 F1
Plas Kynaston La LL14 66 D2
Plas Maen Dr LL12 49 C5
Plas Newton La CH2 36 C6
Plas Newydd Ct*, Woodland Dr CH6 10 B3
Plas Tirion LL14 64 F2
Plas yn Bwl LL12 48 B3
Plassey Cl LL13 57 H6
Plassey Ct LL13 70 C5
Plas-yn-Rhos CH4 28 A4
Platt La CH4 28 C6
Platts La CH3 46 B3
Pleasant La LL11 54 D1
Pleasant Rd LL11 55 F3
Pleasant Vw, Chester CH4 28 C2
Pleasant Vw, Moss LL11 55 F1
Pleasant Vw, Pentre Broughton LL11 55 F3
Plemstall Cl CH2 31 A3
Plemstall La CH2 31 B2
Plemstall Way CH2 31 B2
Plough La, Chester CH3 47 A2
Plough La, Deeside CH5 20 B2
Ploughmans Cl CH66 32 A1
Ploughmans Way CH66 32 A1
Plover Cl CH3 71 D4
Plum Ter CH1 4 A2
Plumley Cl CH3 41 F4
Plymouth St CH5 15 A8
Pont Adam LL14 65 E6
Pont Adam Cres LL14 65 E7
Pont Wen LL13 61 E4
Pont y Capel La LL12 50 B6
Pont yr Afon LL14 64 B4
Pool Bank Bsns Pk CH3 46 C1
Pool St LL14 64 E1
Poolmouth Rd LL11 55 G4
Poplar Av, Deeside CH5 20 A1
Poplar Av, Gresford LL12 51 E5
Poplar Av, Rhosllanerchrugog LL14 64 D2
Poplar Cl, Connahs Quay CH5 13 E8
Poplar Cl, Wrexham LL11 58 C1
Poplar Dr LL12 51 F5
Poplar Gro CH5 19 G4
Poplar Pl LL11 58 C1
Poplar Rd, Chester CH4 43 F2
Poplar Rd, Penycae LL14 64 A4
Poplar Rd, Rhostyllen LL14 59 G6
Poplar Rd, Wrexham LL13 5 C5
Poplar Row LL12 52 B4
Poppy Field Dr CH4 28 B3
Porch La LL12 48 A2
Portal Av LL13 61 E2
Porters Cft CH3 31 B6
Potters Way CH7 24 B3
Pountneys Cnr LL11 55 G2
Powell Rd, Buckley CH7 24 B4
Powell Rd, Wrexham LL12 5 D2
Powells Orch CH4 40 A6
Powys Cl, Buckley CH7 24 C1
Powys Cl, Deeside CH5 20 D1
Powys Ct*, King St CH1 4 A3
Poyser St LL13 5 A5
Precinct Way CH7 24 C4
Pren Av CH7 23 H4
Pren Hill CH7 24 A3
Prenton Pl CH4 4 D6
Prescot St CH2 40 C3
Preston Rd LL13 62 D2
Pretoria St CH4 4 C6
Prices La LL11 56 C6
Primrose Cl, Buckley CH7 18 D1
Primrose Cl, Chester CH3 45 E1
Primrose Hill CW6 46 D4
Primrose St CH5 13 E6
Primrose Way LL11 5 A1
Prince Charles Rd LL13 61 F4
Prince of Wales Av, Flint CH6 10 C2
Prince of Wales Av, Holywell CH8 7 C5
Prince of Wales Ct CH7 25 E3
Prince William Av CH5 21 G2
Prince William Ct CH5 20 A4
Prince William Gdns CH5 20 D4
Princes Av CH1 4 D3
Princes Cl LL11 56 C4
Princes Dr CH6 10 C4
Princes Rd LL14 64 D2
Princes St, Connahs Quay CH5 13 E6
Princes St, Flint CH6 10 C2
Princess Av, Buckley CH7 24 B3
Princess Av, Wrexham LL14 68 E4
Princess St, Chester CH1 4 A4
Princess St, Llangollen LL20 67 B4
Princess St, Wrexham LL13 5 A5
Priors Cl CH5 20 A1
Priory Cl, Chester CH1 40 A1
Priory Cl, Penyffordd CH4 28 B4
Priory Pl CH1 4 C4
Priory St LL13 5 C3
Private Walk CH3 40 D6
Promised Land Rd CH3 47 A4
Propect Cl CH5 20 A4
Prospect Dr LL11 54 B6
Prosser Rd CH2 36 A3
Provan Way CH1 34 D6
Pulford Ct CH4 52 F1
Pulford Rd CH1 35 E6
Pwll Glas CH7 22 B3
Pwll y Hwyaden CH6 10 D4
Pyecroft St CH4 40 B6

Quakers Way LL13 71 B5
Quarry Av CH3 71 C5
Quarry Brow LL12 51 F4
Quarry Cl, Buckley CH7 18 B1
Quarry Cl, Chester CH4 40 A6
Quarry Hill CH3 71 C4
Quarry La, Chester CH3 41 H6
Quarry La, Connahs Quay CH5 13 E7
Quarry La, Tarporley CW6 46 C6
Quarry Rd, Llangollen LL20 70 A2
Quarry Rd, Wrexham LL11 55 F3
Quay Wharf*, Fishermans Rd CH5 13 E6
Queen St, Cefn-mawr LL14 66 C1
Queen St, Chester CH1 4 C3
Queen St, Deeside CH5 20 D1
Queen St, Flint CH6 10 C2
Queen St, Leeswood CH7 30 B2
Queen St, Llangollen LL20 67 C5
Queen St, Rhosllanerchrugog LL14 64 D2
Queen St, Ruabon LL14 65 F6
Queen St, Treuddyn CH7 30 B6
Queen St, Wrexham LL11 5 C3
Queens Av, Chester CH1 4 D3
Queens Av, Connahs Quay CH5 13 C5
Queens Av, Flint CH6 10 D3
Queens Av, Sandycroft CH5 21 G3
Queens Cres CH2 36 C4
Queens Dr, Buckley CH7 24 B4
Queens Dr, Chester CH4 4 D5
Queens Ho CH1 4 D3
Queens La CH7 22 D5
Queens Park Ho CH4 4 C6
Queens Park Rd CH4 4 C6
Queens Park Vw CH4 4 C6
Queens Pk CH7 22 B4
Queens Pl, Chester CH1 4 C3
Queens Pl, Wrexham LL11 58 B1
Queens Rd, Chester CH1 4 D2
Queens Rd, Deeside CH5 15 E7
Queens Rd, Holywell CH8 6 C2
Queens Rd, Wrexham LL11 55 E1
Queens Sq, Rhosymedre LL14 66 E1
Queens Sq, Wrexham LL13 5 C4
Queensbury Dr CH6 10 A2
Queensferry By-Pass CH5 15 E8
Queensferry Ind Est CH5 21 E2
Queensway, Chester CH2 40 C1
Queensway, Connahs Quay CH5 13 F7
Queensway, Gwersyllt LL11 56 A1
Queensway, Hope LL12 48 C2
Queensway, Wrexham LL13 61 E3

Rackery La LL12 48 F3
Radcliffe Cl CH3 46 C1
Radford Cl CH5 13 F6
Radnor Cl CH5 20 D1
Radnor Dr CH4 43 G3
Raewood Av CH5 19 H6
Raikes La CH7 17 A5
Railway Rd, Brymbo LL11 54 D1
Railway Rd, Cefn-mawr LL14 66 D2
Railway Rd, Wrexham LL11 56 C6
Railway Ter, Connahs Quay CH5 13 D6
Railway Ter, Sandycroft CH5 21 G2
Rake La, Backford CH2 32 D6
Rake La, Christleton CH3 47 B1
Rake La, Deeside CH5 21 E6
Rake La, Eccleston CH4 44 A6
Rake Way CH1 34 A3
Ramsden Ct CH4 43 F4
Range Rd LL13 60 D5
Ranscombe Cres LL13 57 E4
Rawson Rd CH1 39 E3
Raymond St CH1 4 A2
Raynham Av LL12 51 F5
Rayon Rd CH8 6 D4
Rectors La CH5 21 E2
Rectory Cl, Chester CH3 71 C4
Rectory Cl, Flint CH6 20 C3
Rectory La CH5 20 C5
Red Rd CH7 24 B1
Red St CH8 9 A4
Redhall Av CH5 13 E7
Redhill Rd, Chester CH4 43 F2
Redhill Rd, Tarporley CW6 46 C5
Redland Cl, Chester CH4 43 G1
Redland Cl, Wrexham LL12 51 E5
Redwither Bsns Centre LL13 63 E3
Redwither La LL13 62 A5
Redwither Rd LL13 62 D4
Redwood Cl, Chester CH4 43 E2
Redwood Cl, Wrexham LL13 71 A5
Reece Cl CH2 31 A2
Reeves Rd CH3 41 E5
Regency Ct CH2 31 A3
Regent Cl LL11 56 A1
Regent St, Llangollen LL20 67 B5
Regent St, Wrexham LL11 5 A2
Regents Cl CH3 41 F3
Renfrew Cl LL11 55 H3
Reservoir Ter CH3 40 D4
Reynolds Rd CH6 8 D6
Rhodfa Cilcain CH7 22 A5
Rhodfa Ganol LL14 64 F2
Rhodfa Ger y Park CH5 13 B8
Rhodfa Kempton LL13 61 G5
Rhodfa Linden LL14 68 D3
Rhodfa Mynydd CH7 22 B5
Rhodfa Taunton LL13 61 G5
Rhodfa Wenlo CH8 6 B3
Rhodfar Bryn LL11 54 B6
Rhodfar Garn LL12 50 C3
Rhone Ct CH3 41 E6
Rhos Av CH4 28 A4
Rhos Berse Rd LL11 58 C3
Rhos Helyg CH7 30 B5
Rhos Rd CH4 28 A4
Rhosddu Ind Est LL11 56 B4
Rhosddu Rd LL11 5 C1
Rhoslan CH8 7 C5
Rhosllanerchrugog Rd LL13 70 H5
Rhosnesni La LL13 57 E6
Rhosrhedyn LL11 55 F5
Rhosrobin Rd LL11 56 B3
Rhoswen CH6 10 D4
Rhuddlan Ct CH4 43 F1
Rhuddlan Rd, Buckley CH7 24 D1
Rhuddlan Rd, Chester CH1 38 D2
Rhyd Broughton La LL11 60 A2
Rhyddyn Hill LL12 48 C3
Rhydymwyn Rd CH7 11 B1
Richard Heights*, Earl St CH6 10 C2
Richards Cft CH3 41 E6
Richmond Cres CH3 41 F4
Richmond Ct CH3 40 D4
Richmond Gdns LL14 68 E3
Richmond Mews*, Hoole La CH2 35 H4
Richmond Pl*, Hoole La CH2 35 H4
Richmond Rd, Connahs Quay CH5 13 E8
Richmond Rd, Wrexham LL12 56 D4
Ridgehill Dr CH6 8 A4
Ridges La CH3 45 F4
Ridgeway Av LL12 51 G4
Ridgeway Cl CH5 13 C8
Ridley Vw LL13 61 G2
Ridley Wood Cl LL13 60 D6
Ridleywood La LL13 63 F2
Ringway CH3 47 C4
River Cl LL13 61 F5
River La, Chester CH4 40 A6
River La, Farndon CH3 71 B4
River La, Saltney CH4 38 D6
River Vw CH5 13 C6
Riverbank CH8 7 E5
Riverdale LL13 61 G5
Riverleigh Ct LL12 48 C1
Riverside Bsns Park LL12 49 D7
Riverside Ct CH7 30 C1
Riverside Ind Pk CH4 43 F1
Riverside Pk CH5 15 F7
Riversmead CH3 44 D2
Rivulet Rd LL13 5 D5
Roberts Cft LL12 48 B3
Roberts La LL14 64 C2
Roberts Rd LL11 55 F4
Robinsons Cft CH3 41 F6
Rock Cotts CH5 13 C5
Rock Hill LL14 66 D1

Rock La, Caer Estyn LL12 48 D3
Rock La, Caergwrle LL12 48 A2
Rock La, Cefn-mawr LL14 66 D1
Rock La, Chester CH1 4 A1
Rock Pl, Cefn-mawr LL14 66 D1
Rock Pl, Coedpoeth LL11 58 B2
Rock Rd LL14 66 E1
Rockcliffe CH7 23 G2
Rockwood Rd LL11 55 F5
Rodens Cl LL12 52 E4
Roebourne Rise CH1 38 D2
Roft Cl LL11 55 H4
Rogers La LL11 55 H3
Roman Dr CH1 35 E5
Roman Way CH7 24 C4
Romans Way CH6 8 C6
Rose Grange LL11 55 F6
Rose Gro LL13 61 F1
Rose Hill, Holywell CH8 7 B6
Rose Hill, Wrexham LL11 55 G5
Rose La CH7 23 G4
Rose Mount CH7 25 E4
Rosedene Cl CH2 36 C3
Roselands Ct LL12 52 E2
Rosemary Cl CH4 27 G4
Rosemary Cres LL14 59 H5
Rosemary La LL12 52 A3
Rosemere Dr CH1 32 A2
Roseneath Vw CH6 8 A4
Roseway LL12 52 A4
Rosewood LL11 55 G5
Rosewood Av, Chester CH2 36 B6
Rosewood Av, Wrexham LL13 61 F2
Rosewood Gro, Buckley CH7 25 F3
Rosewood Gro, Chester CH1 34 B3
Rossett Bsns Village LL12 52 D2
Rossett Pk LL12 52 E2
Rossett Way LL12 56 D3
Rossie Av LL14 64 F3
Rosslyn Cl CH5 21 F4
Rosslyn Rd CH3 41 F2
Rothesay Cl LL11 56 C6
Rothesay Rd CH4 39 G6
Roughlyn Cres CH4 43 E6
Round Hill Mdw CH3 41 F6
Roundel Cl LL13 57 G5
Rowan Cl CH7 25 E3
Rowan Gro CH5 13 C5
Rowan Pk CH3 41 H6
Rowan Pl CH2 41 F1
Rowan Rd CH5 20 A3
Rowcliffe Av CH4 43 G3
Rowden Cres CH5 13 F7
Rowden St CH5 15 A7
Rowen Cl LL12 50 B3
Rowlands Heights CH1 4 D2
Rowlands Rd LL11 55 F3
Rowleys Dr CH5 15 B8
Rowleys Pk Ind Est CH5 15 B8
Rowton Bridge Rd CH3 47 A2
Rowton La CH3 47 A3
Royal Ct, Connahs Quay CH5 13 E6
Royal Ct, Wrexham LL11 55 H3
Royal Dr CH6 10 A2
Royton Cl LL13 60 D6
Ruabon Rd, Ruabon LL14 64 E3
Ruabon Rd, Wrexham LL13 5 A6
Rubery Way LL13 61 E4
Rue St Gregoire CH8 7 B6
Rufus Ct CH1 4 B3
Rumney Cl CH5 19 E1
Rushfield Rd CH4 43 H2
Rushton Dr CH2 36 C5
Russell Gro LL12 61 E1
Russell St, Chester CH3 4 D3
Russell St, Wrexham LL14 66 D1
Ruthin Rd, Bwlchgwyn LL11 53 A2
Ruthin Rd, Gwernymynydd CH7 11 A6
Ruthin Rd, Mold CH7 22 A6
Ruthin Rd, Wrexham LL13 5 A4
Rutland Ct CH5 13 D7
Rutland Pl CH2 40 D1
Rutland Rd LL13 61 E4
Rydal Ct LL13 61 F1
Rydal Dr CH7 24 D2
Rydal Gro CH4 43 G2
Ryder Cl LL13 57 G6
Ryeland St CH5 15 A7

Saighton La CH3 47 A6
St Albans Heights LL11 54 D5
St Albans Rd LL11 54 D5
St Albans Vw LL11 54 D4
St Andrews Cl CH5 20 B5
St Andrews Cres LL13 57 G6
St Andrews Dr CH7 24 A2
St Andrews Walk CH2 31 B2
St Anne St CH1 4 B2
St Bridgets Ct CH4 43 H2
St Catherines Cl CH6 10 C2
St Chads Rd CH1 39 F1
St Christophers Cl CH2 36 A4
St Cynfarchs Av LL12 48 C1
St Davids Cl, Buckley CH7 24 A2
St Davids Cl, Deeside CH5 19 H3
St Davids Cl, Flint CH6 10 C4
St Davids Cres, Llay LL12 50 B5
St Davids Cres, Wrexham LL13 61 E2
St Davids Ct LL13 61 F1
St Davids Dr, Connahs Quay CH5 13 D6
St Davids Dr, Ellesmere Port CH66 32 A2
St Davids Dr, Shotton CH5 15 A8
St Davids La CH7 22 D3
St Davids Pk CH5 19 G5
St Davids Retail Pk CH4 43 E1
St Davids Ter CH4 42 C1
St Ethelwolds St CH5 20 B1
St Georges Av CH66 32 A1
St Georges Cres, Chester CH4 4 D5
St Georges Cres, Waverton CH3 47 B4
St Georges Cres, Wrexham LL13 5 D3
St Giles Cres LL13 61 E2
St Giles Way LL13 5 C4
St Ives Pk CH5 21 G2
St James Av CH2 36 D5
St James Cl CH5 20 B5
St James Ct, Connahs Quay CH5 13 C5
St James Ct, Wrexham LL11 60 C1
St James Ct*, Vicarage Rd CH2 40 D2
St James St CH1 4 C2
St John St CH1 4 C4
St Johns Cl, Buckley CH7 24 C2
St Johns Cl, Chester CH4 28 C1
St Johns Cl, Deeside CH5 20 B5
St Johns Ct CH1 4 C4
St Johns Rd, Chester CH4 4 D6
St Johns Rd, Wrexham LL13 61 E4
St Johns Rear Rd CH4 4 D6
St Johns Way*, Fishermans Rd CH5 13 E6
St Margaret Way LL12 56 D6
St Marks Av CH5 13 C6
St Marks Cres CH66 32 A2
St Marks Rd, Chester CH4 43 F2
St Marks Rd, Wrexham LL11 5 B3
St Martins Mws LL12 50 B3
St Martins Way CH1 4 A3
St Marys Cl, Buckley CH7 18 C1
St Marys Cl, Wrexham LL14 69 D6
St Marys Dr CH7 18 C1
St Marys Hill CH1 4 B5
St Marys Way CH4 27 F3
St Mellion Cres LL13 57 H6
St Mellors Rd CH7 24 A2
St Michaels Cl LL14 65 F6
St Michaels Row CH1 4 B4
St Olave Ct CH1 4 B5
St Olave St CH1 4 B5
St Oswalds Way CH1 4 B2
St Pauls Cl CH5 20 B5
St Peters Pk CH7 17 B2
St Peters Way CH2 31 B2
St Thomas Pathway CH1 4 C3
St Werburgh St CH1 4 B4
Salem Rd LL11 58 B1
Salerno Rd CH2 35 H3
Salisbury Av CH4 43 E1
Salisbury Cl, Ellesmere Port CH66 32 A1
Salisbury Cl, Wrexham LL13 5 C5
Salisbury Rd LL13 5 C5
Salisbury St, Chester CH1 39 H2
Salisbury St, Deeside CH5 15 A7
Salisbury St, Flint CH6 10 C1
Salop Rd LL13 5 D5
Salters La CH2 37 F3
Saltney Ferry Rd CH4 42 B1
Samuel St CH1 4 C3
Sandileigh CH2 40 C2
Sandon Rd CH2 40 B1
Sandown Cl LL13 70 C4
Sandown Ct CH5 20 A1
Sandown Rd, Deeside CH5 20 A1
Sandown Rd, Wrexham LL13 70 C5
Sandown Ter CH3 40 C4
Sandpiper Ct CH4 43 H5
Sandpiper Way CH4 43 H5
Sandringham Av CH3 41 E3
Sandringham Cl LL14 59 G5
Sandringham Rd LL11 56 C5
Sandrock Rd, Chester CH3 47 A2
Sandrock Rd, Wrexham LL12 51 F5
Sandway Rd LL11 56 C6
Sandy Gro CH7 22 B6
Sandy La, Bagillt CH6 8 A4
Sandy La, Chester CH3 40 D6
Sandy La, Deeside CH5 15 E6
Sandy La, Higher Kinnerton CH4 29 G6
Sandy La, Huntington CH3 45 E3
Sandy La, Saltney CH4 42 D2
Sandy La, Wrexham LL12 51 F5
Sandy Way, Connahs Quay CH5 13 B7
Sandy Way, Ewloe CH5 20 A5
Sandy Way, Wrexham LL13 57 H6
Sandycroft Ind Est CH5 21 F2
Sarah Ct CH1 4 C2
Sarl Williams Ct CH1 4 B2
Sarn La LL12 48 B2
Saughall Hey CH1 34 B2
Saughall Rd, Blacon CH1 34 D6
Saughall Rd, Chester CH1 39 H2
Savage St LL14 64 D1
Saxon Rd LL11 55 H3
Saxon St LL13 5 D6
Saxon Way, Chester CH1 35 E6
Saxon Way, Ellesmere Port CH66 32 A1
Scholars Cl CH4 43 E1
School Hill LL12 50 D5
School La, Brynteg LL11 55 F6
School La, Coedpoeth LL11 58 B1
School La, Guilden Sutton CH3 31 A5
School La, Holywell CH8 6 B2
School La, Mickle Trafford CH2 31 A2
School La, Ponciau LL14 64 D1
School Mws, Bangor-on-Dee LL13 70 C4
School Mws, Rhostyllen LL14 59 G6
School Rd, Llay LL12 50 A3
School Rd, Rhosllanerchrugog LL14 64 C2
School St, Chester CH2 40 C2
School St, Rhosllanerchrugog LL14 64 C2
School St, Rhostyllen LL14 59 G6
Scilly Cl CH65 32 D1
Scotch Row CH5 20 D4
Scotts Cl LL13 71 C2
Scotts Rd CH5 20 D4
Sea Hill Rd CH1 34 A3
Sealand Av, Deeside CH5 15 E6
Sealand Av, Holywell CH8 7 D6
Sealand Ind Est CH1 39 F4
Sealand Rd, Chester CH1 34 A6
Sealand Rd, Deeside CH5 16 B5
Seathwaite Way CH5 13 C7
Seaville St CH3 4 D3
Sebring Av CH7 18 D2
Second Av, Deeside CH5 16 A1
Second Av, Flint CH6 10 C3
Second Av, Gwersyllt LL11 55 H3
Second Av, Llay LL12 50 A3
Second Av, Wrexham Ind Est LL13 63 E3
Sedgefield Cl LL13 61 G5
Sedgefield Rd CH1 39 H3
Sedum Cl CH3 45 E2
Sefton Rd CH2 40 D1
Selkirk Dr CH4 43 G1
Selkirk Rd CH4 39 G6
Seller St CH1 4 D3
Selsdon Cl CH7 24 B3
Selsdon Ct CH4 44 A1
Sens Cl CH1 4 A3
Sevenacre Cl CH6 8 C6
Seventh Av LL12 50 B4
Sgwar y Capel CH5 13 E6
Shaftesbury Av CH3 41 F3
Shaftesbury Dr CH6 10 A2
Shaftsbury Av LL11 56 A4
Shakespeare Av CH5 19 G6
Shannon Cl CH4 43 E3
Shavington Av CH2 40 D2
Shaw Cl CH5 19 G6
Sheaf Cl CH3 46 C2
Shed La CH3 41 E4
Sheldon Av CH3 41 F4
Shelley Cl CH5 19 G6
Shelley Rd CH1 35 E5
Shepherds La, Chester CH2 40 B1
Shepherds La, Wrexham LL14 69 E6
Sheraton Rd CH3 47 C4
Sherbourne Av, Chester CH4 43 H3
Sherbourne Av, Wrexham LL11 56 A2
Sheridan Av CH5 19 G5
Sheringham Cl CH4 43 E3
Sherwell Av LL13 57 E3
Sherwood Rd CH1 35 E6
Shields Ct LL13 61 E5
Shipbrook Rd CH2 36 C5
Shipgate St CH1 4 B5
Shire Vw CH7 22 C3
Shocklach Rd CH2 36 C6
Shones La LL12 50 A4
Shordley Cl LL12 52 E4
Short La LL14 66 E3
Shot Tower Cl CH3 4 D3
Shotton La CH5 15 A8
Shotwick Rd CH5 14 D2
Shrewsbury Way CH4 43 F1
Sibbersfield La CH3 71 D4
Sibell St CH1 4 D2
Siddeley Cl CH4 27 G4
Sidney Hall Ct CH5 19 F1
Signal Ct CH2 40 D3
Silver Birch Cft CH4 27 E5
Silver Birch Way CH4 28 B3
Silverbirch Dr LL12 51 F5
Silverbirch Way CH66 32 B2
Silverdale Av CH7 25 F2
Silvermuir CH1 39 E3
Simonstone Rd CH4 27 G3
Simpson Cl CH2 36 A3
Simpson Rd CH2 36 A3
Simpsons Way CH4 27 F4
Sixth Av, Deeside CH5 14 D4
Sixth Av, Flint CH6 10 C4
Sixth Av, Wrexham LL12 50 B4
Skips La CH3 47 A2
Slack Rd CH5 25 H2
Sliverstone Dr CH7 23 H4
Smelt La LL11 54 A6
Smelt Rd LL11 54 A6
Smith St LL14 64 C2
Smithfield Dr LL13 71 A6
Smithfield Grn LL13 71 B6
Smithfield Rd LL13 5 D4
Smithfield St LL13 71 B6
Smithy Cl CH1 34 A3
Smithy La, Ewloe CH7 19 E5
Smithy La, Northop Hall CH7 18 B1
Smithy La, Wrexham LL12 56 D3
Smithy Pathway CH4 43 F4
Smithy Rd LL11 55 E6
Snowdon Av, Connahs Quay CH5 13 C7
Snowdon Av, Mold CH7 23 G2
Snowdon Cres CH4 43 G3
Snowdon Dr, Johnstown LL14 64 F3
Snowdon Dr, Wrexham LL11 56 C4
Somerford Rd CH4 27 G4
Somerset Rd CH2 36 D6
Somerset St CH1 4 C2
Somerville Cl CH7 24 B4
Sontley Rd LL13 5 B6
Sorrel Cl CH3 45 E1
Souters La CH1 4 C4
South Av CH2 4 D1
South Bank CH1 40 A1
South Crescent Rd CH4 4 D5
South Green CH5 16 B6
South La, Buckley CH7 24 B3
South La, Wrexham LL14 64 D1
South St CH3 40 D4
South View Rd CH1 4 A3
South Vw, Buckley CH7 24 C4
South Vw, Chester CH4 40 B6
South Vw, Chirk LL14 68 D4
South Vw, Gresford LL12 51 E6
South Vw, Pandy LL11 56 C3
South Way CH1 39 F1
Southfields Cl CH7 24 B3

Southleigh Dr LL11 56 C5
Southsea Ind Est LL11 55 E5
Southsea Rd LL11 55 F6
Southsea Ter CH3 41 F5
Sovereign Way CH1 39 E3
Sparks Cl CH3 45 F1
Spectrum Bsns Pk LL13 62 D5
Speeds Way CH3 71 B4
Speedwell Cl CH3 45 E2
Spencer Cl CH5 19 G6
Spencer Ind Est CH7 25 E1
Spinney Walk LL14 65 E7
Spital Walk CH3 40 D4
Spon Grn CH7 24 D4
Spring Gdns LL11 5 B1
Spring Rd, Rhostyllen LL11 59 G6
Spring Rd, Wrexham LL11 60 C1
Spring Rise CW6 46 C6
Spring St CH5 13 F7
Springdale CH5 19 H5
Springfield CH5 20 C6
Springfield Cl, Chester CH4 29 H4
Springfield Cl, Connahs Quay CH5 13 B7
Springfield Ct, Chester CH4 29 G3
Springfield Ct, Wrexham LL12 51 E5
Springfield Dr, Buckley CH7 24 A3
Springfield Dr, Chester CH2 40 C2
Springfield La LL12 50 D5
Springfields, Chester CH2 31 A3
Springfields, Holywell CH8 8 D2
Springwood Cl CH1 38 C2
Squirrel La CH2 33 E5
Stablegates LL14 64 F2
Stabler Cres LL11 56 C4
Stables Rd LL11 55 F1
Stadium Ind Est CH1 39 G2
Stadium Way CH1 39 G3
Stafford Rd CH5 15 F7
Stainton Gro CH5 13 C6
Stamford Ct CH3 41 G4
Stamford La CH3 47 B1
Stamford Rd CH1 35 E6
Stamford Way, Deeside CH5 19 E2
Stamford Way, Holywell CH8 7 C8
Stancliffe Av LL12 51 G5
Stanley Est CH7 24 A4
Stanley Gro LL14 65 F6
Stanley Park Ct CH4 43 E2
Stanley Park Dr CH4 43 E2
Stanley Pl, Chester CH1 4 A4
Stanley Pl, Deeside CH5 15 A8
Stanley Place Mews CH1 4 A4
Stanley Rd, Buckley CH7 24 A3
Stanley Rd, Wrexham LL14 64 E1
Stanley St, Chester CH1 4 A4
Stanley St, Mold CH7 22 C5
Stanley St, Wrexham LL11 60 D4
Stanney Woods Av CH65 32 D1
Stansty Chain Rd LL11 56 A4
Stansty Cl LL11 56 B6
Stansty Dr LL11 56 B6
Stansty Lodge Rd LL11 56 A5
Stansty Rd LL11 56 B5
Starling Cl CH3 71 D4
Station App LL11 5 B1
Station Av LL14 69 C6
Station Ct LL11 56 A2
Station Dr CH2 36 B6
Station La, Deeside CH5 20 B5
Station La, Guilden Sutton CH2 31 B3
Station La, Mickle Trafford CH2 31 A3
Station Rd, Backford CH1 35 F1
Station Rd, Bagillt CH6 8 B4
Station Rd, Bangor-on-Dee LL13 70 C4
Station Rd, Buckley CH7 25 F4
Station Rd, Chester CH1 4 D2
Station Rd, Chirk LL14 69 C6
Station Rd, Hawarden CH5 20 C5
Station Rd, Holywell CH8 6 D2
Station Rd, Llangollen LL20 66 B1
Station Rd, Marchwiel LL13 71 C2
Station Rd, Pentre Broughton LL11 55 E2
Station Rd, Queensferry CH5 15 D8
Station Rd, Rhostyllen LL14 59 G5
Station Rd, Rossett LL12 52 C4
Station Rd, Ruabon LL14 65 E7
Station Rd, Sandycroft CH5 21 G4
Station Ter LL14 65 F7
Station Ter*, Station Rd CH5 21 G4
Station Vw CH2 40 D4
Steam Cl LL11 54 D2
Steam Mill St CH3 4 D3
Steam Mull St CH3 40 C4
Stearns Cl CH1 35 G6
Steel Cl LL11 54 D2
Steele St CH1 4 C5
Stephens La*, School Rd LL14 64 C2
Steven Ct CH3 4 D3
Steven Gray Rd CH7 22 D6
Stile End CH2 31 B2
Stirling Av LL11 56 C5
Stirling Cl CH3 41 E3
Stocks Av CH3 41 E5
Stocks La CH3 41 E5
Stockwell Gro LL13 60 D5
Stone Cft CH3 41 E6
Stone Pl CH2 40 C2
Stone Row*, Cable St CH5 13 E6
Stoneleigh Cl CH5 15 F7
Stonewalls LL12 52 B3
Straight Mile LL12 50 B2
Strand Cres CH8 7 B5
Strand La CH8 7 B5
Strand Pk CH8 7 B6
Strand Walk CH8 7 B6
Stratford Cl LL12 57 E6
Stratford Rd CH1 39 E2
Strawberry Dr CH1 32 C1
Strawberry Flds CH3 41 F6
Strawberry Grn CH1 32 C1
Stretton Cl LL13 60 D6
Strickland St CH5 15 A8
Stryd Fawr CH7 22 C4
Stryd Gaer CH7 22 C4
Stryd Henardd CH7 22 C5
Stryd Newydd CH7 22 B4
Stryd Wrecsam CH7 22 C4
Stryt Isa, Chester CH4 28 A5
Stryt Isa, Wrexham LL14 64 B3
Stryt Las LL14 64 D3
Stryt Maelor LL11 53 D1
Stryt y Bydden LL11 59 G1
Stryt y Scwelar LL11 58 A2
Stuart Cl CH3 41 F2
Stuart Pl CH1 4 C2
Stuart St LL13 5 D6
Stuart Way LL13 5 D6
Stubbs Pl CH1 39 E2
Sullivans Rise*, Fishermans Rd CH5 13 E6
Summerdale Rd CH5 20 A2
Summerfield Cl CH4 27 E5
Summerfield Rd CH3 31 A6
Summerfields LL14 59 H5
Summerhill Rd LL11 55 G3
Summerville Cl CH5 13 D6
Sumner Rd CH1 39 E1
Sumpter Pathway CH2 40 D2
Sun La LL13 63 G6
Sunbury Cres CH4 43 F2
Sundawn Av CH8 7 C6
Sunhill Dr LL12 48 C3
Sunningdale CH7 24 A2
Sunningdale Cl LL13 57 G6
Sunny Vw LL11 55 H2
Sunnyacre LL11 56 A3
Sunnyhill LL11 55 G5
Sunnyridge Av LL12 51 G4
Sunnyridge Rd CH7 22 B2
Sunnyside CH5 20 D3
Sunnyside Cl CH6 7 F5
Surrey Rd CH2 36 D6
Sussex Gdns LL11 56 D4
Sussex Rd CH2 40 D1
Sussex Way CH2 40 D1
Sutherland Way CH3 41 F2
Sutton Cl, Chester CH2 31 B3
Sutton Cl, Connahs Quay CH5 13 C8
Sutton Dr, Chester CH2 36 B6
Sutton Dr, Wrexham LL13 61 G1
Swain Av CH7 24 D4
Swallow Dr CW6 46 C5
Swan La CH7 11 D6
Swan St LL14 64 C1
Swinchiard Walk CH6 10 B2
Swinleys Hey CH3 41 E6
Swn y Gwynt CH6 10 D4
Swn y Nant CH7 22 B5
Sycamore Av CH5 13 D7
Sycamore Cl CH5 19 H6
Sycamore Dr, Chester CH4 43 F3
Sycamore Dr, Chirk LL14 68 E3
Sycamore Dr, Gresford LL12 51 F5
Sycamore Dr, Leeswood CH7 30 B1
Sycamore Gro CH4 27 F5
Sycamore Rd LL13 61 F2
Sydney St CH1 39 H3
Sydney Walk CH6 10 C2
Sylester Ct LL13 61 E5
Sylvan Mews CH1 35 E6

Tabernacle St CH7 24 B3
Tabor Hill LL11 58 B1
Tai Chapel*, Summerhill Rd LL11 55 G3
Tai Nestig CH7 11 B2
Talbot Ct LL13 5 C6
Talbot Rd LL13 5 C6
Talbot St CH1 4 C1
Talfryn Cl CH5 13 C5
Talgarreg Dr CH5 19 E1
Taliesin LL13 71 B1
Taliesin Av CH5 13 F8
Talwrn Rd LL11 54 A6
Tan Llan La LL11 58 D1
Tan y Bryn, Buckley CH7 24 B2
Tan y Bryn, Holywell CH8 6 C2
Tan y Bryn, Rhosllanerchrugog LL14 64 D3
Tan y Bryn, Soughton CH7 17 B5
Tan y Bryn, Wrexham LL13 61 F3
Tan y Clawdd LL14 64 F2
Tan y Coed, Holywell CH8 8 B2
Tan y Coed, Johnstown LL14 64 F1
Tan y Coed, Llangollen LL20 67 C6
Tan y Coed, Mold CH7 22 B5
Tan y Coed, Soughton CH7 17 B6
Tan y Coed, Wrexham LL13 61 G5
Tan y Craig CH7 22 A4
Tan y Ddol LL20 67 A4
Tan y Felin CH8 6 B3
Tan y Hafod CH7 11 A2
Tan yr Allt LL12 49 C7
Tan yr Ysgol CH7 17 B5
Tanat Way LL13 61 G3
Tanydre LL13 61 F1
Tanyfron Rd LL11 54 C5
Tanylan LL14 65 F7
Tapley Av LL12 57 F5
Tarporley Rd CH3 46 C2
Tarrant Ct CH1 35 F3
Tarvin Rd, Chester CH3 40 D4
Tarvin Rd, Christleton CH3 41 H3
Tatham Rd LL14 65 E6
Tatton Cl CH4 43 E3
Taunton Cl LL13 5 B5
Taylors Vw CH5 20 A1
Taynton CH5 13 B7
Teak Ct CH5 13 D7
Tecwyn Dr CH5 13 C5
Tegan LL14 64 F2
Tegfan Ct*, High St LL12 48 B3
Tegid LL14 65 C8
Tegid Dr LL11 55 G6
Tegid Way CH4 42 D3
Telford Av, Llangollen LL20 66 B2
Telford Av, Wrexham LL14 69 D8
Telford Way CH4 43 F1
Temperance Rd LL11 55 E5
Temple Row LL13 5 C4
Tennyson Ct CH5 19 G6
Tennyson Walk*, Shelley Rd CH2 35 G6
Tenters La LL13 5 B4
Tenters Sq LL13 5 B4
Tenth Av LL12 50 B4
Terrace La CH4 28 C3
Terrig Cres CH7 24 C4
Terrig St CH5 20 B1
Terrig Way LL11 55 H4
Tewkesbury Cl, Chester CH2 36 D5
Tewkesbury Cl, Ellesmere Port CH66 32 A2
Thackeray Dr CH3 41 F3
Thackeray Twrs CH1 4 D3
The Acorns CH2 36 C4
The Anchorage CH3 47 C4
The Avenue CH5 20 C5
The Barnyard CH5 20 B3
The Bars CH1 4 D3
The Beeches, Chester CH2 36 D5
The Beeches, Deeside CH5 25 F1
The Beeches, Holywell CH8 7 B8
The Beeches, Hope LL12 48 C1
The Beeches, Wrexham LL12 56 D6
The Beechlands LL12 57 E6
The Belvedere LL11 53 D1
The Birches CH4 27 F5
The Borders CH4 42 D1
The Boulevard CH4 27 G4
The Brackens CH7 24 B4
The Brambles, Deeside CH5 15 A8
The Brambles, Wrexham LL11 55 G6
The Bridgeway Centre LL13 62 C4
The Bruen CH3 46 C1
The Bryn CH6 10 B3
The Bye Pass CH3 41 H4
The Cedars CH7 23 H4
The Channel CH2 32 D5
The Chase CH4 29 G3
The Close, Blacon CH1 38 D2
The Close, Deeside CH5 20 A4
The Close, Holywell CH8 6 C3
The Close, Mold CH7 22 B6
The Close, Saughall CH1 34 B3
The Cobbles CH4 44 A1
The Conifers LL12 51 E5
The Coppergate CH5 20 C5
The Coppice CH5 19 H4
The Copse, Deeside CH5 19 H6
The Copse, Wrexham LL12 52 C4
The Courtyard CH2 36 D5
The Crescent CH2 40 B1
The Croft CH2 36 B6
The Crofts CH3 71 C5
The Cross, Chester CH1 4 B4
The Cross, Wrexham LL13 71 B5
The Dale Barracks CH2 36 A3
The Dell, Chester CH3 31 A6
The Dell, Tarporley CW6 46 C6
The Elms, Chester CH2 36 D5
The Elms, Deeside CH5 19 H6
The Firs CH7 22 D6
The Forge CH4 28 B2
The Forum CH1 4 B4
The Furrows CH66 32 A1
The Glen, Chester CH1 39 E1
The Glen, Wrexham LL13 71 B2
The Green, Mold CH4 29 H3
The Green, Wrexham LL12 56 D4
The Grosvenor Precinct CH1 4 B4
The Grove CH7 18 B1
The Grove*, Bridge St CH5 15 A7
The Groves, Chester CH1 4 C5
The Groves, Ellesmere Port CH66 32 B1
The Groves, Wrexham LL13 71 C2
The Haven LL14 64 E1
The Hawthorns LL12 57 E6
The Headlands CH1 4 D4
The Hedgerows CH5 19 H5
The Heywoods CH2 40 A2
The Highcroft CH5 13 B7
The Highway CH5 20 A4
The Holkham CH3 41 E4
The Hollies CH7 24 C2
The Homestead LL14 60 A4
The Hopyards CW6 46 C6
The Larches CH5 25 F1
The Larches*, Park St LL14 64 E2
The Laurels LL12 57 E6
The Limes LL12 52 D4
The Links, Mold CH7 11 A2
The Links, Wrexham LL13 57 H5
The Meadows, Deeside CH5 20 A1
The Meadows, Flint CH6 10 B2
The Meadows, Gwersyllt LL11 56 A4
The Millyard LL12 52 E2
The Moorings CH3 47 A2
The Mount, Chester CH3 40 D4
The Mount, Gwernymynydd CH7 11 D6
The Mount, Holywell CH8 7 C8
The Mount, Wrexham LL12 61 E1
The Nook, Backford CH2 32 D5
The Nook, Chester CH2 40 B1
The Nook, Deeside CH5 20 D4
The Nook, Guilden Sutton CH3 41 G1
The Nook, Saltney CH4 43 E1
The Nurseries, Chirk LL14 69 E5
The Nurseries, Flint CH6 10 B4

The Nurseries,
Gresford LL12 51 E6
The Oaks,
Deeside CH5 25 F1
The Oaks,
Wrexham LL14 64 B3
The Oaks Dr CH2 36 A4
The Old Gdns LL13 61 G1
The Old Orchard
CH5 20 D6
The Orchards,
Chester CH4 43 E1
The Orchards,
Deeside CH5 19 E1
The Orchards,
Holt LL13 71 B5
The Orchards,
Rossett LL12 52 E3
The Orchards,
Wrexham LL13 61 F5
The Oval LL13 62 C5
The Paddock,
Chester CH4 39 H6
The Paddock,
Christleton CH3 41 H6
The Paddocks,
Deeside CH5 20 D3
The Paddocks,
Wrexham LL11 58 C1
The Parade CH1 35 E6
The Park CH3 47 A1
The Park CH7 22 B5
The Parks,
Connahs Quay CH5 13 B7
The Parks,
Wrexham LL11 54 D5
The Pavilions CH4 43 H5
The Pines,
Deeside CH5 19 H6
The Pines,
Wrexham LL12 56 D6
The Pinfold LL13 71 B5
The Poplars CH5 19 H6
The Pryors CH3 46 C1
The Quad CH1 39 E3
The Quadrant CH1 39 E3
The Rest LL14 66 E2
The Ridgeway,
Buckley CH7 18 B1
The Ridgeway,
Chester CH3 46 C1
The Ridgeway,
Deeside CH5 20 A4
The Ridgeway,
Holywell CH8 7 C8
The Ridgeway,
Wrexham LL13 71 C2
The Ridings CH1 34 B3
The Rookery CH4 27 F4
The Ropeworks CH1 39 H3
The Rowans CH4 27 E5
The Serpentine CH4 39 H6
The Small Woods
LL14 65 E7
The Spinney,
Gwynfryn LL11 53 D3
The Spinney,
Marford LL12 51 F2
The Square,
Chester CH1 4 D3
The Square,
Christleton CH3 41 H5
The Street CH2 37 F5
The Sycamores LL11 55 G2
The Triangle LL13 57 G5
The Vetches CH3 31 B6
The Waltons CH4 44 B2
The Warren CH4 26 A4
The Wharf CH1 39 H4
The Wiend CH2 40 B1
The Wigdale CH5 20 C6
The Willows LL12 56 D6
The Woodlands CH5 25 H4
The Wynd CW6 46 B6
The Yonne CH1 4 A3
Third Av,
Deeside CH5 16 A2
Third Av, Flint CH6 10 C3
Third Av,
Gwersyllt LL11 55 H3
Third Av, Llay LL12 50 A3
Thirlmere Ct LL11 56 A2
Thirlmere Rd CH2 40 D1
Thistledown Ct LL14 59 H5
Thomas Av CH5 19 G6
Thomas Brassey Cl
CH2 40 C3
Thomas Cl,
Chester CH1 35 F6
Thomas Cl,
Mickle Trafford CH2 31 B2
Thomas Ct LL13 61 E5
Thomas St CH6 10 C1
Thornberry Cl CH1 34 B3
Thornfield Av CH5 13 E7
Thornfields CH5 20 A1
Thornhill Cl CH4 26 D5
Thornhill Dr LL14 60 A4
Thornhurst Dr LL13 57 H6
Thornleigh LL13 61 G1
Thornleigh Dr LL12 51 F5
Thornton Dr CH2 36 B6
Threos Ct CH5 19 E1
Thursfield Ct CH1 39 H4
Thurston Rd CH4 43 E3
Tilers Cl CH7 24 B3
Timberfields Rd CH1 34 B3
Tintern Av CH2 36 D6
Tir Wat CH7 23 H4
Titian Cl CH5 13 B6
Tivaton Cl CH5 13 C8
Tiverton Cl CH2 36 C6
Toft Cl CH4 43 E3
Toll Bar Rd CH3 41 F5
Tollemache Ter CH2 40 D4
Tomkinson St CH2 4 D1
Toogood Cl CH2 31 A3
Top Rd LL11 55 G1
Totland Gro CH2 40 B1
Tower Cl LL13 63 E3
Tower Gdns*,
High St CH8 7 B6
Tower Rd,
Chester CH1 4 A3
Tower Rd,
Llangollen LL20 67 A3
Tower Vw LL13 61 F2
Tower Wharf CH1 4 A3
Towergate*,
Thursfield Ct CH1 39 H4
Towers Way CH4 28 B3
Town Hall Sq CH1 4 B3
Town Hill LL13 5 C4
Townfield Av CH3 71 B4
Townfield La,
Chester CH3 71 B4
Townfield La,
Miollington CH1 34 D1
Townfield La,
Tarvin CH3 46 B2
Townsend Av LL12 57 F5
Trafalgar Cl LL13 60 D4
Trafford St CH1 4 B2
Tram Rd CH7 24 C2
Tramway St CH1 4 D2
Trebor Av CH6 8 C6
Treborth Rd CH1 38 D2
Trefoil Cl CH3 45 E1
Tregele Cl CH1 38 D3
Trehowell Av LL14 69 C8
Trelawney Av CH6 10 D3
Trelawney Sq CH6 10 C2
Trelech Ct CH5 19 E1
Trem Afon CH7 23 G3
Trem Dolydd LL14 66 D2
Trem Eryri LL11 56 C5
Trem y Berwyn LL14 64 C4
Trem y Gardden
LL14 64 C4
Trem y Gwernant
LL20 67 C5
Trem y Mynydd LL11 53 F4
Trem y Nant LL11 55 F3
Trem yr Eglwys LL13 60 C5
Trem yr Ysgol LL20 67 C6
Tren y Nant LL13 60 C5
Trevalyn Hall Vw
LL12 52 E4
Trevalyn Way LL12 52 D4
Trevenna Way LL13 61 E2
Trevor Av LL14 59 H6
Trevor Rd,
Llangollen LL20 67 D4
Trevor Rd,
Wrexham LL14 69 D6
Trevor St LL13 5 C6
Treweryn Cl LL12 50 A4
Trident Way LL13 57 G5
Trinity Cl LL14 59 G6
Trinity Rd CH8 6 C3
Trinity St,
Chester CH1 4 A4
Trinity St,
Rhostyllen LL14 59 H6
Trinity St,
Wrexham LL11 5 C3
Trofryn LL14 64 C4
Troon Cl LL13 57 G6
Tros yr Aber CH8 6 B3
Truemans Ct CH5 20 C5
Truemans Way CH5 20 C5
Trum yr Hydref CH7 18 C1
Tryweryn Pl LL13 61 G3
Tudor Av, Flint CH6 10 C4
Tudor Av,
Gwersyllt LL11 56 A2
Tudor Av,
Rhostyllen LL14 59 G6
Tudor Cl,
Buckley CH7 18 B1
Tudor Cl,
Deeside CH5 20 B1
Tudor Cl,
Ellesmere Port
CH66 32 A1
Tudor Ct, Hope LL12 48 B1
Tudor Ct,
Johnstown LL14 64 F2
Tudor Grn CH1 35 E6
Tudor Rd LL13 60 D5
Tudor St LL11 58 B1
Tudor Way CH3 45 E1
Turnberry Av LL13 57 H6
Turner Cl LL13 57 G6
Turnpike La LL12 51 F4
Tuscan Way CH5 13 D6
Tushingham Cl CH3 45 E1
Tuttle St LL13 5 C4
Twain Cl CH5 19 G6
Tweedsmuir CH3 41 E3
Ty Cerrig Dr LL12 48 B3
Ty Gwyn La LL11 56 C4
Ty Newydd Ct LL14 65 F7
Ty Wesley*,
Ausralia St LL14 64 D1
Tyddyn Messham
CH6 8 C6
Tyddyn St CH7 22 C4
Tyn Dwr Rd LL20 67 D5
Tyn Twll La CH6 7 E7
Tyn y Celyn Dr LL20 67 D5
Tyn y Plas*, Hall St
LL20 67 A5

Ullswater Cres CH2 36 D6
Ullswater Rd CH7 24 D2
Union Hall Bldgs CH1 4 C4
Union Rd LL13 5 A2
Union St CH1 4 D4
Union Ter CH1 4 C3
Union Walk CH1 4 C3
Unity Pl CH1 4 B5
Uplands Av CH5 13 C8
Upper Aston Hall La
CH5 20 A4
Upper Bryn Coch
CH7 22 B6
Upper Bryn Coch La
CH7 22 A6
Upper Cambrian Rd
CH1 39 H3
Upper Northgate St
CH1 4 B2
Upper River Bank
CH8 6 E4
Upton Dr CH2 36 A5
Upton La CH2 36 A4
Upton Pk CH2 36 B5
Uwch y Dre CH7 11 D5
Uwch y Nant CH7 23 F3

Vale Av CH5 25 F1
Vale Cl CH4 27 G4
Vale Dr CH7 23 F3
Vale Vw,
Brynteg LL11 55 F5
Vale Vw, Llay LL12 50 B5
Valley Dr CH2 36 A6
Valley Way LL13 60 D5
Vaughan Way CH5 19 F1
Vaughans La CH3 41 E6
Vauxhall
Ind Est LL14 **64 F4**
Venables Rd CH1 39 F1
Vermeer Cl CH5 13 B5
Vernay Gdns CH4 43 H2
Vernon Cl CH1 34 A3
Vernon Rd CH1 39 H4
Vernon St LL11 5 B2
Vicarage Cl,
Chester CH3 31 B6
Vicarage Cl,
Wrexham LL11 55 G2
Vicarage Ct LL13 71 B5
Vicarage Dr CH6 8 B6
Vicarage Hill,
Minera LL11 53 F4
Vicarage Hill,
Rhostyllen LL14 59 G6
Vicarage Hill,
Wrexham LL13 5 C4
Vicarage La LL12 51 E6
Vicarage Rd,
Bagillt CH6 8 B5
Vicarage Rd,
Chester CH2 40 D2
Vicarage Rd,
Llangollen LL20 67 B5
Vicars Cross Ct CH3 41 F4
Vicars Cross Rd CH3 41 F4
Vicars La CH1 4 C4
Vickers Cl CH5 20 C3
Victoria Av,
Buckley CH7 24 C3
Victoria Av,
Wrexham LL14 64 E2
Victoria Cres,
Chester CH2 4 B1
Victoria Cres,
Deeside CH5 15 A7
Victoria Cres,
Queens Park CH4 4 D5
Victoria Ct CH2 4 B1
Victoria Pathway CH4 4 D6
Victoria Pk CH8 7 E5
Victoria Pl CH1 4 C3
Victoria Rd,
Bagillt CH6 7 F5
Victoria Rd,
Brynteg LL11 55 F5
Victoria Rd,
Buckley CH7 24 C3
Victoria Rd,
Chester CH2 4 B2
Victoria Rd,
Coedpoeth LL11 58 B1
Victoria Rd,
Deeside CH5 15 A7
Victoria Rd,
Mold CH7 22 C4
Victoria Rd,
Saltney CH4 43 E1
Victoria Rd,
Wrexham LL13 5 A5
Victoria St LL14 64 D2
Victoria Ter CH7 22 D3
Victory Ct CH7 22 D5
Victory Pl LL12 50 B4
Viking Cl LL11 55 H3
Viking Way CH5 13 C6
Villa Rd CH5 16 B5
Village Ct LL11 56 D5
Village Mdw LL14 65 F7
Village Rd CH3 41 H6
Village Walks LL12 51 G3
Villiers St LL13 5 A4
Vincent Dr CH4 43 H2
Vincent St LL14 65 F6
Vine Rd CH66 32 A1
Vinegar Hill LL14 64 D1
Virginia Dr CH1 38 C1
Volunteer St CH1 4 C5
Vounog Hill CH4 28 B3
Vownog CH7 17 B4
Vownog Newydd
CH7 17 B5
Vron Cl LL11 54 D2
Vyrnwy Cl LL11 55 H4
Vyrnwy Rd CH4 42 D2
Vyrnwy Way LL13 61 G3

Waen Rd LL11 54 B6
Walden Cres LL14 69 E5
Walker Cl LL13 57 G6
Walker St CH2 40 C3
Walkers La,
Farndon CH3 71 C4
Walkers La,
Rhosllanerchrugog
LL14 64 D1
Walls Av CH1 39 H4
Walmoor Hill CH2 40 D5
Walmoor Pk CH2 40 D5
Walnut Cl,
Penyffordd CH4 28 B3
Walnut Cl,
Upton CH2 36 B4
Walnut Cotts LL13 71 B5
Walnut Gro LL12 50 B3
Walnut St LL11 60 C1
Walpole Av CH5 19 H5
Walpole St CH1 4 A2
Walter St CH1 4 C1
Waltham Pl CH4 43 G2
Walton Pl CH1 39 E2
Walwen Uchaf CH8 7 E5
Wared Dr CH7 18 B2
Waring Ct LL13 61 E5
Warren Cres CH7 25 F4
Warren Dr CH4 27 E5
Warren Hall Ct CH4 26 C5
Warrenwood Rd LL12 57 F5
Warrington Rd CH2 37 F6
Warwick Av LL13 61 E4
Warwick Rd CH1 39 F1
Washington Dr CH5 20 A4
Waste La CW6 46 D5
Water St*,
Brook St CH5 22 C4
Water Tower St CH1 4 A3
Watergate Sq CH1 4 A4
Watergate St CH1 4 A4
Waterloo Cl LL13 60 D5
Waterloo Rd CH2 40 A2
Waters Reams CH3 41 E6
Waterside Ct CH2 47 A3
Waterside Vw CH1 4 C3
Watertower Vw CH2 40 D4
Waterway CH3 47 C5
Watery Rd LL13 5 A3
Watkin St CH5 21 F3
Watling Cres CH4 44 B1
Watling Ct CH3 41 F4
Wats Dyke Av,
Holywell CH8 7 B5
Wats Dyke Av,
Mold CH7 23 G3
Wats Dyke Way,
Soughton CH7 17 B5
Wats Dyke Way,
Wrexham LL11 56 C4
Watson Cl CH4 27 G4
Watts Ct CH7 24 A3
Watts Dyke LL12 50 A4
Watts Rd CH4 28 B4
Wavell Rd LL13 61 E
Wavells Way CH3 45 E
Waverley Cres LL12 52 E
Waverley Ter CH2 40 B
Waverton Mill Quays
CH3 47 C
Wavertree Rd CH1 38 D
Waynnstay
Ind Est LL14 **65 D**
Wayside Ct CH2 31 B
Weal Stone La CH2 36 B
Weale Ct LL13 61 E
Wealstone Ct CH2 40 C
Weaver Gro CH2 31 A
Weaver St CH1 4 B
Webster Cl CH4 27 G
Wedgewood Heights
CH8 8 D
Wedgewood Rd CH5 20 A
Weighbridge Rd CH5 12 F
Well Cotts CH3 46 C
Well House Dr CH4 28 C
Well La, Chester CH2 40 C
Well La,
Mollington CH1 35 F
Well St, Holywell CH8 7 B
Well St, Mold CH7 23 H
Well St,
Wrexham LL14 66 D
Welland Dr CH5 13 C
Wellington Cl CH5 19 H
Wellington Pl CH1 4 C
Wellington Rd,
Chester CH4 27 F
Wellington Rd,
Wrexham LL13 5 B
Wellington St CH5 15 B
Wells Cl,
Chester CH2 31 A
Wells Cl,
Ellesmere Port
CH66 32 A
Wellswood Rd LL13 57 E
Welsh Rd CH5 15 E
Wemyss Rd CH1 39 E
Wenfryn Cl LL20 66 E
Wenlock Cres CH5 21 E
Wenlock Way CH4 43 E
Wens St LL14 64 C
Wentworth Cl CH7 24 A
Wentworth Rise
LL13 57 H

Wepre Ct CH5 13 D8
Wepre Dr CH5 13 F7
Wepre Hall Cres CH5 13 E8
Wepre La CH5 13 D8
Wepre Pk CH5 13 E8
Wepre Vw CH5 15 A7
Wern LL14 68 D4
Wern Av CH6 8 B5
Wern La LL14 64 D2
Wern Las LL14 64 D3
Wern Rd, Llangollen LL20 67 B4
Wern Rd, Wrexham LL11 53 E4
Wern Ucha CH6 8 B5
Wervin Rd CH2 33 G4
Wesley Rd LL11 53 C1
Wesley St CH5 13 E6
West Bank CH1 40 A1
West Bank Rd LL12 50 A3
West Circle LL13 61 E2
West Dr CH8 7 A6
West Gro LL14 59 G6
West Lorne St CH1 4 A2
West Park Dr CH66 32 A1
West St, Chester CH2 4 D1
West St, Llangollen LL20 67 B4
West St, Wrexham LL11 60 B1
West View Dr CH7 23 F4
West Vw, Buckley CH7 24 C4
West Vw, Chester CH4 28 B5
West Vw, Mold CH7 22 B4
West Way, Deeside CH5 20 D3
West Way, Wrexham LL12 52 E4
Westbourne Cres CH7 24 B3
Westbourne Dr LL14 59 H5
Westbourne Rd CH1 39 G1
Westbrook Dr CH7 24 C5
Westbury Dr, Buckley CH7 25 E4
Westbury Dr, Wrexham LL11 56 C3
Westbury Way CH4 43 F2
Western App CH2 40 C2
Western Av CH1 38 D2
Western Ct CH2 40 C2
Western Vw LL11 56 C3
Westfield Cl CH4 39 H6
Westfield Ct LL13 61 G5
Westminster Av CH4 43 H1
Westminster Cl LL12 60 D1
Westminster Cres CH5 15 B8
Westminster Ct*, Westminster Rd CH2 40 D3
Westminster Dr, Gresford LL12 51 F5
Westminster Dr, Wrexham LL12 60 D1
Westminster Grn CH4 40 A6
Westminster Rd, Broughton CH4 27 E5
Westminster Rd, Chester CH2 40 C2
Westminster Rd, Wrexham LL11 55 F2
Westminster Ter CH4 40 A6
Weston Cl CH5 15 E7
Weston Dr LL11 56 B6
Weston Gro CH2 36 C5
Weston Rd LL11 59 G1
Westward Rd CH3 41 E5
Westwood Dr LL13 57 G6
Wetherby Cl CH1 39 H3
Weybourne Cl CH4 43 E3
Whaddon Dr CH4 43 F4
Whalleys Way LL14 65 B8
Wharf Hill LL20 67 B4
Wharfdale Av CH5 13 C7
Wharton Ct CH3 40 C4
Whayley Ct CH1 34 A3
Wheat Cl LL11 55 H4
Wheatsheaf La LL11 55 G3
Wheatsheaf Mws LL11 55 H3
Wheldon Cl CH2 36 B4
Whipcord La CH1 39 H3
Whitby Av CH2 36 B6
Whitby La CH1 32 B2
Whitchurch Rd, Chester CH3 41 E5
Whitchurch Rd, Wrexham LL13 70 C5
White Friars CH1 4 B5
White La CH3 41 G6
White Lion Cl LL11 55 G2
White Oaks LL11 53 D1
White Oaks Dr CH7 18 D2
White Rock Cl CH4 28 C1
Whitecroft Cl CH5 13 B6
Whitegate Flds LL13 71 B5
Whitegate Light Ind Est LL13 61 F4
Whitegate Rd LL13 61 E4
Whitehurst Link LL14 68 D2
Whites Mdw CH3 41 E6
Whiteway Dr LL12 51 E4
Whiteway Gro CH5 15 E7
Whitford St CH8 7 A5
Whitland Way LL13 61 F5
Whittle Cl CH5 21 G2
Whitton Dr CH2 36 C6
Wicker La CH3 31 B6
Wilde Cl CH5 19 G6
Wildmoor La WA6 31 D1
Wilkinson Dr LL14 59 G5
Willan Rd CH1 39 E2
William St, Boughton CH2 40 C3
William St, Chester CH1 4 C2
William St, Wrexham LL14 64 E2
Williams Cl, Chester CH2 40 A2
Williams Cl, Penyffordd CH4 28 C2
Williams Ter LL14 64 E1
Williams Way LL12 52 D4
Willington La CW6 46 C6
Willington Rd CW6 46 C6
Willow Av LL12 48 C2
Willow Cl, Buckley CH7 25 E4
Willow Cl, Chester CH2 36 B4
Willow Cres, Chester CH2 41 E1
Willow Cres, Connahs Quay CH5 13 D7
Willow Cres, Ewloe CH5 19 H6
Willow Ct, Bangor-on-Dee LL13 70 C4
Willow Ct, Chester CH4 29 H4
Willow Ct, Wrexham LL13 61 G1
Willow Ct*, Pen y Llan CH5 13 D5
Willow Dr, Chester CH1 34 D6
Willow Dr, Flint CH6 10 A3
Willow Dr, Gresford LL12 51 F5
Willow Dr, Llay LL12 50 B3
Willow Gro, Buckley CH7 24 B1
Willow Gro, Chester CH2 41 E1
Willow Gro, Ellesmere Port CH66 32 B1
Willow La CH5 20 D2
Willow Lea CH1 35 F2
Willow Lea Cl LL11 56 A4
Willow Rd, Chester CH4 43 F2
Willow Rd, Wrexham LL11 54 B6
Willow St LL20 67 B5
Willow Walk CH7 30 B1
Willow Way CH4 27 F5
Willoway Rd CH3 41 F4
Willowdale Way CH66 32 A1
Willowherb Cl CH3 45 E2
Wilson Av LL13 61 E2
Wilton Rd CH5 20 D3
Winchester Sq CH4 43 F3
Winchester Way LL12 51 E5
Windermere Av, Chester CH2 36 D6
Windermere Av, Connahs Quay CH5 13 E6
Windermere Rd LL12 56 D3
Windmill Cl CH7 24 B3
Windmill La CH3 41 H5
Windmill Rd CH7 24 C3
Windmill Rise CH2 36 B5
Windrush Cl LL13 61 E4
Windsor Av, Connahs Quay CH5 13 E7
Windsor Av, Shotton CH5 15 A8
Windsor Av, Wrexham LL12 48 A2
Windsor Ct CH1 4 C5
Windsor Dr, Chester CH4 27 E5
Windsor Dr, Flint CH6 10 A2
Windsor Dr, Wrexham LL11 60 B1
Windsor Rd, Chester CH4 43 F1
Windsor Rd, New Broughton LL11 55 G6
Windsor Rd, Rhosllanerchrugog LL14 64 D2
Winkwell Dr CH4 43 G3
Winscombe Dr CH3 41 G3
Winsford Way CH1 39 F4
Winston Ct*, Mannings La South CH2 37 E6
Wirral Vw, Connahs Quay CH5 13 D7
Wirral Vw, Ewloe CH5 20 A4
Wirral Vw, Holywell CH8 9 B3
Withy Cft CH3 41 E6
Witter Pl CH1 4 D3
Woburn Cl LL13 61 G1
Woburn Dr CH2 36 D5
Wold Ct CH5 20 C5
Wood Cft, Buckley CH7 25 E1
Wood Cft, Chester CH3 31 A6
Wood Grn CH7 22 D4
Wood Gro CH7 30 B1
Wood La, Chester CH4 27 E4
Wood La, Deeside CH5 19 H6
Wood La, Holywell CH8 7 D5
Wood St CH5 21 F3
Woodall Av CH4 43 E1
Woodbank Rd CH5 13 D8
Woodberry Cl LL14 60 A4
Woodfield Av CH6 10 D3
Woodfield Cl, Chester CH4 27 E5
Woodfield Cl, Connahs Quay CH5 13 E7
Woodfield Gro CH2 41 E1
Woodfields CH3 41 H6
Woodland Bank CH2 31 B2
Woodland Ct CH6 10 A3
Woodland Dr, Flint CH6 10 B3
Woodland Dr, Holywell CH8 6 B3
Woodland Gro, Llangollen LL20 66 C4
Woodland Gro, Wrexham LL13 61 F1
Woodland Rd LL11 55 F2
Woodland Rise CH7 19 E6
Woodlands Av CH1 39 H1
Woodlands Cl CH7 22 D4
Woodlands Cres CH5 13 F7
Woodlands Ct, Hawarden CH5 20 B5
Woodlands Ct, Mancot CH5 20 D4
Woodlands Ct, Wrexham LL11 54 D5
Woodlands Dr, Chester CH2 40 C2
Woodlands Dr, Deeside CH5 25 F1
Woodlands La CH3 40 D4
Woodlands Rd, Chester CH4 43 G1
Woodlands Rd, Huntington CH3 44 D1
Woodlands Rd, Llangollen LL20 66 B4
Woodlands Rd, Mold CH7 22 D5
Woodlands Rd, Wrexham LL12 51 F4
Woodlands St CH5 13 F7
Woodlea Av CH2 36 C5
Woodridge Av LL12 51 F4
Woodside Cl CH5 20 A4
Woodside Ct LL14 59 H5
Woodside Ct*, Abbots Pk CH1 40 A1
Woodside Rd CH1 38 D1
Woodville Av CH5 20 D4
Woodville Gdns CH7 17 A6
Woodward Walk CH3 46 C1
Woodwards Walk LL14 65 C8
Worcester Pl CH1 39 G1
Worcester Rd LL13 70 C4
Wordsworth Cl CH5 19 G5
Wordsworth Cres CH1 35 F6
Wordsworth Mews CH1 39 G1
Wordsworth Sq CH1 35 G6
Worsley Av, Chester CH1 34 A3
Worsley Av, Wrexham LL14 64 F2
Wrekin Way CH4 43 F2
Wrexham Bsns Pk LL13 62 D3
Wrexham By Pass 59 G6
Wrexham Ind Est LL13 63 F3
Wrexham Rd, Brynteg LL11 55 G4
Wrexham Rd, Caergwrle LL12 48 B3
Wrexham Rd, Chester CH4 43 G6
Wrexham Rd, Holt LL13 71 A6
Wrexham Rd, Mold CH7 22 C5
Wrexham Rd, Penyffordd CH4 28 B5
Wrexham Rd, Rhostyllen LL14 59 G6
Wrexham Rd, Rossett LL12,CH4 52 E2
Wrexham Rd, Wrexham LL13 57 H6
Wrexham St CH7 22 C4
Wroxham Cl CH2 4 B1
Wycliffe Ct CH2 40 D3
Wylfa Av CH7 23 F4
Wyndam Gdns LL13 61 G3
Wyndham Dr LL12 49 C5
Wyndham Rd CH1 38 D1
Wynn Av, Ruabon LL14 65 F6
Wynn Av, Wrexham LL11 56 C6
Wynnstay Av LL13 61 F2
Wynnstay Cres LL14 59 H6
Wynnstay La LL12 51 G5
Wynnstay Rd CH4 27 F3

Y Berllan LL11 54 A6
Y Cedrwydd CH7 23 G4
Y Dolydd CH7 22 B5
Y Dreflan CH8 9 B4
Y Fron LL14 64 F2
Y Gamer LL20 70 C2
Y Gerdd CH8 9 C5
Y Gesail LL14 64 F3
Y Gilfach CH7 22 C5
Y Gorlan LL14 64 D3
Y Maes LL20 70 C1
Y Parc CH7 22 B5
Y Stryt Fawr LL11 58 B1
Y Waen CH7 11 A2
Y Wern LL13 61 F3
Yale Gro LL12 56 D6
Yale Pk LL11 60 B1
Yale St LL14 64 E2
Yarrow Cl CH4 27 F5
Yarwood Dr LL13 57 E3
Yeld La CW6 46 D4
Yerburgh St CH2 40 B2
Yew Tree Cl CH4 27 F4
Yew Tree Ct LL12 51 E5
Yewdale Dr CH66 32 B1
York Av CH5 15 A8
York Cl LL13 61 G5
York Dr CH2 31 A2
York Rd CH5 13 C5
York St CH1 4 C3
Yorke Av LL13 71 B1
Yorke Cl LL13 71 C2
Yorke St LL13 5 D4
Yowley Rd CH5 19 H3
Yr Helfa LL14 68 E3
Ystad Goffa*, Albert Av CH6 10 D3